Left Hand Financing

Left Hand Financing

An Emerging Field of Corporate Finance

Editors

Thomas L. Chrystie

Frank J. Fabozzi

DOW JONES-IRWIN
Homewood, Illinois 60430

ISBN 0-87094-342-1
Library of Congress Catalog Card No. 82-72366

Printed in the United States of America

1 2 3 4 5 6 7 8 9 0 K 0 9 8 7 6 5 4 3

Foreword

It is a fundamental tenet of double-entry bookkeeping that a company's statement of assets and liabilities will always be in balance at any particular point in time, even if some creditors are represented only reluctantly. A principal focus of the financial manager's task has been to anticipate what kinds and volumes of assets will be necessary in the future to carry out the company's strategic plan and then to go out and raise the funds necessary to make the funds sources on the right hand side of the balance sheet equal the projected investment requirements on the left hand side.

For many years that task was relatively straightforward for most businesses. After allowing for expected internal cash generation, the financial manager would negotiate the flotation of sufficient term debt and equity capital to balance corporate sources and uses, using the overall standing of the business as the credit backing. In recent years, however, fundamental alterations in the economic environment and consequent changes in the capital markets have complicated corporate financing arrangements. Long-term funds have often been either unavailable or perceived by many businesses to be prohibitively expensive. Short-term debt has been increasingly relied on to "balance up" the sources and uses but at the cost of a growing disparity in the maturity patterns of corporate assets and funding liabilities.

The editors and authors of *Left Hand Financing: An Emerging Field of Corporate Finance* have focused on a rapidly expanding cluster of "solutions" to these corporate financing complications—solutions which will likely be relevant to a broad swath of growing businesses during the 1980s. They have documented the ways in which segmented capital markets, increasingly differentiated tax and accounting treatments for selected financing instruments, and the likelihood of some out-and-out market inefficiencies have created opportunities to solve the equation of balanced assets and liabilities by focusing on unique characteristics of individual asset investments rather than on the general credit yielded by the corporation's total portfolio of individual asset investments.

This is therefore an important reference book for executives with corporate financing responsibilities. It does not offer pat solutions that can be used to bail out every company with a capital rationing problem. What it does provide is a framework of analysis so managers can more readily identify and structure financing arrangements which will likely be less costly and preserve greater flexibility for the capital-seeking business.

Samuel L. Hayes III
Jacob H. Schiff Professor of
Investment Banking
Harvard University Graduate
School of Business Administration

Preface

This book is designed for the chief financial officer of a growth-oriented, asset-intensive corporation. It should be of keen interest to the executives to whom he reports, corporate directors, and all those that provide financial services to corporations. As a book that should both be read and serve as a reference, it will aid the career development of those aspiring to the increasingly demanding position of chief financial officer.

Troubled markets have made it increasingly difficult for corporations to sell long-term, fixed-rate debt and equity securities at prices that are fair to current shareholders. In such an environment, investment bankers must be creative in matching the investment objectives of savers with the needs of users of capital. We believe the emerging field of corporate finance set forth in this book is fundamental to meeting this challenge and has far-reaching implications for corporations and the capital markets.

We can summarize the new approach as follows. An asset-intensive line of business really has two facets—operating assets for a profit and investing in those assets. Many asset-intensive corporations may be better off redefining their business to be primarily operating or managing assets. Income-producing corporate assets can be structured to have the investment characteristics that are increasingly in demand. Current shareholders may be better off in the long run if investors purchased some of the direct ownership benefits of assets used in the business, thus avoiding the need to incur high, fixed-rate debt and/or issue additional common stock. In so doing, the corporation can continue to grow by using its earnings from managing assets to increase rather than dilute its return on equity.

What do we call this emerging new field of corporate finance? To draw the chief financial officer's attention to the asset side of the balance sheet, we call it *left hand financing*. We believe left hand financing is the most significant development in corporate finance in the 20th century.

We have divided the book into three basic parts. The first part gives the reasons why the chief financial officer should consider left hand financing and actual examples of such transactions. In the second part, tax, financial reporting and marketing considerations for left hand financing are discussed. There is also a chapter on the factors that should be considered in selecting an investment banker. In the last part of the book, specialty financing techniques that constitute the roots of left hand financing are described.

We are indebted to many individuals who provided direct or indirect assistance in this project. To all the contributors we extend our deep thanks and appreciation. The following individuals gave generously of their time to read portions of the manuscript and provide valuable suggestions:

Arthur Blutter, Attorney at Law
Frederick J. C. Butler, Merrill Lynch Leasing Inc.
Niles L. Citrin, Laurence M. Brown & Company
Arnold Civens, Laurence M. Brown & Company
Richard A. Hanson, Merrill Lynch Industrial Resources
Dennis J. Hess, Merrill Lynch, Hubbard Inc.
Richard J. Hoffman, Merrill Lynch, Pierce, Fenner & Smith Inc.
Robert C. Kline, Merrill Lynch White Weld Capital Markets Group
Harry C. Pinson, Merrill Lynch White Weld Capital Markets Group
James D. Price, Merrill Lynch White Weld Capital Markets Group
Robert R. Rivett, Merrill Lynch Industrial Resources
Christopher Ryan, Ruskin, Schlissel, Moscou & Evans
Melvyn Stein, Stein, Rubine & Stein
W. Joseph Wilson, Merrill Lynch White Weld Capital Markets Group
Michael G. Wolfson, Brown, Wood, Ivey, Mitchell & Petty
John A. Zwald, Merrill Lynch Industrial Resources

We also made good use of the talents of the following individuals:

Sylvan Feldstein, Moody's Investors Service
Valda A. Gowing, Merrill Lynch Capital Resources Inc.
Richard Granat, Granrich Capital Corp.
Nicholas J. Letizia, Donaldson, Lufkin & Jenrette Real Estate Inc.
Thomas R. Robinson, Merrill Lynch Economics, Inc.
Jaime Romero, American Express International Banking Corporation
Jane Rountree, Merrill Lynch, Pierce, Fenner & Smith Inc.

Last, but far from least, we wish to express our appreciation to those readers of this book who carry forward with the development of the emerging field of left hand financing. They will be enhancing the viability of capitalism and private enterprise.

Thomas L. Chrystie
Frank J. Fabozzi

Contributors

Mathias Bowman Managing Director, Merrill Lynch White Weld Capital Markets Group, New York

Douglas Carleton Associate, Merrill Lynch White Weld Capital Markets Group, New York

Richard W. Carrington Assistant Treasurer, Corporate Finance, American Airlines, Inc.

Thomas L. Chrystie Chairman, Merrill Lynch Capital Resources Inc., New York

Frank J. Fabozzi, PhD, CFA, CPA Professor of Economics, Fordham University, New York

William Gremp Managing Director, Merrill Lynch White Weld Capital Markets Group, New York

Carolyn G. Hubsch Vice President, Merrill Lynch Leasing Inc., New York

Peter K. Nevitt Chairman and Chief Executive Officer, BankAmerilease Group, BankAmerica Companies, San Francisco

John Niehuss Vice President, Merrill Lynch White Weld Capital Markets Group, Washington, D.C.

Philip Peller, CPA Arthur Andersen & Company, New York

Walter Perlstein Vice President, Merrill Lynch Capital Resources Inc., New York

Lester Schoenfeld Executive Vice President, Merrill Lynch Leasing Inc., New York

Frank J. Schwitter, CPA Arthur Andersen & Company, New York

Janet G. Spratlin, PhD Assistant Vice President, Merrill Lynch, Pierce, Fenner & Smith Inc., New York

John L. Steffens Director of Marketing, Merrill Lynch, Pierce, Fenner & Smith Inc., New York

David N. Thrope, CPA Arthur Andersen & Company, New York

Kevan Watts H.M. Treasury, London, U.K., on secundment to Merrill Lynch White Weld Capital Markets Group, New York

Daniel W. West President, Macrolease International Corporation, New York

Maynard I. Wishner President, Walter E. Heller & Company, Chicago

Contents

PART THREE

SPECIALTY FINANCING–THE ROOTS OF LEFT HAND FINANCING

bonds. Commercial paper. Floating- and adjustable-rate bonds. Put bonds. Convertible and deep discount bonds. Summary.

Independent, third-party financing. Third-party financing: *Benefits to user.* Pricing of vendor financing programs. Summary.

Accounts receivable financing. Inventory financing. Fixed assets and secured financing packages. Cost of secured borrowing. Factoring. Conclusion.

PART 1

Overview

CHAPTER 1

Left Hand Financings

THOMAS L. CHRYSTIE
Merrill Lynch Capital Resources Inc.

THE NEW FIELD OF CORPORATE FINANCE

A new field of corporate finance is emerging in the 1980s. Its driving forces are the current costs of the inflation of the 1970s and the present unpredictability of future inflation. Corporate executives are responding to these driving forces by redefining their business as the employment of income-producing assets. The corporation can own those assets, but so can investors. These investors could be domestic institutions, corporations, and individuals or international investors.

Conventional corporate finance involves the right hand side of the balance sheet. It achieves long-term financing of assets through the issuance of long-term debt or equity. There are numerous variations and combinations of conventional debt or equity, but they all involve expanding the capitalization of the corporation.

Unfortunately, the inflation of the 1970s decreased investor confidence in the growth trend (and quality) of corporate earnings. The resulting low price-earnings ratios have made common equity costly. At the same time, the unpredictability of future inflation and the related volatility of the debt markets have sharply increased the cost of long-term debt to the corporate user of capital (see Exhibit 1).

Increasing shares of common stock outstanding at low price-earnings ratios can result in a lower overall return on equity and lower earnings per share. Very high fixed charges on long-term debt can increase the volatility of net earnings and can even result in negative leverage. Faced with less than satisfactory alternatives stemming from study of the right hand side of the balance sheet, chief financial officers

4

EXHIBIT 1
Trends in the Cost of Corporate Finance (percent)

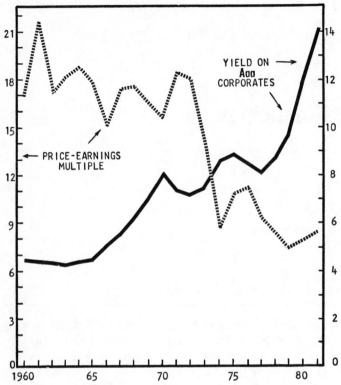

YIELD ON →
Aaa
CORPORATES

← PRICE-EARNINGS
MULTIPLE

Source: Moody's Investors Services; Standard & Poor's Corp.;
Merrill Lynch Economics Inc.

and their investment bankers are turning to the left hand side of the balance sheet to develop alternatives.

The left hand, or asset, side of the balance sheet has typically been the province of the assistant treasurer. For certain defined types of assets, he would calculate the cost of alternatives to buying. These alternatives include renting, leasing, and borrowing. Financings stemming from the left hand side fill special needs and are referred to by terms with narrow and variously defined meanings. Among these terms are:

— Asset-based financing.
— Lease financing.
— Off-balance sheet financing.
— Project and joint venture financing.
— Secured financing.
— Tax-free bond financing.

   — Tax-shelter financing and tax-benefit-transfer leasing.
   — Vendor financing.

   Left hand financing borrows many of the techniques of the above specialty areas. However, it meets the chief financial officer's broader need for alternatives to the least painful of the conventional financing possibilities that he has developed from study of the capitalization on the right hand side of the balance sheet.

   Left hand financing is any financing that provides resources to a corporation if the financing (a) draws its investment characteristics from the left hand side of the balance sheet and (b) avoids or lowers the cost of expanding the capitalization of the corporation.

   Left hand equity financing provides investors with direct ownership interests in assets. Left hand debt financing uses assets as direct security for nonrecourse debt or as indirect security for fixed obligations.

   The possible variations of left hand financing are infinite in number, challenging the creativity of all involved.[1] To better understand why employers of funds need left hand financing, let us examine the cumulative effect of inflation, and the current unpredictability of future inflation.

INFLATION

In the 1950s and 1960s, inflation was generally ignored as a planning factor because of its low rate compared to the real growth of the economy. The 1970s were different. The inflation rate accelerated, and annualized inflation rates at times hit double-digit levels. Clearly, as a sharply larger percentage of nominal GNP growth, inflation could not be ignored, but how did it influence corporate planning? (See Exhibit 2.)

   For the most part, the presumption throughout the 1970s was that we were seeing the delayed results of trying to fight an unpopular war in Vietnam without making concurrent sacrifices on the domestic front. The United States financed both guns and butter with deficit spending and a related increase in the money supply. The conventional wisdom was that inflation would subside to manageable levels after a couple of years of painful readjustment.

   High inflation and interest rates, combined with low price-earning ratios, made long-term financing expensive. The tendency in the 1970s was to use short-term debt to postpone long-term financing for a year or two, when inflation was expected to subside. However, with inflation increasing costs at an annual increment approximating the annual interest cost, there was little reason to postpone capital expenditures.

---

[1] Actual examples of left hand financing are provided in the next chapter.

EXHIBIT 2
Critical Dimensions on Inflation

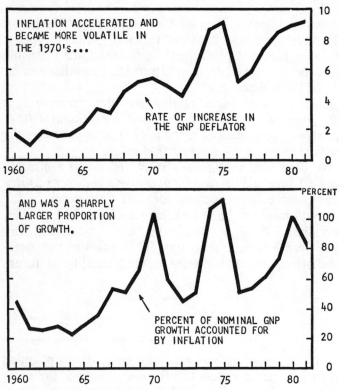

Source: U.S. Department of Commerce; Merrill Lynch Economics Inc.

When short-term debt became burdensome, it was typically refinanced with long-term debt.

Sale of common stock to revive capital was unfortunately not an alternative for most industrial companies. Unanticipated surges in inflation disrupted cost structures, causing growth of real earnings to be interrupted. Inventory and depreciation charges were well below replacement costs (see Exhibit 3).

During the 1970s, corporate debt grew much faster than book equity increased through retained earnings. Market equity, the aggregate market value of shares outstanding, too often decreased while debt increased. Hence, capitalization ratios of many corporations deteriorated to the point where a major capital expenditure program could not be conventionally financed without expanding all layers of capitalization (see Exhibit 4).

Added to investor concern over earnings was the widened gap between dividend yields and interest rates, which caused the prices of stocks to fall or lag well below any reflection of the stocks' earning

EXHIBIT 3
Perspectives on Corporate Profitability ($ billions)

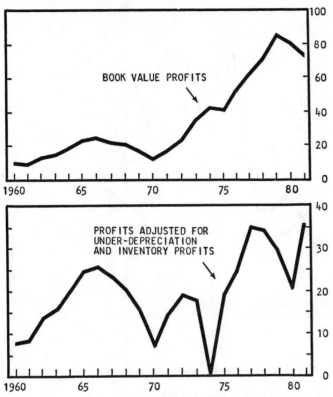

Source: *Economic Report to the President* p. 246; Merrill Lynch Economics Inc.

power over the long term. The parts (shares of stock) were selling at deep discounts from the replacement value of the whole company.

The cumulative effect of inflation from the mid 1970s to the early 1980s doubled the cost of a given increment of capacity. The need to consider inflation in planning capital expenditures in the 1980s is widely recognized. But what is the current trend of inflation?

When there is a confluence of air or water currents, there is turmoil. The early 1980s are a period of economic turmoil. There is a major confluence of forces that will determine the future trend of inflation, but the outcome is unpredictable.

The economic program of the Reagan administration just may succeed in reducing government spending as a percentage of GNP, stimulating savings and investment, controlling the money supply so that it expands at the same rate as productivity, and reregulating the economy on a cost-effective basis. If all of this is achieved, the inflation rate could subside to 4 percent in the 1980s. If it doesn't?

EXHIBIT 4
Trends in Corporate Debt and Equity (percent)

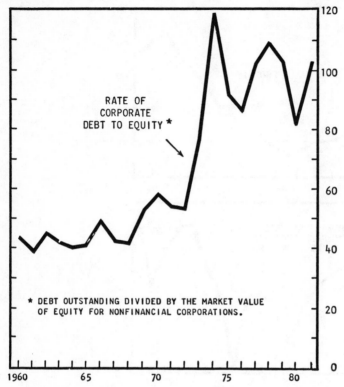

RATE OF
CORPORATE
DEBT TO EQUITY *

* DEBT OUTSTANDING DIVIDED BY THE MARKET VALUE
OF EQUITY FOR NONFINANCIAL CORPORATIONS.

Source: Board of Governors of the Federal Reserve System;
Merrill Lynch Economics Inc.

Reduced tax receipts, high defense spending, and lack of carry-through by Congress in cutting back on costly, inefficient social programs could create another inflation surge to 14 percent. If the industrial world is caught in an upward spiral, inflation in the United States could soar to 24 percent. At that rate, hyperinflation could destroy the value of fiat currencies in circulation throughout the world.

Let us presume that after examining all turbulent crosscurrents in the economy, a corporation decides to use the following planning assumptions:

	Probability Assigned to
	Three-Year Average Annual Inflation
Inflation	*Mid to Late 1980s*
4%	20%
8	40
14	25
24	10
Hyperinflation	5

With the range of possibilities so wide, an entire financing program should not be built around a most probable assumption of high single-digit inflation. The well-positioned corporation should be financed to retain viable alternatives for realizing opportunities if inflation rates of 4 percent or 14 percent and above eventuate.

The emerging field of left hand financing can add flexibility and balance to a financing program. For this reason, we are witnessing the emergence of financing plans that draw their strength from newly acquired assets or undervalued assets carried at historical depreciated costs. Funds with attractive current costs can be raised by allowing an investor certain or all benefits of an asset's ownership while retaining the full use of the asset for the corporation. Such left hand equity financing can be and is being weighed against right hand alternatives. An overall plan with a mix of conventional financing and left hand financing usually provides the optimum balance between current cost and future flexibility.

To better understand the advantages of the infinite variations of left hand financing design to the user of capital, let us turn to the profile of investment characteristics that investors, the providers of capital, find desirable. An understanding of these characteristics plus flexibility of design leads to maximum benefit at minimum cost.

INVESTMENT CHARACTERISTICS DESIRED

Investors providing resources to U.S. corporations may be:

- Corporations (financial or industrial).
- Individuals.
- Institutions (tax-free or taxable).
- International (individuals or institutions).

Historically, investors of all types have sought investments with some combination of:

- Appreciation, or growth.
- Income.
- Liquidity.
- Safety.
- Stability.

There is a new investment characteristic that is being sought in varying but increasing degrees by investors in the 1980s. *It is the ability to retain real value of purchasing power and principal no matter what results from the turmoil in the economy that is causing high and unpredictable rates of inflation.* No longer do investors assume that long-term growth, appreciation, high fixed income, or price increases of non-income-producing assets will preserve real values. A new solution is being sought to provide protection against inflation.

Ownership interests in income-producing assets can provide the most reliable protection against high and unpredictable inflation rates. It is this new investment characteristic, combined with the desired profile of traditional characteristics, that can provide a broad, growing market for carefully structured left hand equity financings.

Left hand debt financing uses assets as direct security for non-recourse debt or as indirect security for fixed obligations. Such security is being increasingly recognized as less vulnerable to the ravages of high inflation than corporate cash flow and earning power. Left hand financings with both debt and equity characteristics have a large market among investors of many types.

We will outline examples of left hand financing vehicles that could serve as prototypes to meet many corporate needs. First, let us enumerate some of those needs that must be satisfied in the 1980s.

CORPORATE FINANCING NEEDS OF THE 1980s

Acquisitions, of which at least a substantial portion were for cash, were a major capital outlay in the 1970s and into the 1980s. The cumulative effect of inflation and low equity values has already been referred to. As a result of these conditions, even at premiums of 50 to 100 percent above the prevailing market value of the common stock, existing net assets became a bargain versus the replacement value of those assets. This was particularly true when the assets acquired were net assets subject to long-term debt with low coupons. However, realignments of corporate ownership don't by themselves create additional capacity or increase productivity. Much of the revenue growth of corporations in the 1970s was a result of inflation, not of more units sold.

The 1980s will see a substantial increase in capital expenditures compared to the previous decade because of:

- Facilities for research and development of products resulting from new or only partly explored technologies.
- Increased demand in excess of what idle capacity can produce.
- Increased need to offer financing support to dealers or franchisees.
- Increased need to offer financing to customers.
- "Office of the future" equipment provided to white-collar workers at all levels.
- Real growth in sales.

- Reindustrialization, or automation, of plant facilities to increase productivity.
- Retirement of inefficient capacity.
- The need to participate in major project financing to assure supply of needed resources.

Increasing international competition and steadily climbing labor costs have made expenditure for increased productivity an economic imperative for many corporations. It is likely that the decade of the 1980s will see substantial real growth under almost all inflation scenarios. Greater control of essential energy and raw material resources has become a high-priority need for many industries.

The 1980s will see considerable long-term financing to improve corporate liquidity and to refund short-term borrowing for capital expenditure made in previous years. However, the new depreciation and investment tax credit provisions effective for purchases of assets in 1981 and subsequent years will lessen the need for raising external capital. Overall, the demand of externally generated capital in the 1980s should be of record proportions. Both private institutional supplies of capital and the public markets use balance sheet and earnings coverage ratios that will act as constraints on financing needed assets (see Exhibit 5).

The relative weight that the corporate user of capital puts on trade-offs among the various cost elements of capital, and knowledge of the

EXHIBIT 5
Ratio of Long-Term to Short-Term Debt, Nonfinancial Corporate Business

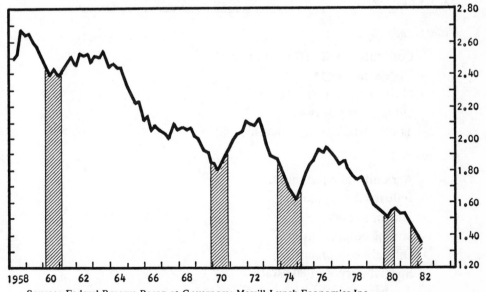

Source: Federal Reserve Board of Governors; Merrill Lynch Economics Inc.

market for investments, must be coupled with a study of assets to design a left hand financing. Let us examine these assets themselves as a resource.

ASSETS AS FINANCING RESOURCES

Any income-producing corporate asset can be the basis of a left hand financing. In balancing the characteristics desired by investors against the objectives of the corporate client, it may be preferable to use *existing* assets as a resource to fund the acquisition of *additional* assets. Hence, the entire left hand side of the balance sheet should be studied in designing left hand financing alternatives.

Left hand financing is an emerging field. Acquisition of ownership interests by Investors has been widely accepted for certain types of assets. However, the degree and variation of ownership interests are changing as part of the current trend. Listed below are examples of categories of corporate assets which could be the basis for left hand financing. They are grouped roughly in order of the degree to which ownership interests have been held by investors as a result of the specialty financings that are the roots of the emerging field of left hand financing.

DEGREE OF OWNERSHIP INTERESTS HELD BY INVESTORS

Widespread

- Computers and office equipment.
- Hotels and motels.
- Multipurpose real estate.
- Oil and gas reserves.
- Transportation equipment.

Not unusual

- Agricultural equipment.
- Industrial gas plants.
- Machine tools.
- Mining equipment.
- Oil field equipment.
- Special-purpose real estate.
- Timber.

Unusual

- Coal reserves.
- Electric generating plants.
- Film libraries.
- Ore reserves.
- Patents and research development equipment.
- Raw land.
- Resort accommodations.
- Special-purpose manufacturing equipment.
- Steel plants.

Rare or not at all

- Agricultural land.
- Aluminum plants.
- Amusement parks.
- Automotive plants.
- Bottling plants.
- Food processing plants.
- Hydroelectric projects.
- Original equipment plants.
- Steel plants.
- Refineries.
- Synfuel projects.

To illustrate the versatility and significance of the emergence of left hand financing, the key terms of a hypothetical left hand financing involving some of the assets listed above should be examined. However, it will simplify the presentation to first comment on some of the legal formats that can be the vehicles for left hand financings.

LEFT HAND FINANCING VEHICLES

No corporation executive or investment banker wishes to take unnecessary risks or create uncontrollable delays in connection with an innovative financing. One logical result of this is that new fields of finance are rare and emerge over time. Another is that any innovative financing uses established legal and regulatory formats to the extent possible.[2]

If established vehicles are used, the form and predictable results of the contract, offering documents, legal rights of the investors and the

---

[2] Part 3 of this book covers specialty financing.

issuer, regulatory procedures, state blue-sky considerations, tax considerations, and aftermarket private sales or trading procedures are all relatively well established. Vehicles that have been or can be used to structure left hand financing are:

- Corporation—regular; taxed as partnership; special-purpose (minimum equity).
- Grantor trust.
- Joint venture.
- Lease—all types.
- Limited partnership.
- Participation certificate.
- Special-purpose REIT.

The Economic Recovery Tax Act of 1981 has added to the flexibility of left hand financing.[3] The determination of which party receives residual values, the cash flowing back to the provider of funds, and tax benefits can be based on the profile of the investment characteristics most broadly or eagerly desired by investors and on the needs of the corporation. The tax laws and regulations involving leasing have been effectively reregulated on a cost-effective basis, so that intended incentives to save and invest can be more effective.

LEFT HAND FINANCING ALTERNATIVES

To grasp the exciting potential, to users and providers of capital alike, of the emerging new field, we must understand what can be accomplished through left hand financing. The following hypothetical examples of financing needs and simplified outlines of the key terms of left hand financings are presented to stimulate the imagination of the reader. (Some actual transactions are presented in the next chapter.) Since the legal vehicles for a left hand financing should be selected after the preliminary outline of key terms has been determined, the hypothetical left hand financing alternatives that follow will not focus on the legal vehicles but on the economic effect on the user and provider of funds.

Grocery Stores

Need
A grocery store chain needs to finance the construction of stores and

---

[3] See Chapter 3.

related land. Unless a high rate of inflation is assumed, the fixed rent on a financing lease is too high to start up stores except at a loss for an unacceptably long period.

Financing
A public offering to individual investors is made of shares in a trust that represent undivided ownership in a group of newly opened stores purchased at cost from the chain. The trust leases, net of all costs, the stores to the chain for 15 years at a variable rent of 7 percent of sales. At the end of the lease, the investors own the stores and land free and clear.

Left hand feature
The chain uses a fixed percentage of the revenues from the stores owned by the investors to pay for the use of those assets. The capitalization is not increased.

The investor establishes an income stream that should purchase a constant amount of groceries for 15 years. If those years prove to be a period of high inflation, the stores and related land will probably increase in dollar value, at least in nominal terms.

In a period of low inflation, the investor would still realize the objective of a real rate of return. The grocery store chain would benefit by a low-cost financing versus a high-fixed-rate lease. In a period of high inflation, the grocery store chain would have a fixed cost in relation to sales but one that proved more expensive than a fixed-rate lease.

Joint Venture Coal Gasification Plant

Need
A synfuels joint venture has a long-term supply of coal and is building a gasification plant which it needs to finance. Both partners wish to minimize their equity investment.

Financing
The joint venture sells 25-year subordinated debentures with an 8 percent coupon at par. An index of the cost of gas is established to equal 100 at the issue date. Every six months, the coupon and par are adjusted to parallel the index if at that time the index is above 100. The bonds are redeemable at the index price anytime after 15 years.

Left hand feature
The joint venture uses its "inventory" of coal at historical cost and its plant at embedded cost to lower the coupon cost of adding long-term debt to the capitalization. In a period of significantly rising gas prices,

the joint venture will do well but not as well as it would have if the participants had put in more equity and if it had used fixed-rate debt. In a period of stable or lower gas prices, the reverse would be true.

The investor earns an attractive real rate of return over the increase in the cost of gas. This is of minor benefit if the cost of gas is relatively stable, but it is a valuable protection against a rapidly rising cost of gas.

Timberlands

Need
A paper company needs to assure itself of a supply of suitable timber within economic distance of a new plant. Unless it relies on an assumption of large increases in product prices, the company can finance only half of the needed timberlands without increasing equity to the point that it has an unattractive return at current paper prices.

Financing
Foreign investors purchase a 50 percent joint venture interest in the required timberlands. The investors give a management contract to the paper company to grow and cut timber on their 50 percent undivided interest for a percentage of the sales price of the timber. The sales price is the current market price at the time the timber is cut.

Left hand feature
The paper company shares ownership of its timberland assets with investors. The company avoids overrelying on price increases in paper to make the plant economical. The paper company will improve its quality of earnings, achieving more stable growth over cycles of price increases and price lags or declines.

The foreign investors with little need for current income acquire a renewable natural resource which protects their purchasing power in the event of inflation.

Mature Manufacturing Company

Need
A manufacturing company with geographically dispersed facilities needs to undertake a major automation of its historical business in order to reverse profit margin deterioration resulting from the competition of companies with more automated plants. Only intermediate-term or floating rate debt is available at other than "junk bond" rates. The stock is selling well below book value at five times depressed earnings.

Financing
The company makes an installment sale at a capital gain of its multipurpose real estate—regional office building, distribution centers, and certain assembly plants. It leases the real estate back for various terms at escalating rentals geared to current interest rates and the fair market value of comparable property.

Left hand feature
The company uses its equity ownership of multipurpose real estate to increase current earnings during the transition years and to raise cash for the automation program. In the years ahead, it will benefit by renewed growth of operating earnings which should be sufficient to absorb inflationary escalations.

The real estate investors gain a portfolio of real estate with sound residual value and income that keeps pace with the current real estate market.

Young Manufacturing Company

Need
A young manufacturing company with products gaining new applications is faced with a new, long-term demand for its products that would require doubling its manufacturing capabilities. A large equity offering, at a discount from the current depressed market, would be an essential component of a conventional right hand financing.

Financing
Three plants near the company's new customers' facilities are built with industrial revenue bond financing, providing the company with a fair market purchase option. The equipment is leased, giving the lessor the residual values. Working capital is raised based on long-term contracts for the plants' output.

Left hand feature
The company avoids any sale of equity, giving up the residual value of the new machinery in order to lower current fixed costs and a fixed-purchase option on the real estate to keep it off the balance sheet. The company uses the employment potential of its new plants to gain tax-exempt financing secured by the asset and a lease. A long-term contract with limited price flexibility is used to gain the asset of output of finished product to its new customers. The high profitability of the new product line makes the trade-off attractive for the company's shareholders under all scenarios other than depression, when no expansion would have been preferable.

The investors in the industrial revenue bonds get a high rate due to the company's low credit rating, but they are secured by well-located modern plants producing a desired product. The equipment lessors get a kicker of residual values for undertaking a credit risk that is more difficult to appraise. The working capital lender is well secured based on proven ability to manufacture the product line and the long-term contract.

Steel Company

Need
A major steel company wishes to build a new plant which would provide both lower cost production and increased capacity.

Financing
Straight debt financing would lower the company's credit rating below the A level, increasing other borrowing costs. The common stock sells below book value and at a low multiple of depressed earnings. The company would be unable to utilize the tax benefits of ownership.

The left hand financing approach is utilized as follows:

    a. The land is sold and leased back from a pension fund, subject to a fair market purchase option.

    b. The plant is sold to taxpaying investors and leased back, leveraged with nonrecourse debt.

    c. Debentures are placed with insurance companies, and they have a fixed rate plus a variable rate indexed to price increases in steel above the current rate.

Left hand feature
The inflationary impact on land values, the residual value of plant, and the price of steel are given up by the company to investors. In return, the company retains its A debt rating and avoids giving up an equity interest in the overall business. Both the investors and the company will gain under other than extreme conditions. Severe depression would cause both to lose versus no expansion, although the company would be better off than under the conventional alternative financing. A very sharp escalation in the price of steel would make the left hand approach of variable-rate debt more expensive than the alternative of selling fixed-rate debt and equity in the company.

Vendor Financing

Need
A machine tool company has historically sold its products mostly to

major corporations that provided their own financings. A leasing subsidiary has been able to handle the demand from creditworthy smaller customers.

To satisfy a major capital expenditure boom driven by the need for both additional capacity and less labor-intensive facilities, the machine tool company is selling automated assembly lines complete with computer controls and robots. Regular customers have large capital demands for new plant facilities and working capital. They have a new requirement of supplier financing for their machine tool purchases just when the surge of business makes it unpalatable for the machine tool company to build its investment in its leasing subsidiary.

Financing
Third-party vendor financing is made available, so the machine tool company gets a cash sale instead of lease receivables. The vendor financing company has three main variables to use in designing a financing attractive to the machine tool buyer: (1) imputed interest rate, (2) tax benefits, and (3) the residual value. The Economic Recovery Tax Act of 1981 has added flexibility to the design and separate marketing of these three left hand financing features.

Left hand feature
The buyer of the machine tools can obtain 100 percent financing on or off its balance sheet. The vendor receives cash for the sale, eliminating the need to expand the equity investment in its leasing subsidiary. The third-party vendor financing company builds assets that include the inflation hedge of some residual values with upside potential.

Windpower Plants

Need
Utilities need both additional power capacity and additional sources of energy. They are limited in their ability to raise capital and conduct extensive research and development. They have limited ability to utilize tax benefits.

A manufacturer of windmills wants to develop the existing utility market for its product. Technological risk and uncertainty over the outlook for alternative energy costs eliminate most third-party financing. Its own balance sheet will not permit the manufacturer to finance the sale of its products.

Financing
Limited partnership interests are offered in a partnership established to own windpower plants and sell the electricity generated to the local public utility. The manufacturer installs, manages, and maintains the

windpower purchased by the partnership from the proceeds of the partnership offering plus some debt financing. The company is compensated for the services it provides to the partnership by a royalty on the partnership's gross revenues from the sale of electricity.

Left hand feature

The utility gets a new source of purchased power without a capital commitment through its willingness to absorb all power generated by the windmills. The utility's ability to adjust the output from its owned assets gives it the needed flexibility. The windmill manufacturer succeeds in expanding its sales to the electric utility market. It sells its product but helps assume the responsibility for its success retaining the right to operate the plant and recovering part of the revenue as a fee.

Film Partnership

Need

A film production company finds that the expansion of its business is constrained by escalating production costs, limitations on additional leverage, and difficulty in selling its equity at a price that is fair to current shareholders.

Financing

A partnership is established to participate in a joint venture with the film company for the production, ownership, and exploitation of a number of films. The company agrees that the joint venture will have the right to produce and exploit each film meeting certain criteria that the company intends to produce. The joint venture exercises that right until it has spent a fixed amount on film production. The partnership funds its share of the joint venture's commitment from the proceeds of a public offering of limited partnership interests and additional borrowing up to a fixed proportion of the capital contributions of limited partners. Once the joint venture undertakes to produce a specific film, it engages the film company to complete and deliver the film at a price equal to the direct costs plus an allowance for overhead. The distribution of completed films is managed under a further agreement between the joint venture and the film company.

Left hand feature

The film production company is able to maintain and expand its film production and distribution activities despite escalating production costs and balance sheet constraints.

The investors have the opportunity to acquire direct ownership interests in a number of films produced and distributed by an established motion-picture studio. They receive the portion of aggregate revenues from their films similar to that generated by a film studio. In addition, the partnership generates tax losses in the early years that enable the investors to deduct from their taxable income a substantial proportion of their investment in the partnership.

SELECTING THE ALTERNATIVE

A corporation considering left hand financing alternatives can study their effect on the corporation under different economic scenarios and develop an appropriate mix of these alternatives with conventional right hand financings. Computer models are useful tools for such an exercise. They can be used to compare the effects of letting investors have ownership interests in assets versus issuing additional debt and common stock under various assumptions. The alternatives alone can be modeled or reflected in a model of the corporation since varying economic assumptions would affect many elements of revenue and cost.

We have described the economic background that has been the driving force for the emergence of left hand financings. The new field has been defined, and the ingredients and some illustrations have been set forth. Left hand financing is by far the most significant new development in corporate finance in the 20th century. It rivals in significance the public markets in stocks and bonds that emerged in the 19th century. The chief financial officer of a growth-minded asset-intensive corporation must stay current with the most favorable alternatives that draw their strength from the left hand side as well as the right hand side of the balance sheet.

CHAPTER 2

Examples of Left Hand Financings

MATTHIAS B. BOWMAN
R. DOUGLAS CARLETON
KEVAN V. WATTS
Merrill Lynch White Weld Capital Markets Group

INTRODUCTION

In the previous chapter, the attributes and origins of the newly emerging field of corporate finance, referred to as left hand financing, are discussed. The discussion in Chapter 1 draws upon hypothetical examples in order to demonstrate the concepts involved. The purpose of this chapter is to provide the reader with actual examples of left hand financings that have occurred in the last few years.

No one area of business can claim preeminence in the development of left hand financing techniques. The concept has evolved in businesses ranging from established real estate development companies to start-up computer manufacturing operations. Further, no one legal structure has dominated the field. The techniques used include partnerships, trusts, common stock corporations, and specially constructed debt instruments. Perhaps of greatest significance, the use of left hand financing techniques has not been limited to corporations of any single credit standing. Corporations with high credit ratings as well as corporations with low credit ratings have found it desirable to undertake left hand financings for a variety of reasons. In some cases, the underlying reason for using the financing techniques is to simply raise cash without expanding the company's capitalization. Often, the motivation behind the financing method goes deeper and includes such objectives as changing the corporation's mix of businesses or changing the risk profile of one or more of its businesses.

The most significant examples of left hand financings can be roughly divided into the following six categories:

1. Leasing/asset management.
2. Oil and gas.
3. Commodities.
4. Real estate.
5. Research and development.
6. Project financing.

While there are some conceptual overlaps in the above categories (e.g., a timber-related financing may be viewed as a project financing or a real estate transaction or even, depending on its structure, a commodity-related transaction), the categories provide a convenient method for cataloging the financings which will be discussed here.

LEASING/ASSET MANAGEMENT

In recent years, a number of left hand financings have involved leasing and/or asset management structures. These financings have usually involved either private or public offerings of partnership interests in some kind of durable equipment, most commonly transportation equipment, such as barges, railcars, helicopters, or buses. Most of the financings have involved new equipment, with the result that a significant portion of the yield to the investor has been in the form of tax benefits. A few of these financings have involved used equipment, where most of the yield to the investor has been in the form of cash. From the standpoint of the investor, investment in hard assets, whether new or used, provides a significant hedge against inflation.

In this section, we will discuss two examples of left hand financing that fall into the leasing/asset management category. The first, North American Railcar Partners, Ltd., 1981-I, involved a predetermined and discrete pool of used railcars, while the second, MLL Equipment Investors-I, involved a highly diversified "blind pool" of new equipment.

North American Railcar Partners, Ltd., 1981-I

General description
Beginning in March 1981 and ending in July 1981, approximately 9,210 limited partnership interests in North American Railcar Partners, Ltd., 1981-I, were sold to investors. The purpose of the partnership was to purchase from North American Car Corporation (NAC) a fleet of approximately 1,000 used tank and covered hopper cars and the leases to which the cars were subject. NAC, a Delaware corporation whose

principal office is located in Chicago, furnishes and provides services with respect to specialized types of railcars for industrial companies in the United States, Canada, Mexico, and Western Europe. NAC is the third largest lessor of privately owned, managed railcars in the world, and in 1981 it controlled a fleet of approximately 60,000 railcars.

Traditionally, NAC has owned the railcars which it leases to its shipping customers. It has generally financed the acquisition of these railcars through the issuance of equipment trust certificates or other types of indebtedness.

In the late 1970s, NAC began to enter into a number of left hand financings which involved predominantly new railcars. These financings involved an outside investor who purchased new railcars which were then managed by NAC as a part of its fleet.

The North American Railcar Partners transaction, which entailed selling to an investor partnership cars already in NAC's fleet, was a logical continuation of NAC's strategy of moving away from direct ownership of its managed cars. The covered hopper cars purchased by the partnership carried grain fertilizer and other dry products, while the tank cars carried corn syrup, petroleum products, and other nonexplicit commodities. NAC warranted that all the cars would be in a condition suitable for railroad interchange service except for certain incidental repairs to be made at no cost to the partnership. All the cars were sold "as is where is," with NAC representing that the cars had been maintained like other railcars in NAC's fleet and in accordance with NAC's customary maintenance policies and procedures. The partnership paid NAC approximately $16,557,000 for the cars and the leases, which was a cost significantly less than the fair market value of the cars established by an independent appraiser. Approximately 53 percent of the purchase price of the cars and the leases was financed through an institutional lender.

The partnership entered into a management agreement under which NAC is to act as the partnership's manager for purposes of initiating new leases for the cars, collecting rents from the lessees, arranging for maintenance of the cars, paying state taxes, acquiring insurance, and handling certain administrative responsibilities. Also, as part of the management agreement, NAC is to arrange for the sale of the cars, supervise repair of damaged cars, arrange for collection of lessee railroad indemnity insurance proceeds, and generally provide services necessary to the leasing and eventual disposition of the cars. An essential element of the transaction is the requirement that NAC apply to the partnership's cars the same standards as those it applies in the management of its own railcars. The management agreement will be in force until the termination of the last lease in effect at the end of its 15th year, but it could be ended earlier depending on certain events or extended in 5-year increments up to an additional 15 years. Further, the management agreement is terminable, among other things, (*a*) with respect to any car upon the sale or destruction of the car; (*b*) by one party if the other party materially breaches the management agreement; and (*c*) by the partnership if certain minimum operating income levels are not met.

NAC is to receive a management fee equal to 7½ percent of the rentals earned on the cars and an incentive management fee equal to 50 percent of the extent to which operating income from the cars exceeds specified base levels. In addition, if the operating income falls below the base levels, NAC is required to repay the partnership 50 percent of the deficiency from its management fee.

During the term of the management agreement and for six months thereafter, NAC will have exclusive right of sale with respect to any or all of the railcars (if the partnership elects to sell) and will receive a sales commission equal to the then prevailing fair market value of such services, determined as set forth in the management agreement. Under certain circumstances, NAC has a right to purchase the cars at the higher of fair market value or the highest bona fide independent offer for the cars.

The cars that NAC sold to the partnership were selected according to general guidelines arrived at in negotiations between the investment banker and NAC. These guidelines specified the number and general car type, age, lease expiration date, and type of service to which the cars were assigned. After taking these factors into consideration, the cars were selected in a random manner from NAC's fleet. As a result, they tended to approximate the composition of NAC's fleet within the above guidelines.

As part of NAC's fleet, the cars were leased at the time of the financing and were to continue to be leased to major U.S. industrial companies in the agricultural, food, chemical, and petroleum industries. The expiration dates of the leases varied considerably, some extending as far as seven years into the future. Further, the cars had widely varying ages in order to provide a good cross section of NAC's portfolio and reduce the risk of owning all cars of a single age.

Advantages to NAC

From the point of view of NAC, the transaction can be viewed on a number of different levels. First, on the most basic level, it can be viewed as a financing method to raise capital. Second, it can be viewed as a method to increase NAC's return on its capital. By selling the cars to the partnership but continuing to earn a management fee on the operations, NAC will experience a significantly higher return on the remaining small amount of capital which it has invested with respect to these railcars. Consequently, NAC's overall return on capital should be increased. Third, the transaction can be viewed as a means of increasing the number of cars under NAC's management and thereby obtaining economies of scale. Sale of these cars frees capital which can be used for additions to NAC's fleet. A larger fleet may be managed with relatively modest increases in the size of NAC's management and in the systems which it has developed to track and control railcar maintenance, leasing, and usage. Fourth, the transaction can be viewed as a strategic move by NAC to change its mix of businesses. NAC can be regarded as participating in two businesses—the ownership of railcars and the management of railcars. The financing allows NAC to shift its business focus toward the management of railcars.

Left hand features
The NAC transaction is a good example of an equity-related left hand financing. NAC had a need to raise capital in order to expand its operations. Rather than attempting to increase the right hand side of its balance sheet, that is its capitalization, NAC elected to exploit the economic value of the assets reflected on the left hand side of its balance sheet. While NAC is obligated to manage the cars owned by the partnership, this obligation does not constitute a financial obligation, and hence NAC's overall balance sheet has been strengthened by the financing. Further, the assets were used as security to raise debt financing nonrecourse to NAC, another common element of left hand financings.

The investors are able to participate in an investment that produces an attractive cash return but also has two significant inflation-hedging characteristics. First, when the lease on any particular car is renegotiated, approximately every five years, the renewal lease rates tend to increase in line with the prevailing lease rates. Prevailing lease rates generally reflect the cost of new cars, which is in turn dependent on the cost of labor and steel. Second, the investors will have the benefit of the car's residual value when the cars are sold at the end of the 15-year management agreement.

Risk elements
Like many other left hand financings and consistent with the greater upside return that investors may realize, this investment exposes investors to different elements of risk than would an investment in fixed-income securities or equities. The investors in North American Railcar Partners are exposed to the following risks:

1. *Demand for railcars.* The profitability of the investment depends on the extent to which the railcars are leased and can be re-leased at favorable rates. The ability to re-lease the cars may be affected by a myriad of economic and business factors, including general economic conditions, the supply of and demand for railcars generally, the supply of fuel, increases in maintenance costs, and conditions affecting the supply of and

demand for the commodities normally transported by such cars.

2. *Residual value.* The ultimate cash return from the investment depends partly on the residual value of the cars at the time of sale. This will be affected by such factors as the cost of new railcars, the condition of the cars, the supply of and demand for similar types of railcars, and developments in transportation technology.

3. *Leverage.* Since the partnership financed a portion of the purchase price of the cars with borrowed funds, the sensitivity of the yield on the investment to adverse developments is increased.

4. *Capital additions.* The ownership of railcars is subject to extensive regulation by governmental authorities which from time to time issue orders requiring modification of or capital improvements to railcars. The investors, as owners of railcars, may be required to produce additional funds to cover these costs.

5. *Casualty losses.* Railcars are subject to the risk of casualty losses. There can be no assurance that insurance proceeds will be adequate to repair or replace cars which suffer such casualties.

6. *Competition.* The railcar leasing industry experiences competition from alternative transportation sources, including the trucking, barge, maritime, and pipeline industries. Further, the partnership will face competition from railcars of the same type owned by other lessors, including NAC itself. This introduces a potential conflict of interest not uncommon in left hand financings.

MLL Equipment Investors-I

General description

The second example of left hand financing that falls into the leasing/asset management category is an offering of limited partnership interests. MLL Equipment Investors differs from North American Railcar Partners in several significant aspects, and in some ways it must be considered a newer development in the evolution of left hand financing. For example, the partnership is designed to own a variety of new equipment which has not been specified or identified at the time of the offering and will be leased to a wide range of lessees who will either use the equipment themselves or will manage it and sublease it to others. It is similar to North American Railcar Partners in that it represents a type of left hand financing for the users or managers of the equipment. However, instead of representing the financing of a single company, it originated with an intermediary financial institution and enables a number of companies to obtain left hand financing in relatively small amounts. Because of the relatively small size of each of their participations, the companies would be unlikely to undertake this kind of public left hand financing on their own.

From the point of view of the investor, the investment provides the opportunity to participate in the returns from leasing a variety of equipment to a variety of lessees. The partnership has been structured to give investors the benefit of depreciation deductions and investment tax credits, but these tax advantages are not expected to be essential for a satisfactory return. The offering is for a maximum of $25 million in 25,000 limited partnership interest units which will provide approximately $21.2 million for equipment purchases after the deduction of public offering expenses, equipment acquisition fees and expenses, and the necessary working capital reserve. The terms of the offering leave open the possibility of leveraging the partnership's interest subsequently up to a maximum of half the aggregate equipment acquisition cost.

The partnership plans to acquire an inventory of equipment falling into the following categories:

a. Transportation equipment, including railroad rolling stock, corporate or commercial helicopters or aircraft, tractors and trailers, intercity buses, and intermodal containers and chassis.
b. Production, extraction, generating, and office machinery and equipment ranging from drilling rigs and cranes to machine tools and photocopying equipment.
c. Miscellaneous equipment and property, the acquisition of which would normally entitle the partners to claim investment tax credits.

The sole limitations on the types of equipment that may be purchased are that computers may only be purchased for direct financing leases (to safeguard against the probability of low residual values) and that investments in any one type of equipment are restricted to $10 million. Within this broad range of possible purchases, the partnership plans to concentrate on equipment which is expected either to have a long, useful life and continuing value for operation or sale or to have a high level of current revenues. As a noncorporate lessor, the partnership will need to structure its leases to meet specific criteria in order to entitle the partners to depreciation deductions and investment tax credits. Consequently, many of the leases will be for a term less than one half of the present ADR midpoint life of the equipment and will require the partnership to pay ordinary and necessary expenses relating to the equipment in an amount of at least 15 percent of the gross rentals. This means that the partners will be more exposed to the uncertainty of realizing the residual value of the leased equipment than they would be if the partnership concentrated on long-term "net" leases. The focus on equipment with a long useful life is intended to reduce this risk.

Initially, the partnership will finance all its equipment purchases from capital contributions. However, if interest rates fall and more favorable borrowing possibilities emerge, the general partner may borrow funds on the security of the partnership's initial equipment inventory. If this recapitalization occurs within the first two years of the partnership's life, it is likely that the borrowing will be used to finance additional equipment purchases. While no borrowing limit has been set on any particular item of equipment, it is intended that any aggregate borrowings undertaken will not exceed 50 percent of the total cost of all equipment bought by the partnership. If the recapitalization occurs after the first two years, the proceeds will be distributed to the partners as a return of capital.

The partnership may both lease equipment and operate equipment to perform services for others. In both cases, it will act through agreements with operators or managers retained by the partnership. The equipment managers will typically be third parties, but affiliates of the general partner are not precluded from acting in this role.

It is intended that the partnership will make regular quarterly distributions of cash from operations and that, as a consequence of depreciation deductions and investment tax credit, the taxable income from these distributions will be less than the taxable income from cash distributions. The general partner's capital contribution will be 1 percent of the partnership's total capitalization, but cash from operations (and profits and losses) will generally be divided between the limited partners and the general partner on the basis of 98 percent and 2 percent shares, respectively, after the deduction of a 5 percent partnership management fee payable to the general partner. Proceeds from the sale of equipment (or any loan financing raised in substitution for limited partners' capital) will be distributed on a similar basis except that the general partner has a subordinated incentive interest in such proceeds. This comes into effect when the limited partners have received cash from operations (or from the sale of equipment or refinancing) together with an investment tax credit not subject to recapture, equal to their original capital contributions plus an aggregate return of 10 percent per year, cumulative but not compounded. Thereafter, distributable sale or refinancing proceeds will be divided 85 percent to the limited partners and 15 percent to the general partner, after the payment at that stage of sales commissions to the general partner not exceeding 5 percent of the gross sales price of the equipment.

Distributions of cash (and allocations of profits and losses) among the limited partners will be determined on the basis of their individual proportionate shares in the total limited partnership interests outstanding.

In addition to the partnership management fee, the general partner's partnership interest in distributable cash, and the sales commission payable to the general partner, ML Leasing Partners, Inc. (the general partner and a subsidiary of Merrill Lynch Leasing, Inc.), will also be entitled to certain acquisition fees and reimbursement of actual out-of-pocket organizational, offering, acquisition, and management expenses.

Since there is no provision for the partnership to make any equipment purchases after the first two years, these distribution arrangements ensure that the partnership will be self-liquidating.

Left hand features

The left hand financing features of MLL Equipment Investors are similar in many respects to those of North American Railcar Partners. Capital is provided to the participating corporations based on assets which they are managing. There is also an intent to raise debt financing which will be nonrecourse to the corporations and will be used to leverage the equity funds supplied by investors.

As is often the case with left hand financings, the investors will enjoy direct ownership of assets with several inflation-hedging characteristics. The partnership's leases will not in general be long-term "net" leases, and accordingly the rentals received on individual items of equipment will not typically be fixed for their useful life. In addition, the residual value of the partnership's equipment will reflect price increases arising during the partnership's ownership of the equipment.

There are a number of differences between MLL Equipment Investors and North American Railcar Partners, which, as already suggested, establish MLL Equipment Investors as a newer and more flexible form of left hand financing. These differences include the following:

1. MLL Equipment Investors represents a left hand financing for a number of companies yet to be identified, that is, the operators of the equipment owned by the partnership. North American Railcar Partners is a left hand financing for one corporation.

2. The equipment owned by MLL Equipment Investors will be determined by investment decisions yet to be made by the general partner, whereas the North American Railcar transaction involves a fixed group of assets.

3. The funding of the partnership in the MLL Equipment Investors transaction in advance of equipment decisions increases the flexibility of the vehicle in two respects:

    a. It enables relatively small pieces of equipment to be purchased and leased in a cost-effective manner.

      b. It enables the partnership to rapidly fund attractive equipment investment opportunities.

Risk elements
Like the limited partners in North American Railcar Partners, the limited partners in MLL Equipment Investors-I will face risks different from those typically arising in conventional debt and equity securities. First, they will be subject to the usual business risks arising from owning and operating equipment, in particular, the possibility that the partnership will be unable to keep the equipment fully leased at rentals that provide an acceptable return after the deduction of operating expenses. The partnership has been structured to reduce this risk by providing the general partner with considerable flexibility over the choice of the equipment to be purchased. However, all the investments must be made within a two-year period, so that whatever range of equipment is selected, there will remain a risk that the partnership may find its equipment obsolete before an economic return has been achieved.

    Second, the limited partners face the risk that the tax advantages will not materialize if the IRS successfully challenges some part or all of the basis for the limited partners' entitlement to depreciation deductions and investment tax credits. The partnership meets this risk by not relying on these benefits to generate an acceptable return on the limited partners' investment.

    Third, the general partner is given considerable freedom to manage the partnership's affairs, which is necessary for practical reasons but could lead to conflicts of interest because of the general partner's affiliation with other companies active in the same field.

OIL AND GAS

Not surprisingly, the oil and gas development and exploration industry has developed its own peculiar forms of left hand financing, the most outstanding examples of which have used a royalty trust type of ownership and investment structure. The royalty trust mechanism itself dates back to the 1950s, but originally royalty trusts were established for the benefit of existing shareholders and were not used to expand the sponsoring corporation's activities. Royalty-producing assets were transferred to a trust, and interests in the trust were distributed to shareholders as a form of dividend. Only in recent years has the structure been used as a means of left hand financing. The following example demonstrates the use of the royalty trust as a means of raising capital in the public market rather than as a means of distributing ownership to shareholders.

Houston Oil Royalty Trust

General description

In April 1980, underwriters offered 2.4 million units of beneficial interest in an oil royalty trust at $25 a unit. Houston Oil & Minerals Corporation received the proceeds of the offering ($60 million gross, $56 million net), and the trust itself acquired an interest in overriding royalties in both productive and exploratory oil and gas properties in which the company had a working interest. The properties were chosen both to give investors income out of current production from proven reserves and to enable them to participate in the returns from future exploratory wells of the company. The trust itself was structured as a grantor trust so that the investors would be treated for federal income tax purposes as if they owned the assets of the trust directly. This means that investors will be entitled to depletion deductions and any abandonment losses.

Houston Oil & Minerals Corporation benefited by being able to reduce its outstanding long-term debt by 15 percent while only surrendering ownership to a much smaller percent of its total proven oil and gas reserves at the end of 1979. Thus, the transaction was a means of exploiting the economic value of the company's proven reserves, value not fully reflected in its balance sheet, where oil and gas properties owned by the company are recorded at the historic cost of acquisition, exploration, and development.

The royalties in which the trust acquired an interest relate to 12 productive and 40 exploratory properties and constitute percentage interests in the gross production of oil and gas therefrom, free of the expense of drilling, completion, development, and other operating costs. Assuming 8 percent annual price and cost increases, the trust's projected revenue from the productive properties had at the time of the offering a discounted present value of $50 million using a 10 percent per annum discount rate. In cash terms, the projected revenue from the productive properties should equal approximately 1½ times the aggregate public offering price for the units.

The royalties on the productive properties were calculated to produce estimated revenue for the trust equal to certain percentages of the company's estimated net revenue from the properties. The percentage was 5.5 percent initially, rising to 12 percent in 1982, 15 percent in 1983, and finally to 16 percent in 1984 and for the remaining economic life of the properties. The royalties on the exploratory properties were fixed at 3 percent of the company's net revenue interest in these properties on February 22, 1980.

In order to give cash and accrual taxpayer similar tax treatment and to avoid excessive administrative costs, title to the overriding royalty interests is held by a partnership in which the trust has a 99 percent share and the company has 1 percent. The partnership will recognize income for federal income tax purposes on the date of receipt of payment. Distributions of income are made monthly.

It is anticipated that neither the trust nor the partnership will be treated for tax purposes as an association taxable as a corporation and that the trust will be regarded as a grantor trust. This means that the unit holders should be treated for federal income tax purposes as if they owned the assets of the trust directly. As a consequence, unit holders will be entitled to depletion deductions and any abandonment losses with regard to the exploratory properties.

The aggregate offering price of $60 million was determined by taking account of the following factors:

1. Independent estimates of proven reserves and future net revenues on the productive properties.
2. Evaluation by the company of the potential for the discovery of reserves on the exploratory properties.
3. The expertise of the company in the exploration, development, and operation of oil and gas properties.
4. The tax treatment of unit holder.
5. The future prospects for appreciation in the value of oil and gas reserves.

Left hand features

The Houston Oil Royalty Trust is a true example of an equity-related left hand financing. The sponsoring corporation had a need for additional capital to finance expansion and was able to raise this competitively by exploiting the economic value of its principal assets. The units of beneficial interest in the trust do not represent any obligation of the company, and hence the financing results in a strengthened balance sheet.

The investors have the advantage of an effective floor to their downside risk through the inclusion of productive properties in the royalty base. The upside, and hence the hedge against inflation, is provided through the exploratory properties.

Risk elements

Like investors in other left hand financings, the investors are exposed to more direct risks than would generally be the case for investors in fixed-income securities and equities. In particular, in the Houston Oil Royalty Trust, the following risks arise:

a. Risks inherent in the exploration for, and production of, oil and gas.
b. Uncertainties inherent in estimates of oil and gas reserves.

c. The effect of government regulation and legislation in this area.
d. The possibility that the tax treatment of unit holders might vary from the company's expectations.
e. The absence of any contractual obligation on the company to develop the exploratory properties.
f. The operation of "nonconsent" provisions in operating agreements which may reduce revenues.
g. Potential conflicts of interest between the company and the trust in the exploration and development of the properties.
h. Potential exposure of the unit holders to the possibility that they might be held liable under Texas law for the obligations of the trust.

COMMODITIES

One of the most interesting recent developments in left hand financing has been the creation of securities whose return is in some way dependent on the future value of a specific kind of commodity. The commodities most often used have been gold, silver, and oil. Recent examples include Mexican oil bonds that were brought to market in 1980 and an Ecco Bay Mines offering in the fall of 1981 of units consisting of one preferred stock share and four warrants to purchase gold produced at Ecco Bay's Lubin Mine near the Arctic Circle. The warrants entitle the holders to purchase gold at a fixed price for a period of three years beginning in 1986. For purposes of this chapter, we shall focus on yet another example, an offering of silver-indexed bonds by Sunshine Mining Company in 1980.

Sunshine Mining Company—Silver-Indexed Bonds

General description

Sunshine Mining Company made two separate offerings of 8½ percent silver-indexed bonds in 1980. The first issue was originally filed as a $50 million offering payable at maturity or redemption at the greater of $1,000 per bond or a specified average market price of a predetermined number of ounces of silver. With the price of silver soaring at the time, initial demand was high, and the issue was raised to $100 million. However, the SEC required considerable time to review the registration statement, and before the registration became effective, the price of silver plummeted. Consequently, the final offering on April 11, 1980, was reduced to $25 million, although $30 million of the bonds were eventually sold. At the pricing, Sunshine valued the silver at $20 an ounce (compared to the then current spot price of $16 an ounce), so that each $1,000 bond was backed with 50 ounces of silver.

In December 1980, the company offered a further $25 million on a similar basis—a coupon of 8½ percent, a final maturity of 15 years, payable at the greater of $1,000 or the value of 50 ounces of silver. At the time of this second offering, the spot price for silver was $14.81 an ounce, so that the terms for the second issue were rather more aggressive. The silver price implicit in the offering represented a 35 percent premium over the market price compared with the 25 percent premium for the first transaction.

Advantages for Sunshine Mining

In 1979, Sunshine Mining Company adopted a new business plan intended to transform the company from a conglomerate into an integrated precious metals company with primary emphasis on silver. This required new capital to finance increased exploration, development, and acquisition of mining properties; accelerating expansion of the company's existing production capacity; and developing and constructing a precious metals refinery. Some funds were realized on a gain arising from the disposal of discontinued oil and gas operations, but Sunshine needed additional external financing.

At the beginning of 1980, the company's capital consisted entirely of stockholders' equity, so that there was no immediate inhibition on leveraging the company's capitalization. However, the planned concentration on silver, which was intended to exploit more effectively Sunshine's management capabilities and resources in this area, increased the likelihood that the company's future results would be influenced significantly by the market price of silver. From this standpoint, the silver-indexed bonds had two major advantages for Sunshine Mining Company. First, by offering investors the possibility of substantial capital gains through the link with silver prices, the company was able to issue bonds with a significantly lower coupon than would otherwise have been available. Second, by using silver rather than some other commodity as the inflation hedge, Sunshine was able to avoid exposing itself to increases in the effective cost of its debt that would not be reflected in corresponding increases in its earnings. So long as the company was able to use the proceeds of each bond to produce more than 50 ounces of silver, the linkage to silver could be hedged within the company in the course of its usual operations.

Detailed terms

Some more details on the terms of the issues must be given to explain fully how the bonds are related to silver prices. For this purpose, the terms of the second issue will be described.

The value of each $1,000 face amount bond is fixed at the greater of $1,000 or a specified average of the market price of 50 ounces of silver (the "indexed principal amount"). The company has the option of calling the bonds at the indexed principal amount at any time after

5 years if that amount exceeds $2,000 for a period of at least 30 consecutive calendar days. In addition, a sinking fund will begin to operate two years from the issuing date. Under this, the company will retire at least 7 percent per annum of the original issue less any bonds retired by the company other than through the operation of the sinking fund. The bond indenture gives Sunshine the option of meeting its obligations with respect to the sinking fund, or at redemption or maturity, by delivering silver in the event that the indexed principal amount exceeds $1,000 plus an amount of money equal to accrued interest. This option is, however, subject to the right of each bondholder to elect to receive cash rather than silver, and the bondholder also has the right to elect not to have his bonds redeemed if called before final maturity.

In addition to the use of silver in the repayment provisions, the bonds are also secured by a continuing mortgage and security interest on the company's interest in the Sunshine Mine. The company owns interests in various areas of this mine, all amounting to at least 50 percent of the total interests and rights to production. The Sunshine Mine itself is the largest primarily silver-producing mine in the United States, and its interests therein represent the company's principal holding. The mortgage relates to 3.627 percent of the gross annual mining production at the Sunshine Mine without charge to the trustee or bondholders of any related mining and production expenses. This is subject to a ceiling in any one year, broadly amounting to the total number of ounces of silver represented by all outstanding bonds on the acceleration date, divided by the number of years remaining to final maturity of the bonds. The bonds are subordinated to all senior indebtedness to the extent that this collateral is insufficient to satisfy the company's obligations.

The indenture places no restrictions on the creation of senior indebtedness, but it does limit the company's issue of new silver-related securities. After any such issue, the company's proven, probable, and economically recoverable reserves of silver must be equal to at least 500 percent of the total number of ounces of silver required by all the company's silver-related securities. In addition, the company must maintain silver reserves equal to at least 400 percent of the total number of ounces of silver represented by its silver-related securities.

Left hand features

Sunshine Mining Company's silver-indexed bonds are a good example of left hand debt financing. They draw their characteristics from silver, the principal asset of the company, and are in fact directly secured by Sunshine's silver reserves. As such, they provide a potential hedge against inflation.

From the point of view of the company, the silver-indexing feature significantly lowers the cost of expanding the company's capitalization.

The company accomplishes this by surrendering some of the appreciation potential of its silver reserves. In this way, the company realizes today some of the benefit from expected future increases in the value of its assets. Further, the company's risk from movements in silver prices is not increased. The reserves provide the company with a hedge that protects it from the additional amounts it must pay to the bondholders.

The bonds vary from many other left hand financings in not drawing their inflation hedge directly from the issuing company's revenue stream. The market price of silver is only one of many factors that will influence Sunshine's future revenues. Even if Sunshine's revenues decline or remain flat, the bondholders might still enjoy a significant gain from an increase in the price of silver. Similarly, Sunshine's revenues may increase dramatically without a significant increase in silver prices.

REAL ESTATE

No area of business can compare with real estate in its proclivity for generating new and different creative financing structures. It is not surprising, therefore, that the real estate industry is replete with examples of left hand financings or of hybrid financings that have some left hand features. One example of left hand financing in the real estate industry is the real estate investment trust (REIT) vehicle structured by Lomas & Nettleton, 2 million common shares of which were offered to the public in the spring of 1981.

L & N Housing Corp.

General description
In May 1981, a group of underwriters offered at $25 a share 2 million shares of common stock of L & N Housing Corp., a recently organized corporation established by Lomas & Nettleton Financial Corporation for the purpose of making investments in multifamily rental projects in the United States. The company was structured to offer an investment vehicle through which substantial individual and institutional investors might invest in residential multifamily rental housing projects on a diversified pool basis. The company's operations have been arranged to provide investors both with regular cash income from fixed-interest mortgage loans and with the possibility of increasing income from the equity participation features of its investments. It is also intended that the company qualify as a real estate investment trust and, accordingly,

that it not be taxed at the corporate level on the net income which it distributes to its stockholders.

L & N plans to invest in multifamily residential rental projects in the United States to be constructed and managed by experienced real estate developers. The projects chosen will typically be located in metropolitan areas where higher than average growth is projected and will be located, designed, constructed, and maintained with a view toward facilitating their eventual sale to owner-occupiers. It is intended that L & N's initial investments will take the form of a 7- to 10-year first-mortgage loan on a project, funded after the completion of construction to avoid any exposure to costs arising from building delays. The loans will provide for monthly interest payments at a fixed rate and for little or no amortization of principal prior to maturity. L & N plans to supplement its mortgage loans with arrangements entitling it to participate in increases in the projects' gross rents and increases in the value of the properties realized through sale or refinancing. These arrangements could take various forms, but their effect will be to treat L & N as though it were the equity owner of a portion of the project

At the time of the offering, it was anticipated that the fixed rate on mortgage loans would be in the range of 11-13 percent per annum. L & N's participation in increases in gross rents were expected to be 20-25 percent of any such increases, with a 40-60 percent share of the increase in the value of the properties on disposition or refinancing. The terms of the company's loans were anticipated to range from 7 to 10 years, with the payment of interest only for a period of from 5 to 7 years.

The prospectus for the offering explained the reasoning behind this investment policy in terms of four basic assumptions:

1. Inflation in the United States is likely to continue during the 1980s at a generally high rate.
2. The price appreciation of housing units in the United States will continue to exceed the general rate of inflation.
3. In areas of above-average economic growth, price appreciation in housing tends to be higher than the national rate.
4. Economic, demographic, and social factors indicate that in the 1980s there will be an increasing need for housing in multi-family residential projects of the type in which the company proposes to invest.

As a part of the investment structure, L & N entered into a management agreement with L & N Housing Managers, Inc., a subsidiary of Lomas & Nettleton, under which L & N Housing Managers will advise L & N on all aspects of its business and administer L & N activities under the supervision of its board of directors. Under this agreement, L & N Housing Managers will bear all costs relating to its investment management services and its day-to-day administration of the company's affairs. L & N itself will meet expenses associated with any use of borrowed funds, architects' fees, and so on. The manager's compensation is structured in terms of a basic annual fee and incentive compensation. The basic annual fee is equal to a percentage of L & N's invested assets—1.25 percent of the portion up to $100 million, falling in stages to 0.75 percent of the portion exceeding $400 million—and this is payable in monthly installments. The incentive compensation arrangements essentially give L & N Housing Managers a share in the company's annual net profits where the average annual net profit from the date of the offering to that time exceeds 12 percent of the company's average net worth for the period. The share is initially set at 10 percent, rises to 15 percent for average profits exceeding 17 percent, and reaches 20 percent for average profits exceeding 22 percent. There is, however, an overall ceiling on management fees equal to the greater of 2 percent of L & N's average net worth or 25 percent of the company's net income.

L & N's investments will originate from an undertaking by Lomas & Nettleton to offer the company a right of first refusal on any mortgage financing projects within the primary investment objectives of the company until the net proceeds of the stock offering have been invested in such projects. This is a significant advantage for L & N, given Lomas & Nettleton's position as the largest mortgage banking firm in the United States.

It is planned that L & N will distribute annually at least 95 percent of its taxable income. Since L & N also intends to qualify for taxation as a real estate investment trust, it should not generally be subject to federal corporate income taxes.

Left hand features

From the standpoint of the sponsoring corporation, this transaction is similar to the leasing/asset management deals described earlier. Lomas & Nettleton is able to expand its real estate financing operations through this REIT without any need for additional capital. For the owner/developer of an apartment project, some of the appreciation potential of ownership is given up for lower cost debt.

From the investors' standpoint, L & N has an interesting mixture of debt and equity features. The investors enjoy both a fixed-income form of return through the mortgage loans and the possibility of a hedge against inflation through participation in increases in rentals and property values.

RESEARCH AND DEVELOPMENT

Left hand financing has most often been used to finance the acquisition of new property, as with the real estate example just described, or to realize a portion of the value of assets already owned by the corporation, as with the Houston Oil Royalty Trust. A relatively recent phenomenon has been the use of left hand financing to fund an R&D program in connection with a start-up corporation or with a new product development effort in an existing corporation. Development of the Lear Fan Aircraft was in part financed through R&D left hand financing, as was some of the development effort for the new DeLorean automobile.

A recent example of R&D left hand financing was initiated by a well-known computer expert, Gene Amdahl, in order to fund the initial R&D efforts of Amdahl's new computer company, Trilogy.

Trilogy Computer Development Partners, Ltd.

General description

Trilogy Computer Development Partners, Ltd., was formed to conduct research and development for the design of a large-scale, high-performance, IBM-compatible, general-purpose computer system. The partnership will attempt to license the computer design, if developed, and will receive royalties under such license from the sale of computer systems incorporating the design. In August 1981, 11,000 units of limited partnership interest with a total value of $55 million were offered, and the offering was oversubscribed. The general partner is Trilogy Systems, a subsidiary of Gene Amdahl's Bermuda holding company, Trilogy Limited.

It is generally estimated that approximately 70 to 80 percent of the current installed base of large-scale, high-performance, general-purpose computer systems are IBM or IBM-compatible. There is therefore a strong economic incentive for users to acquire improved systems that are compatible with this installed base. The primary objective of the partnership's R&D is to develop new technology which is IBM-compatible but is also superior to existing technology in certain performance aspects.

The models in the targeted market segment currently have processing power in a uniprocessor mode over a broad range of applications of approximately 4 to 10 million instructions per second. Recent product announcements indicate that the next generation of models will have a range of 10 to 15 million instructions per second, whereas in 1975, the typical range was 1 to 4 million instructions per second. Against the background of this rapid increase in performance ranges, the partnership's computer design will need to perform substantially better than products now on the market for it to be competitive in 1984, the earliest date by which the project can be completed.

The key to the development project is the general partner's belief that the main technological problem restricting the growth of these computers's performance arises from signal transmission time within the computer logic system. The intention is to reduce signal transmission time by achieving much higher levels of integration.

To this end, the partnership will first attempt to achieve limited volume production capability for semiconductors permitting significant advances in the state of the art relating to very large scale integrated circuits. For this purpose, the partnership has acquired from Trilogy Limited a royalty-free license to use certain semiconductor technology owned by it. It will then endeavor to use semiconductors incorporating this technology to execute a detailed system design which uses the advanced circuits in complex logic structures. The final stage of the project will involve the refinement and debugging of one or more engineering prototype models.

The net offering proceeds of the limited partnership interests amounted to approximately $50.5 million. The general partner contributed 1 percent of the partnership's total capital, so that initially about $51 million was available to finance the development program. Expenditure is expected to be incurred over the period to 1984, with most of the expenses falling in 1982 and 1983. Allowing for interest earnings on unspent capital, over the period to 1984, the partnership should be able to provide $64.5 million for costs arising under the development program.

These costs will arise almost entirely under the terms of a development contract between the partnership and the general partner as contractor to carry out the research and development project. Under this contract, Trilogy Systems will be reimbursed only for actual costs incurred prior to successful completion of the project. If the computer design is successfully developed, Trilogy Systems will be entitled to a profit equal to the difference between the total funds available to the partnership and the costs incurred but not in excess of 15 percent of those costs. The funds available to the partnership are expected to be sufficient to develop the computer design. If this does not prove to be the case, the general partner can either seek additional voluntary capital contributions from the limited partners or borrow funds on behalf of the partnership from third-party lenders.

Upon completing a successful design, Trilogy Limited will have an exclusive option to acquire a license for $250,000 for the purpose of exploiting the design commercially. The option becomes exercisable one year and one day after the partnership reduces the computer design to practice. This delay is necessary to increase the likelihood that the royalties payable under the license agreement will be taxed as capital gains in the hands of the partners. Royalty payments, which will be made annually, will be allocated 99 percent to the limited partners and 1 percent to the general partner. The limited partners' share of the royalty payments will amount to 7.7 percent of revenues from the sale, lease, or other disposition by Trilogy Limited of products incorporating any portion of the design, up to a total of $110 million. Thereafter, the limited partners will receive 3.3 percent of such revenues or 11 percent of the pretax profits of Trilogy Limited, whichever is greater. In lieu of paying periodic royalties, Trilogy Limited may acquire the partnership's entire interest in the computer design at any time for a lump-sum payment. The limited partners' share would be the greater of $220 million less gross royalties paid or $110 million. Alternatively, each partner may elect to receive the payment in the form of shares of Trilogy Limited common stock or a combination of stock and cash. A total of 1,718,750 shares is allocable to the limited partners.

The partnership is not primarily a tax-oriented investment vehicle. Certain provisions of the tax laws may, however, afford the partnership favorable treatment of its expenditures and receipts. In particular, it is possible that payment by the partnership to Trilogy Systems under the development contract may be expensed, so that deductions in excess of partnership income could be used to offset limited partners' income from other sources. In addition, a substantial part of any royalty payment may be taxable as a long-term capital gain. The eventual tax treatment is subject to some uncertainty, as there have been few legal cases involving research and development limited partnerships.

Risk elements

Trilogy Computer Development Partners, Ltd., must be regarded as a high-risk investment. The limited partners derive their return from uncertain tax benefits and the possibility of royalty income that cannot begin before 1985. There can be no assurance that Trilogy Systems, the general partner, will be successful in developing a competitive computer design within the planned schedule and without the need for further finance. Moreover, Trilogy Systems itself is not an established corporation and is heavily dependent on a few key persons, notably Gene Amdahl and his son, Carlton Amdahl. Even if the development program is successfully completed, it is possible that Trilogy Limited will not exercise its option to market the design commercially, in which case the partnership would have to take other steps to secure a return on its investment. The limited partners will necessarily be dependent on the general partner for managing the partnership. This could lead to conflicts of interest in view of the general partner's role as contractor under the development contract and the affiliation of Trilogy Systems with the holder of the option to market any developed design. Finally, the partnership interests will only be transferable subject to various restrictions and it is not anticipated that any public market for the units will develop.

Left hand features

The R&D partnership, although relatively unique in the world of finance, clearly fits the mold of left hand financing. The Trilogy partnership draws its investment characteristics from the asset side of Trilogy Limited's balance sheet in that the partners are receiving a royalty-free license to use certain semiconductor technology owned by Trilogy Limited. Further, by virtue of the partnership undertaking to develop the technology, the financing avoids the need to expand Trilogy Limited's capitalization.

The limited partners may earn extremely attractive returns on their interests if the development of the computer design and its commercial exploitation are realized and if favorable tax treatment of expenses and income is forthcoming. The success of the offering is probably attributable to the rare opportunity it gives individual investors to participate directly in the returns achievable as a result of technological advances. This direct ownership is a typical feature of left hand equity financings.

In some ways, the appeal of the partnership to investors is similar to that of other left hand financings already discussed. Accepting different risks for potential returns with inflation hedge characteristics is encouraged by the uncertainty of real returns available elsewhere due to the unpredictability of future rates of inflation.

PROJECT FINANCING

The final type of left hand financing that we have chosen to discuss is project financing. Project financing must be considered a classic form of left hand financing for several reasons. First, almost by definition, it draws its investment characteristics from the assets in question. Second, as the financing is generally "off-balance sheet," it avoids the need to expand the corporation's capitalization. Finally, project financings almost always involve nonrecourse debt.

One of the most interesting and innovative examples of project financing of which we are aware is the financing for the refuse plant located in Saugus, Massachusetts, which occurred in the mid-1970s.

Refuse Energy Systems Company

General description

Refuse Energy Systems Company (RESCO) was created in 1975 to own and operate the first commercial facility in the United States designed to extract energy from municipal refuse. The plant, located at Saugus, Massachusetts, was designed by Wheelabrator-Frye, Inc., as licensee for Von Roll, Ltd., of Zurich, Switzerland. While new to the United States, such facilities were common in Western Europe and other densely populated areas; more than 50 plants of Von Roll design were in operation when the RESCO facility was constructed.

The impetus for the project arose from two sources: first, the sudden rise in energy costs triggered by the Arab oil embargo had made the latent energy content of municipal waste more valuable; second, increasing urbanization had increased the cost of land used for landfill, the traditional method of disposal, and federal regulations to reduce ground and water pollution caused by landfill operations would cause a further, dramatic cost increase.

The Von Roll system consists essentially of an extremely sturdy moving grate incinerator surrounded by a waterwall boiler. The refuse is incinerated in essentially untreated, as-delivered form. The incineration reduces dramatically the tonnage which must ultimately be landfilled, and the sale of the recovered energy, either in the form of steam or steam-generated electricity, serves to partly offset the operating and capital costs of the plant. The principal remaining source of revenue is the disposal fees paid by private collectors and municipalities delivering waste to the plant. To be commercially viable, these disposal fees must be competitive with the costs of other disposal alternatives in the area, principally landfills.

Wheelabrator-Frye believed that the combination of increasing energy and landfill disposal costs would make systems like the Von Roll design economically feasible in more and more American urban centers in the near future. However, the high capital cost of these plants (the RESCO facility, which could handle the waste generated by a population of approximately 700,000, had a 1975 construction cost of over $38 million) would rapidly outstrip Wheelabrator-Frye's ability to finance additional plants using conventional techniques. A financing technique had to be devised which could be used in successive plants and which would:

1. Minimize the balance sheet impact of plant financing and ownership.
2. Minimize the amount of direct equity investment per plant by Wheelabrator-Frye.
3. Consistent with the first two objectives, minimize the cost of capital raised for each plant.

In the case of RESCO, Wheelabrator-Frye negotiated 20-year disposal contracts with 10 municipalities that collectively produced 6,100 tons of waste per day, or 50 percent of the plant's planned capacity. Other municipalities within the plant's service area generated an additional 2,400 tons per day, from which the remaining plant capacity would be filled by additional short- or long-term contracts. The contracts committed the municipalities to provide a minimum daily tonnage of waste in return for a disposal fee that would be adjusted each year by an inflation escalator. The steam to be generated by the plant was sold to the General Electric Company for use at its plant in nearby Lynn, Massachusetts, under a 15-year contract at a price indexed to GE's cost of fossil fuel.

The combination of long-term contracts covering substantially all of the project's revenues, and a long history of reliable operations by Von Roll plants elsewhere led the investment banker to propose a financing scheme for the project that would rely to a considerable extent on the income-generating power of the project itself rather than the credit-worthiness of Wheelabrator-Frye. The essential elements of the scheme were as follows:

1. RESCO would be owned by a joint venture of a wholly owned subsidiary of Wheelabrator-Frye and M. DeMatteo Constructors, a local company that owned the site on which the plant was built. Each joint venturer would own 50 percent of RESCO. Because Wheelabrator-Frye would not own a majority of RESCO, its ownership interest could be reported on an equity basis, thereby avoiding the weakening of balance sheet ratios that would occur if RESCO and subsequent highly leveraged projects were consolidated on Wheelabrator-Frye's balance sheet. At the same time, the joint venture form of ownership allowed RESCO's parents to make use of the substantial tax benefits, in the form of investment tax credit and depreciation, generated by the project.

2. Upon completion of the financing, RESCO's capitalization would consist of $10 million in equity contributed by the two parents and $30 million in debt. Because of the qualifying nature of RESCO's capital expenditures, the debt could be in the form of long-term tax-exempt revenue bonds issued by the town of Saugus. The lower interest costs associated with tax-exempt debt permitted greater leverage than would have been the case with conventional debt without lowering fixed-charge coverage ratios.

3. The debt would be an obligation of RESCO but not of RESCO's parents. Security for the debt would be RESCO's guarantee, a first-mortgage lien on the facility, and a reserve fund, partly funded from bond proceeds, equal to the next two years' debt service. The final maturity of the bonds would be 20 years, matching the term of the disposal contracts. The "nonrecourse" nature of the debt has two important benefits to Wheelabrator-Frye. First, the reduced capital commitment allows Wheelabrator-Frye to undertake more projects than would otherwise be possible. Second, by reducing the amount of capital considered "at risk" in each project, the profit that a project is required to generate in order to provide a sufficient return on investment may be similarly reduced, thereby making more projects economically attractive.

4. In order to provide an additional source of capital to RESCO, an innovative contract called the "Additional Equity Contributions Agreement" would be entered into by Wheelabrator-Frye (on behalf of both parents) and RESCO, pursuant to which Wheelabrator-Frye would be obligated to make additional investments if RESCO failed to meet certain financial tests. Wheelabrator-Frye's obligation under this agreement is limited by a formula which is intended to represent, as of a given

date, the aftertax value to the owners of RESCO of the cumulative tax credits and net deductions generated by RESCO, reduced by contributions already made and increased by prior distributions of profit to the coventurers. Because of the 10 percent investment tax credit and the very rapid tax depreciation for which the project qualified, the amount represented by this formula is substantial at the outset and grows over time. It also increases as additional capital expenditures are made (or losses incurred) because of the credits and deductions they generate. At the same time, the agreement requires no "net" new investment by Wheelabrator since the formula limits its obligation to the net cash flow generated by its ownership in the project, either in the form of dividends or tax "shelter."

As a result of these security features and in recognition of the long-term disposal and steam sales contracts and the long operating history of similar systems elsewhere, the bonds were given A ratings by both major rating services. A successful public offering was accomplished in August 1975.

Advantages to Wheelabrator-Frye, Inc.

From an accounting point of view, Wheelabrator-Frye was able to reduce the balance sheet impact of a large capital expenditure to the reporting of the company's equity investment in RESCO, a consideration that would be of increasing importance as more projects were undertaken. From a financial point of view, Wheelabrator-Frye was able to raise the major portion of the capital required for the project by exploiting the earning power of the project itself, which allows Wheelabrator to undertake more projects than would be possible if all of the capital had to be raised on its corporate credit.

Left hand features

RESCO is a good example of a true "project financing," wherein certain corporate assets are segregated and their income stream pledged to secure indebtedness incurred to finance the assets themselves. Lenders look to the security provided by the collateral value of the assets and, more important, by the contractual agreements providing income or services to the project. Such contracts are necessarily complicated in that they must anticipate every contingency which might materially affect the economic viability of the project over the length of the financing term. In addition, provision must be made for meeting fixed charges in the event of temporary income shortfalls and for raising additional funds for completion or modifications under circumstances in which third-party lenders would perceive the project to be too risky. In the RESCO case, the long-term disposal and steam sales contracts, reserve funds and the Additional Equity Contributions Agreement were designed to meet these objectives.

PART 2

Tax, Financial Reporting,
Marketing, and Banking
Considerations for
Left Hand Financing

CHAPTER 3

Tax Considerations

WALTER PERLSTEIN
Merrill Lynch Capital Resources Inc.

FRANK J. FABOZZI
Fordham University

In evaluating the opportunities for *left hand financing* discussed in the first two chapters, the chief financial officer should be aware that tax-conscious investors are prepared to enter into risk-taking transactions involving not only the assets now owned by the corporation but those it is to acquire or build in the near future. And these include not only the real estate, plant, and equipment used by manufacturing or commercial enterprises but also the natural resources, timber properties, and hard minerals owned by companies.

Each of these categories of corporate assets is afforded special treatment by the Internal Revenue Code for the express legislative purpose of encouraging capital investment and job creation. With the notable exception of the "safe harbor leases" created by the Economic Recovery Tax Act (ERTA) of 1981 to promote purchases and sales of tax benefits alone, investors are interested in both the economic benefits and the income tax benefits associated with the ownership of physical assets.

The purpose of this chapter is to discuss the tax benefits available under the Internal Revenue Code, the flexibility that the ERTA provides in transferring these tax benefits under certain circumstances, who may take advantage of the tax benefits, and what kinds of transactions are attractive to different types of investors.

TAX BENEFITS AVAILABLE UNDER THE
INTERNAL REVENUE CODE

The Internal Revenue Code (IRC) has long been the repository of tax incentives for investments in particular economic activities. The Economic Recovery Tax Act of 1981 is the latest amendment of the IRC and probably the most sweeping in the changes it has wrought in a twin effort to stimulate corporate investment in capital goods and to free up more investable funds by giving substantial tax relief to high-bracket taxpayers. Lower capital gains taxes and estate and gift taxes assure investors of greater aftertax profits for themselves and their heirs. The reduction in capital gains rates benefits a wide range of investments from real estate and securities to minerals, oil and gas, and timber.

Depreciation (cost recovery)

Specifically, the Economic Recovery Tax Act of 1981 provides for an unprecedented liberalization of depreciation allowances on both real property and tangible personal property acquired and placed in service after December 31, 1980, for business or income-producing purposes. Under the prior law, annual depreciation allowances were based on: (1) the cost of the asset, (2) the useful life of the asset, (3) the permissible depreciation method selected, and (4) the estimated salvage value.

The ERTA substitutes the Accelerated Cost Recovery System (ACRS) for the class life Asset Depreciation Range (ADR) system. Depreciable personal property will now be recovered over periods which are unrelated to and generally substantially shorter than useful lives of assets. The types of assets that fall within the four recovery period classes prescribed by the ERTA for depreciable personal property (3, 5, 10, and 15 years) are as follows:

3-year period:
Automobiles.
Light trucks.
Equipment and machinery used in connection with research and development.
Machinery and equipment with an ADR midpoint class life of four years or less.

5-year period:
All other property not included in the other classes.
Public utility property with an ADR midpoint class life of more than 4 years but less than 18 years.

10-year period:
Public utility property with an ADR midpoint class life of more than 18 years but not more than 25 years.

Railroad tank cars.
Certain "qualified" coal utilization property.

15-year period:
Public utility property with an ADR midpoint class life greater than 25 years.

The new law prescribes the annual recovery rates for each recovery period class. The annual recovery rates also depend on the year the asset is placed in service. Exhibit 1 presents the recovery rates for the four recovery period classes. The lower part of Exhibit 1 indicates how the recovery rates were determined by the Treasury. As can be seen, commencing in 1985, the recovery rates become more favorable, and in 1986 and subsequent years, they become even more favorable.

The following points should be noted concerning the statutory recovery rates for personal property. First, unlike the previous law, the new law does not require a different treatment for new and used prop-

EXHIBIT 1
ACRS Recovery Rates for Depreciable Personal Property

	Property Placed in Service in:											
	1981-1984†				*1985 ‡*				*After 1985 ‡*			
If the Recovery Year Is: *	*3 Years*	*5 Years*	*10 Years*	*15 Years (public utility)*	*3 Years*	*5 Years*	*10 Years*	*15 Years (public utility)*	*3 Years*	*5 Years*	*10 Years*	*15 Years (public utility)*
1 . . .	25%	15%	8%	5%	29%	18%	9%	6%	33%	20%	10%	7%
2 . . .	38	22	14	10	47	33	19	12	45	32	18	12
3 . . .	37	21	12	9	24	25	16	12	22	24	16	12
4 . . .		21	10	8		16	14	11		16	14	11
5 . . .		21	10	7		8	12	10		8	12	10
6 . . .			10	7			10	9			10	9
7 . . .			9	6			8	8			8	8
8 . . .			9	6			6	7			6	7
9 . . .			9	6			4	6			4	6
10 . . .			9	6			2	5			2	5
11 . . .				6				4				4
12 . . .				6				4				3
13 . . .				6				3				3
14 . . .				6				2				2
15 . . .				6				1				1

*The percentages reflect the use of the half-year convention for the first year. Generally, no ACRS deduction is allowed in the year of disposition of personal property.

†Approximates the benefit of using the 150 percent declining-balance method for the early years with a switch to the straight-line method.

‡In 1985, approximates the benefit of using the 175 percent declining-balance method for the early years with a switch to sum-of-the-years'-digits method. After 1985, approximates the 200 percent declining-balance method in the early years with a switch to sum-of-the-years'-digits method.

EXHIBIT 2
Comparison of Present Value of Cost Recovery Allowances Under ACRS and ADRS for a
$1 Asset in the Five-Year Recovery Class: 1981-1984, Personal Property

	Cost of Capital					
	17 Percent	18 Percent	19 Percent	20 Percent	21 Percent	22 Percent
Cost recovery under new law	$.628	$.613	$.599	$.585	$.572	$.559
Prior law and useful life is:						
10 years	.578	.563	.548	.535	.522	.509
15 years	.478	.462	.448	.434	.421	.409
20 years	.405	.390	.376	.363	.350	.339
25 years	.350	.336	.322	.310	.299	.288
30 years	.307	.294	.282	.270	.260	.250

Method: Double-declining balance with a switch to sum-of-the-years'-digits in second year.
This method was permissible when the class life ADR system was adopted. No salvage value is
assumed.

erty. That is, the recovery rates shown in Exhibit 1 apply to new and used depreciable personal property. Second, when the recovery rates are applied, the estimated salvage value is not considered. This is a change from the prior law, which required the taxpayer to consider the estimated salvage value in determining depreciation except when the estimated salvage value did not exceed 10 percent of the original cost. Third, a cost recovery based on straight-line depreciation over the recovery period or a longer recovery period is permitted.[1] Finally, the cost recovery allowances set forth by ACRS are for tax reporting *not* financial reporting purposes.

To demonstrate the liberalized cost recovery allowed under the new law, Exhibit 2 compares the present value of the cost recovery allowances under ACRS and the old law for an asset in the 5-year recovery class but with a longer useful life. For example, assume that the cost of capital of a firm is 19 percent and it purchases an asset for $10 million before 1985. Assume further that the asset falls into the 5-year recovery period class but has a useful life of 15 years. The present value of the cost recovery allowances would be $5.990 million ($10 million times .599) under the new law. Under the prior law, the present value of the cost recovery allowances would have been $4.48 million ($10 million times .448), or 25 percent less than under the new law.

With respect to new or used real property acquired and placed in

---

[1] The optional recovery periods for personal property are as follows:

3-year class	3, 5, or 12 years
5-year class	5, 12, or 25 years
10-year class	10, 25, or 35 years
15-year class	15, 35, or 45 years

service after December 31, 1980, most of which has an ADR midpoint life in excess of 12.5 years, the cost recovery period has been radically reduced to a 15-year life, reflecting a very liberal 175 percent declining-balance method changing to straight-line depreciation. The new law does not permit componential depreciation, as the previous law did, and allows first-year depreciation not on the half-year convention but on the number of months actually in service. Real property having an ADR midpoint life of 12.5 years or less has a 10-year recovery period based on 150 percent declining balance changing to straight line and is subject to the half-year convention.

Exhibit 3 reflects the annual recovery percentages for both 10- and 15-year class real property, assuming that January is the acquisition month. As with personal property, the taxpayer can use straight-line depreciation over the regular or extended period.

In the event of a sale of personal or real property, some or all of the depreciation benefits obtained in earlier years may be recaptured as ordinary income, depending on the type of property involved and the gain or loss results of the sale. In the case of personal property, all depreciation previously claimed will be recaptured to the extent of the gain realized. To the extent that the selling price exceeds the original cost, capital gains treatment will be afforded that excess, the balance of the realized gain being recapturable as ordinary income. In the case of 15-year life real commercial or industrial property, if the accelerated rates provided by the Treasury tables are used, *all* of the depreciation previously claimed will again be recaptured. However, when an election taking straight-line depreciation has been made, all of the gain will be treated as capital gain with no recapture. Analysis discloses that the straight-line election is more desirable if the holding period of the asset is expected to be less than 20 years; rapid depreciation would work out more profitably for longer holding periods.

EXHIBIT 3
ACRS Recovery Rates for Real Property

Year	10-Year Real Property	15-Year Real Property
1	8%	12%
2	14	10
3	12	9
4	10	8
5	10	7
6	10	6
7	9	6
8	9	6
9	9	6
10	9	5
11-15	–	5

Investment Tax Credit

The investment tax credit (ITC) is another substantial incentive to capital investment which produces an immediate dollar reduction on the purchase of eligible property. Under the prior law, the taxpayer was entitled to a 10 percent ITC for property with a useful life of at least seven years. Property with a useful life of five but less than seven years entitled the taxpayer to two thirds of the ITC, while one third was allowed for property with a useful life of three but less than five years. The ERTA allows the full 10 percent ITC for eligible property in the 5-year, 10-year, and 15-year recovery period classes and a 6 percent ITC for eligible property in the 3-year recovery period class.

There are limitations on the amount of acquisition costs on which ITC can be claimed. These limitations are based on the taxpayer's tax liability and on maximums imposed on used property.[2] The ITC can now be carried forward 15 years instead of 7 years.

A sale may also trigger a recapture of investment tax credit if it occurs before the five- or three-year recovery period elapses. There is a ratable giveback based on the number of years that have elapsed—2 percent for each year under five years or three years.

The ERTA strongly supports the "substantial" rehabilitation of existing buildings by allowing the following investment tax credits:

Type of Structure	Credit (percent)
Nonresidential buildings 30-39 years old	15%
Nonresidential buildings 40+ years old	20
All certified historic structures, whether residential or otherwise	25

"Substantial" as used above requires that qualifying expenditures over the current tax year and the preceding year must exceed the adjusted cost basis of the property before rehabilitation. The expenditures must be capitalized and written off over 15 years straight line except that where the 15 percent and 20 percent credits are applicable, the capitalized expenditures must be reduced by the credits claimed.

An additional 10 percent ITC is available for qualified energy property. This tax credit resulted from the enactment in 1978 of the Energy Tax Act. The expiration date for this tax credit is December 31, 1982.

Energy property is defined as property which is:

— Alternative energy property.

— Solar or wind energy property.

— Specially defined energy property.

---

[2] For used property, the ERTA expands the maximum allowed from $100,000 to $125,000 for 1981 through 1984. After 1984 it is increased to $150,000.

– Recycling equipment.

– Shale oil equipment.

– Equipment for producing natural gas from geopressured brine.

The property must be depreciable and have a useful life of at least three years.

To stimulate research and experimentation by business, the ERTA allows a nonrefundable tax credit based on incremental research expenditures paid or incurred after June 30, 1981, and before January 1, 1986.

THE FLEXIBILITY OF TRANSFERRING TAX BENEFITS UNDER ERTA

The liberalized recovery allowances do not generate a dollar-for-dollar reduction in the taxpayer's liability. Instead, the tax shield or cash flow engendered by ACRS allowances will be equal to the dollar allowance times the firm's marginal tax rate. Consequently, for firms not currently in a taxpaying position or in a low marginal tax rate (such as steelmakers, airlines, utilities, and new firms), the accelerated cost recovery would not encourage capital investment. Similarly, the ITC will encourage capital investment only if the taxpayer can take advantage of the carrot offered by the government. Since the ability of the taxpayer to utilize the ITC is based on its tax position before the ITC is taken, some firms not in a taxpaying position or with ITC carry-forwards cannot take advantage of the ITC.[3] For example, at the beginning of fiscal 1981, Ford Motor Company had $340 million in tax credits that it could not utilize.

In recognition of the substantial value of the ITC and the accelerated cost recovery provisions applicable to personal property, the ERTA has expressly made it possible through the "safe harbor" lease provisions for corporations not able to use these benefits to maximum advantage to sell them to corporations fully able to do so. Under prior law, and *it still is the law for lease transactions not qualifying for safe harbor treatment,* sale-leaseback transactions were governed by rigid rules which required that the purchaser enter the transaction with a provable pretax motivation and possibility, that there be no option to purchase or sell the asset at the lease expiration for any price other than fair market value, and that the asset be capable of being moved from its location at lease termination and hence not be a single-purpose asset for a single user (i.e., so-called limited use property).

---

[3] A possible solution to this problem that was proposed during the Carter administration was to make the ITC refundable. However, due to the projected cost estimates by the Treasury, President Reagan rejected this approach. No doubt, the ring of "business welfare" was also a driving force in the rejection of a refundable ITC.

The new law provides that if a sale-leaseback of new qualified personal property is consummated within three months after purchase for a price equal to the seller's adjusted cost basis, the purchaser's equity is at least 10 percent, and the lease term is no longer than the greater of 90 percent of economic useful life or 150 percent of ADR midpoint class life, then the lease will meet the safe harbor requirements and will be treated as a valid lease for tax purposes even if there is no pretax profit motive, put or call options for less than market exist, and immovable, single-purpose assets are involved. In the typical transaction, the purchase price is between 17 percent and 30 percent of asset cost, depending on the length of the lease, the time value of money, and the creditworthiness of the lessee; the balance is represented by a third-party mortgage debt or a purchase-money mortgage note to the seller, in either case—nonrecourse to the buyer. No other cash changes hands since the lease rental exactly equals the debt service on the note and since the lessee has a $1 purchase option at the maturity of the lease.

Let us examine how each side of the transaction fares. A numerical illustration is provided in Chapter 7. The seller surrenders tax benefits it cannot use and pockets the equity payment, thereby effectively reducing its cost of acquiring and using the asset over its entire useful life. The buyer generally recovers its cost in two taxable years by reason of the 10 percent investment credit and depreciation deductions totaling 37 percent of cost. The tax savings over the next three years plus reasonable sinking-fund accumulations more than cover the tax on phantom income reportable over the remainder of the lease term. The aftertax yield on unrecovered cost is in the area of 20 percent or better. The buyer's only risk in these transactions is a default by the lessee where third-party lenders hold a lien on the asset. Should there be a foreclosure, the buyer will find itself in an involuntary sale for a price equal to the unpaid balance of the note and recapture of depreciation and possibly investment tax credit will result to an extent which depends on how many years of the lease have elapsed. Under the circumstances, the buyer is well advised to deal only with an acceptable credit risk lessee or to obtain an agreement from the third-party lenders that the safe harbor lease will be honored in the event of default or bankruptcy by the lessee.

Individuals, Subchapter S corporations, and personal holding companies are not eligible to enter into safe harbor leases. Nor, as a practical matter, are closely held corporations. While such corporations are not expressly excluded by the statute, they are nonetheless effectively prevented from doing so by reason of the at-risk rule applicable to individuals, Subchapter S corporations, and closely held corporations. A closely held corporation is defined as one in which five or less unrelated persons own 50 percent or more of a corporation's outstanding common stock. Since nonrecourse debt is at the heart of the safe harbor lease, the tax losses resulting from the transaction far exceed the equity at risk, so that the full tax benefits are not achieved for such an investor.

One important implication of the safe harbor provisions is that they allow the lessee to purchase property subject to the safe harbor lease for a nominal amount. Prior to the ERTA, and at present for leases that do not satisfy the safe harbor rules, any purchase option had to be for the fair market value at the time the option was exercised. In fact, it was the handsome residual value due to inflation that made lease transactions attractive to lessors. The expectations of lessors as to the future residual of the leased property was embodied in the lease terms. In safe harbor leases, lessees may now place their bets on the wheel of fortune by negotiating for the right to the residual value for a nominal amount. This will not come without a cost, however. The lessor will consider the loss of the residual value in pricing the lease. The lessee must therefore weigh the trade-off between retention of the residual value and the less attractive lease terms offered by the lessor. Other implications of the safe harbor rules for leasing transactions are discussed in Chapter 7.

The provisions of the ERTA that allow qualified parties to buy and sell tax benefits have been strongly criticized in two quarters—on the one hand, by those who think it obscene that wealthy companies are encouraged and permitted to avoid paying taxes to the exclusion of individuals and closely held corporations; on the other hand, by those who oppose granting corporate welfare to economically troubled companies.

We cannot help but speculate that a refundable ITC, although economically inefficient, might have been more palatable to some critics of the new law. It might be easier for these critics to accept giving a tax break to a company with financial difficulties and not a large, well-heeled corporation. Yet, an understanding of the requirements for a safe harbor lease would clearly establish why it provides an economically efficient vehicle for transferring tax benefits to the entity in need of assistance. The competition for tax benefits by qualified buyers resulting from the more efficient procedures for transferring tax benefits ensures that the sellers will receive the full incentives to invest inherent in the ACRS. The regulations set forth by the Treasury for a safe harbor lease ensure that tax benefits cannot be "manufactured" by the parties and that leasing cannot be used to encourage uneconomical investments.

Keep in mind that the Treasury spent many years watching over the candy store to make sure that taxpayers entering into lease transactions were not doing so just to take advantage of Uncle Sam. The Treasury now is attempting to comply with the mandate of the ERTA, which is to provide an efficient means for getting the tax benefits set forth in the ERTA to those for whom it was intended. This may require giving away some candy to encourage future business, but the Treasury doesn't want to give away the entire store! At the time of this writing, the Senate Finance Committee has proposed modifications which would restrict purchasers of tax benefits to a 50 percent reduction in their annual tax liability and similarly limit eligible property transfers by sellers to approximately 50 percent thereof.

WHO IS THE BUYER OF TAX-ADVANTAGED INVESTMENTS?

The character of the purchaser will largely be determined by the availability of tax benefits under the IRC. It has been clearly observed in the area of safe harbor leases that widely held corporations alone are able to take advantage of them.

In general, the corporate investor fares considerably better than the individual investor insofar as tax-advantaged investments are concerned. Every attempt has been made by the Congress over the past five years to divert the individual from such ventures, including lowering his marginal tax rates to 50 percent and his maximum capital gains tax to 20 percent so as to make it costlier for him to risk his money in such programs. The corporate investor gets a 10 percent ITC without any restrictions when it acquires eligible property, whether it leases the asset for its entire useful life in a leveraged financing lease or in an operating lease. The individual investor may not avail himself of the ITC where property is leased unless two conditions are satisfied. First, the lease must be for a period less than half of the ADR class life of the asset, and second, operating costs associated with the property, not counting interest and taxes, must equal 15 percent of the gross income during the first 12 months of ownership. Hence, the individual is in effect limited to operating lease investments, whereas the corporation is not.

In addition, the individual is subject to the at-risk rule in all investment areas except real estate, whereas the widely held corporation is not. This means that aggregate losses stemming from an investment may not exceed what the individual has actually invested or has at risk. The new tax law extends the at-risk concept to the investment tax credit as well. Thus, if nonrecourse debt is utilized in a purchase of new equipment, the ITC will be limited to 10 percent of the purchase price paid in cash or with obligations with respect to which the purchaser is at risk. The balance of the credit will be allowed as the nonrecourse debt is paid down. If the nonrecourse debt is borrowed from a qualified lending institution, that is, a bank, insurance company, and so on, it will not be treated as nonrecourse debt, provided the investor's equity is at least 20 percent.

Furthermore, the individual's deductibility of interest in all net lease transactions involving personal or real property is limited to $10,000 per annum plus his investment income from interest, dividends, and net rental income from other net lease transactions. The corporation is not so limited.

In the area of developmental real estate transactions, the individual is required to amortize construction interest and real estate taxes over a 10-year period, while the corporation is permitted immediate write-offs as incurred.

Finally, the IRC imposes a minimum tax on tax preferences that is harsher for individuals than for corporations. The minimum tax is an add-on tax to the regular tax liability of an individual or a corporation and is computed by taking 15 percent of the tax preferences for the year less an exemption equal to the greater of $10,000 or 50 percent of the regular tax liability in the case of an individual, 100 percent of the regular tax in the case of a corporation.

The excess of accelerated recovery costs of real estate over straight-line depreciation is a tax preference for both individuals and corporations, as is the excess of percentage depletion over the adjusted basis of the property at year-end. However, tax preferences for intangible drilling costs, to the extent that they exceed net income from oil and gas and the excess of accelerated recovery costs over straight-line depreciation on all leased personal property, are applicable only to individuals and not to corporations.

Finally, the alternative minimum tax is imposed on individuals and not on corporations. It basically prevents an individual from taking full advantage of tax shelter investments in a year in which he has realized substantial capital gains. It is to be noted, however, that $^{18}\!/_{46}$ of long-term capital gains are to be treated as a tax preference by corporations for purposes of the minimum tax.

TYPES OF TRANSACTIONS

The kinds of transactions that are attractive to different types of investors are:

- Safe harbor leases.
- Conventional leveraged lease financing of personalty and realty.
- Operating leases involving personal property.
- Management programs involving personalty not under lease, oil and gas.
- Joint venture—personalty, realty.
- Unleveraged net leases ("single investor" or "direct leases")—personalty, realty.

Safe harbor leases have been discussed earlier in this chapter because they are part of the new tax law. The other transactions are discussed in Part 3. However, in the remainder of this chapter we will provide an overview of these transactions with respect to their attractiveness to investors.

In traditional leveraged net lease transactions, yield is derived from a combination of tax benefits (ITC, depreciation, and interest expense) and residual values, there being very little, if any, cash flow over the lease term. Since these are, in effect, financing transactions, the price paid reflects the credit rating of the lessee as well as the anticipated resale or re-lease value of the particular personal or real property and, of course, the going market return on alternative investment opportunities. It should be noted that the IRS rules on traditional leases are still in effect notwithstanding the existence of the safe harbor rules. As previously noted, real property cannot be made the subject of a safe harbor lease.

It might be desirable for the corporate CFO to enter into a net lease financing transaction involving real estate to be constructed with a partnership of individuals rather than a corporate investor since the corporation itself may claim the construction write-offs of interest and taxes and sell the completed building to the investor partnership. In any event, the internal rate of return for the individual investor must be a satisfactory one, reflecting the faster depreciation write-offs but also the lower marginal tax rate benefits brought about by the new law.

The corporation in need of personal property assets in its business may, if its needs so dictate, lease such assets in a short-term operating lease, from an individual or a partnership of individuals, provided the transaction is cast in conformity with the ITC requirements for noncorporate lessors that have been outlined. If the present inflationary environment continues, it is likely that investors will be attracted to the inflation-hedging characteristics of such an investment.

For corporations that own fleets of assets, such as cars, trucks, buses, supply vessels, helicopters, airplanes, drilling rigs, and railcars, which they do not want to own, net lease long term or short term, transactions may be structured as joint ventures or pools whereby an individual investor group buys the newest addition to the fleet and shares with the corporation in the bottom-line results of the operation of the combined assets on some equitable pooled basis. This may or may not require some minimum guaranteed utilization rate or cash return to the investor group to assure that the investment will be made. The corporation's benefits are obvious: it obtains control of the assets it needs in its business; it reduces the overhead on its own assets; and it usually obtains an incentive management fee for its performance. The tax benefits for the investor group are exactly the same as in the operating lease situation, while the economic risks are somewhat higher. Again, the investor group must have sufficient confidence in the corporation, the industry, and the business prospects of the enterprise. The willingness of the individual investor to participate in both of the above programs is contingent on his ability to obtain recourse financing at an aftertax interest rate which produces positive leverage.

Corporations owning chains of retail stores or department stores have used traditional leveraged net long-term lease financings with investor groups to reduce their financing costs and also to keep their obligations off-balance sheet. However, it is possible, theoretically at least, to structure the transactions on an unleveraged basis, provided the corporation is willing to pay a high enough fixed rental with opportunity for overages to produce a sufficiently attractive aftertax yield for the investor group. This is a case where the tax depreciation benefits are relatively small in comparison with the anticipated economic advantages.

Companies in the natural resources industry have been financing speculative and development drilling operations for many years by permitting individual investors to obtain the benefits of intangible drilling write-offs and percentage depletion subsequently in exchange for their capital contributions. These development programs call for a reversion to the corporation of most of the economic benefits after the investor has recovered his original dollar investment. The risk-return ratio for the investor is very modest in that historically 7 out of 10 development wells are successful. Accordingly, the return in dollars is in the area of 1.5 to 2 to 1 over a 10-year period.

Where speculative drilling programs are involved, the risk-reward return is greater since approximately only 1 in 13 wells is commercially successful. These investments have been structured to place all of the financial risk on the investor and, of course, to assign him all of the tax benefits. The corporation obtains a promotional, carried interest of approximately 25 percent.

Timber investment programs may be structured by corporations in that industry to permit the individual investor to obtain capital gain treatment on economic benefits realized. The key to the success of such a program is, of course, the attractiveness of the aftertax yield.

SUMMARY

In this chapter we have explained the tax benefits associated with various types of assets and the channels available for transferring some or all of these benefits to other tax entities. Finally, we provided an overview of the kinds of transactions that are attractive to different types of investors. These transactions are discussed in more detail in Part 3 of this book. The chief financial officer must be familiar with the tax factors discussed in this chapter in order to evaluate opportunities for left hand financing.

CHAPTER 4

Financial Accounting and Reporting Considerations

PHILIP R. PELLER
FRANK J. SCHWITTER
DAVID N. THROPE
Arthur Andersen & Co.

INTRODUCTION

The introductory chapter of this book outlines a number of methods used in *left hand financing*. These methods are elaborated and explained more fully in subsequent chapters. This chapter discusses the accounting principles and reporting requirements that apply to such left hand financing methods as investments in related parties, lease financing, and off-balance sheet financing.

As noted elsewhere in this book, many left hand financing techniques are not recent innovations. Rather, a shift in emphasis to such techniques has occurred over an extended period of time due to changing investment objectives in which persistently high inflation and interest rates have been significant factors. Similarly, most of the accounting principles and practices that apply to these techniques have also been around for a long time. Nevertheless, the shift to the use of left hand financing techniques is likely to be accompanied by a reexamination of the various accounting methods and practices now in use.

It should be borne in mind that several of the accounting principles and reporting requirements discussed in this chapter are under active review by the Financial Accounting Standards Board and others within the accounting profession and are therefore subject to change. Although the text makes note of several changes that could occur, the accounting treatment of particular transactions should be periodically checked for current applicability.

INVESTMENTS IN RELATED ENTITIES

Joint Ventures–Accounting and Reporting

A joint venture is an entity owned and operated by a small group of investors as a separate business or project for the mutual benefit of the investors. An entity which is more than 50 percent owned by any one investor is not a joint venture. Several legal entities are commonly used in forming joint ventures. These include:

1. Incorporated joint ventures (i.e., stock ownership).
2. Unincorporated joint ventures, in which each participant has an undivided interest.
3. General or limited partnerships.

Selecting the right entity entails legal and financial considerations that include the limitation of legal liability, the necessary financial commitment by the investor, income tax consequences, and the control of the investee retained by the investor.

The major issues in accounting for an investor's interest in a joint venture relate to:

1. The timing of recognition of income.
2. The form of financial statement presentation.
3. The financial statement disclosures.

Timing of recognition of income

In general, an investor in a joint venture that is *not* a subsidiary (see the subsequent section on subsidiaries) can account for its interest using the cost method or the equity method of accounting. Under the more commonly used equity method, the investor records its share of the investee's aftertax income or loss regardless of whether that income is distributed. Under the cost method, the investor records income as it is received through dividends or other distributions and records losses only when it is determined that a permanent impairment in the carrying amount of the investment has occurred.

Accounting Principles Board (APB) Opinion No. 18, the primary professional standard for joint venture accounting, requires that the equity method be applied to investments in corporate joint ventures as well as to other investments of 20 percent to 50 percent in the common stock of investee companies when the investor is able to exercise "significant influence" over the operating and financial policies of the investee. (Consolidation is generally required when ownership exceeds 50 percent, while the cost method is typically used for investments owned under 20 percent.) The ability to exercise significant influence may be indicated by representation on the investee's board of directors, by a commonality of managerial personnel, by technological dependence, or by some other participation in the investee's decision-making process. Although the investor's ownership has to be related to that of other shareholders, a substantial or majority ownership by another shareholder does not preclude the investor from exercising significant influence.

To achieve a reasonable degree of uniformity in application, *APB Opinion No. 18* states that ownership of 20 percent or more of the voting stock of an investee should lead to the presumption, in the absence of contrary evidence, that an investor has the ability to exercise significant influence. The percentage of an investor's voting interest is based on outstanding securities that have voting privileges. Excluded from the calculation are voting privileges that may become available to holders at a later date (through options, nonvoting convertible securities, etc.). While *APB Opinion No. 18* does not apply to unincorporated joint ventures and partnerships, the accounting guidance provided in that opinion is commonly used in accounting for these types of entities.

The cost method is appropriate for investments in partnerships and other noncorporate joint ventures and in those corporate ventures where the investor is likely to encounter significant problems in receiving distribution of income. For example, the cost method would be appropriate for corporate joint ventures where the investor is unable to exercise significant influence over the investee's operating and financial policies (e.g., bankruptcy), where the investment is temporary, where the investee is legally subject to restrictions, or where severe political risks in the investee's country impair the investor's ability to exercise significant influence over the investee's assets and operations.

When the equity method of accounting is used, the investor should provide deferred income taxes on its share of the investee's undistributed earnings. Deferred taxes would not be provided where the earnings of a joint venture are defined as "indefinitely invested" by *APB Opinion No. 23.*

The cost of an investment and the investor's underlying equity in the net assets of the investee may be different. Normally, this difference would be allocated to the investee's individual assets and liabilities (based on fair market values at the time the investment was acquired) and would affect the determination of the investor's share of earnings over the same period as the related assets and liabilities are reflected in income by the investee. If the difference can't be related to specific assets and liabilities of the investee, it is normally considered goodwill by the investor and amortized over a period not to exceed 40 years.

Form of financial statement presentation

The following alternative methods may be used in presenting joint ventures and other 20 to 50 percent-owned investments in an investor's financial statements:

1. One-line equity.

2. Expanded equity.
3. Proportionate consolidation.

The one-line equity method, which is required by *APB Opinion No. 18* and in reports filed with the SEC, is generally used, unless authoritative literature or industry practice permits use of another method. Essentially, the one-line method presents the investment at original cost, plus or minus the investor's share of net earnings or net losses and minus any distributions received. Losses would not ordinarily reduce the carrying amounts to below zero. The investor's share of earnings or losses is shown as a single amount in its income statement, except that extraordinary items recorded by the investee are also classified as extraordinary items by the investor unless the amounts are immaterial. Intercompany profits and losses resulting from transactions between the investor and the investee are excluded from the investor's income, based on the investor's percentage ownership.

Under the expanded-equity method, the investor's proportionate share of the investee's assets, liabilities, revenues, and expenses are presented separately in the investor's financial statements. An alternative is to present separate current and noncurrent balance sheet categories for the investor's equity in the assets and liabilities of the venture.

Under the proportionate consolidation method, the investor combines its proportionate interest in each of the investee's assets, liabilities, revenues, and expenses on a line-by-line basis with its own assets, liabilities, revenues, and expenses.

The application of these alternative methods is illustrated in Exhibits 1 and 2. To illustrate how these alternative methods are applied, it

EXHIBIT 1
JOINT VENTURE
Balance Sheet

Assets

Current assets:

Cash	$ 1,000
Inventory	2,000
Total current assets	3,000

Property, plant, and equipment:

Land	6,000
Building	14,000
	20,000
Less: Accumulated depreciation	6,000
	14,000
Total assets	$17,000

Liabilities and Stockholders' Equity

Current liabilities:

Current maturities of long-term mortgage loan	$ 500
Accounts payable and accrued liabilities	1,000
Total current liabilities	1,500
Long-term mortgage loans	15,000
Stockholders' equity	500
Total liabilities and stockholders' equity	$17,000

EXHIBIT 2
INVESTOR
Balance Sheet

Assets	One-Line Equity	Proportionate Consolidation	Expanded Equity Alternative I	Expanded Equity Alternative II
Current assets:				
Cash	$ —	$ 500	$ —	$ —
Inventory	—	1,000	—	—
Company's share of current assets of joint venture	N/A	N/A	1,500	N/A
Total current assets	—	1,500	1,500	—
Property, plant and equipment:				
Land	—	3,000	—	—
Building	—	7,000	—	—
		10,000		
Less: Accumulated depreciation	—	3,000	—	—
	—	7,000	—	—
Company's share of property, plant and equipment of joint venture	N/A	N/A	7,000	N/A
Investment in joint venture	250	N/A	N/A	N/A
Company's share of assets of joint venture:				
Current assets	N/A	N/A	N/A	1,500
Property, plant and equipment	N/A	N/A	N/A	7,000
Total assets	$250	$ 8,500	$8,500	$8,500

Liabilities and Stockholders' Equity	One-Line Equity	Proportionate Consolidation	Expanded Equity Alternative I	Expanded Equity Alternative II
Current liabilities:				
Current maturities of long-term mortgage loans	$ —	$ 250	$ —	$ —
Accounts payable and accrued liabilities	—	500	—	—
Company's share of current liabilities of joint venture	N/A	N/A	750	N/A
Total current liabilities	—	750	750	—
Long-term debt:				
Mortgage loans	—	7,500	—	—
Company's share of long-term debt of joint venture	N/A	N/A	7,500	N/A
Company's share of liabilities of joint venture:				
Current liabilities	N/A	N/A	N/A	750
Long-term debt, less current maturities	N/A	N/A	N/A	7,500
				8,250
Stockholders' equity	250	250	250	250
Total liabilities and stockholders' equity	$250	$8,500	$8,500	$8,500

is assumed that the investor has no assets and liabilities other than a 50 percent interest in the joint venture.

Financial statement disclosures
Financial statement disclosure requirements for investments in joint ventures and other 20 to 50 percent-owned investments are prescribed by *APB Opinion No. 18* and include:

1. The name of the investee and the investor's percentage ownership.
2. The accounting method used (i.e., the equity or cost method).
3. Any differences between the amount at which the investment is carried and the investor's underlying equity in net assets and how that difference is treated.
4. The reasons for not using the equity method when the investor owns more than 20 percent of the investee.
5. The reasons why the equity method is used when the investor owns less than 20 percent of the investee. (However, the SEC generally does not allow the equity method of accounting if less than a 20 percent equity position is held.)

When investments in joint ventures are material to the investor's consolidated financial position or results of operations, summarized financial information that includes the joint venture's assets, liabilities, and results of operations would normally be presented in a note to the investor's financial statements.

In addition, the SEC requires the filing of separate financial statements for significant unconsolidated subsidiaries and affiliates (based on asset and pretax earnings tests). In addition, the computation of the ratio of earnings to fixed charges, which disclosure is frequently required by the SEC, must include amounts that relate to unconsolidated subsidiaries or affiliates.

Exhibit 3 illustrates an investor's disclosure of joint venture investments.

Subsidiaries—Consolidated Financial Statements

Form of financial statement presentation
The previous section discussed the accounting and reporting of investments in which ownership is 50 percent or less. The accounting for investments in which ownership is greater than 50 percent is prescribed by *Accounting Research Bulletin (ARB) No. 51*. That bulletin states:

> There is a presumption that consolidated statements are more meaningful than separate statements and that they are usually necessary for a fair presentation when one of the companies in the group directly or indirectly has a controlling financial interest in the other companies.

EXHIBIT 3
Illustration of Notes to Consolidated Financial Statements

Investments in joint ventures, at equity: At December 31, 1981, the Company owned 50 percent of ABC, Inc., and XYZ, Inc. These investments are stated at cost of acquisition plus the Company's equity in the undistributed net income since acquisition. A summary of the combined financial position and results of operations of joint venture companies follows:

Summary of Financial Position

	1981	1980
Current assets	$14,000	$13,300
Property, plant and equipment	1,900	1,500
Goodwill	500	500
Other assets	200	200
Total assets	16,600	15,500
Current liabilities	8,100	8,600
Other liabilities	400	200
Long-term debt	1,700	1,700
Total liabilities	10,200	10,500
Net assets	$ 6,400	$ 5,000
Company's equity in net assets	$ 3,200	$ 2,500

Summary Statement of Income

	1981	1980	1979
Net revenues	$25,500	$21,500	$17,400
Cost and expenses	23,100	20,100	16,200
Provision for income taxes	800	600	400
Income before extraordinary credit	1,600	800	800
Extraordinary credit: Income tax benefit arising from utilization of net operating loss carry-forwards	–	100	–
Net income	$ 1,600	$ 900	$ 800
Company's equity in net income	$ 800	$ 450	$ 400
Company's portion of dividends declared and paid	$ 100	$ 100	$ –

The Company engages in various transactions with its 50 percent-owned companies. Agreements with these companies generally provide for a price structure projected to result in a reasonable return to the respective parties. Significant transactions with the companies that are accounted for on the equity method for the three years ended December 31, 1981, were as follows:

	Sales to	Royalties Charged to	Purchases from	Receivable from	Payable to
1981	$590	$ 50	$150	$200	$10
1980	640	230	50	210	20
1979	180	230	50	110	10

Consolidated financial statements combine the assets, liabilities, revenues, and expenses of the parent company (the investor) with those of its subsidiaries. Intercompany transactions and balances are eliminated from consolidated financial statements. *ARB No. 51* defines a subsidiary (including unincorporated ones) as an enterprise that is controlled through the ownership of more than 50 percent of the enterprise's voting shares.

ARB No. 51 specifies certain circumstances under which a subsidiary should not be consolidated. For example, a subsidiary should not be consolidated when control is likely to be temporary or when it does not rest with the majority owners (as in bankruptcy). Also, separate statements would be preferable for a subsidiary or a group of subsidiaries if such separate presentation of financial information would be more informative to shareholders and creditors of the parent company. For example, separate statements may be presented for a subsidiary which is a bank, insurance company, or finance company if the parent and its other subsidiaries are engaged in manufacturing or in some other nonfinancial business. Separate presentations of such dissimilar operations provide useful information on items such as revenues, costs, assets, and debt—items that would most likely be obscured by consolidation. Also, this prevents distortion of the results of the parent and its other subsidiaries which could result if the dissimilar operation were consolidated.

Under present rules, however, there are essentially two gradations of subsidiaries that might not be consolidated—a wholly owned finance subsidiary that makes loans exclusively to its parent's customers and a similar finance subsidiary that makes loans to outsiders who have no connection with the parent. In the first instance, it can be argued that the finance subsidiary should be consolidated. Nonconsolidation would allow the parent company to finance sales but record them as if they were cash sales, and exclude the debt used to finance the sales from its balance sheet.

Some in the accounting profession have argued that a finance subsidiary should be consolidated if its principal activity is to purchase receivables from its parent and affiliated companies or otherwise finance the sales of these companies. *ARB No. 51,* however, does not require consolidation in this instance. An exception to this lack of specific criteria is a leasing subsidiary which is principally involved in leasing to its parent or other affiliates. Such a subsidiary is required to be consolidated.

A clear sentiment appears to have developed within the accounting profession that the consolidation criteria should more clearly specify the types of subsidiaries that should not be consolidated. The Financial Accounting Standards Board (FASB) has placed the broad subject of consolidation accounting on its active agenda.

Financial statement disclosures

The disclosure requirements applicable to unconsolidated subsidiaries are essentially the same as those for investments in joint ventures. In addition, the extent to which a parent company guarantees the obligations of an unconsolidated subsidiary must be disclosed in the parent's financial statements.

As with corporate joint ventures, the SEC requires that separate financial statements of significant unconsolidated subsidiaries (as measured by asset and pretax earnings tests) be included in a parent company's filings with the SEC.

Research and Development (R&D) Partnerships

Many high-technology companies have recently financed their research and development activities through such innovative vehicles as general partnerships, limited partnerships, and corporate joint ventures.

An R&D partnership might be a limited partnership which has been formed to finance the R&D of the sponsor corporation (the general partner). Commonly, the sponsor will contribute its preliminary R&D to the partnership. The limited partners contribute the capital for the R&D program and are allocated the partnership's profits or losses. The partnership often contracts with the sponsoring corporation to conduct the R&D on a cost-plus basis. If a product is successfully developed, the sponsor is usually required to market the product and pay a royalty based on sales. The sponsor may also have the option to purchase the developed product.

The accounting literature does not provide specific guidance on accounting for these partnerships by the general partner, and in practice various alternative methods have been used. Some within the profession view an R&D partnership as an integral part of the sponsor and would treat the limited partner's interest as that of the sponsor (this implies that the sponsor consolidates the partnership). Others view the partnership as a separate entity that should not be consolidated by the sponsor. One factor that appears to be critical to this determination is whether the general partner or the limited partners assume the risks of the R&D effort.

The SEC has indicated its concern about the accounting for R&D partnerships. In some cases, the SEC has required that the money raised from the limited partners be considered a loan to be shown on the sponsor's balance sheet. In other cases, where the parties could demonstrate that the limited partners were at risk in essentially the same manner as an outside party, the SEC has accepted off-balance sheet accounting.

In April of 1982, the FASB issued an exposure draft of a proposed statement, "Research and Development Arrangements." The exposure draft provides that the liability, and the corresponding R&D expense, be recorded by the sponsor of an R&D arrangement to the extent that it is obligated to repay any of the funds provided by the outside parties even though the R&D project is unsuccessful.

LEASE FINANCING

Lease Accounting and Reporting

General

In 1976 the Financial Accounting Standards Board (FASB) issued *Statement No. 13,* "Accounting for Leases." This statement mandated that a lease which transfers substantially all the benefits and risks incident to the ownership of leased property to the lessee be accounted for by the lessee as the acquisition of an asset and the incurrence of an obligation and by the lessor as a sale with financing. While the FASB could have taken a strict legalistic approach in determining whether a lessee had acquired an asset and assumed an obligation, it leaned in this instance to the substance of the transaction rather than its legal form. Certain accounting commentators believed that an asset should be recorded only if, in essence, an installment purchase had occurred and a legal obligation had arisen. The FASB chose to set the criteria on the basis of whether the lessee, in fact, assumes the risks and benefits of an owner. The requirements of *Statement No. 13* for determining whether a lease must be capitalized are specific, and one would think that its application would be mechanical. But as practice has shown, interpretations of the *Statement* have varied considerably and there remains some latitude in determining whether capitalization is required. Perhaps for this reason, the FASB has amended and interpreted *Statement No. 13* many times in attempts to clarify the application of its mechanical rules to varied and complex transactions.

Essentially, *Statement No. 13* requires that a lease be classified as a capital lease if it meets *any* of the four following tests:

1. The lease transfers ownership of the property to the lessee by the end of the lease term.
2. The lease contains a bargain purchase option.
3. The lease term is equal to 75 percent or more of the estimated economic life of the leased property.
4. The present value of the minimum lease payments equals or exceeds 90 percent of the fair value of the leased property (net of any investment tax credit to be retained by the lessor) at the inception of the lease.

Leases that do not meet any of the above criteria should be accounted for as operating leases.

Accounting

Accounting by lessees employs either the operating- or capital-lease method. Under the operating-lease method, rental payments are expensed as they become payable. If rental payments are not made on a straight-line basis, rental expense should nevertheless be recognized on a straight-line basis or on some other systematic and rational basis. If a lease is determined to be a capital lease, the leased asset and the related lease obligation would be recorded as an asset and a liability, respectively, at an amount equal to the present value of the minimum lease payments. The lower of the lessee's incremental borrowing rate or the interest rate implicit in the lease, if known, is used to discount the minimum lease payments. The implicit interest rate is that rate which, at the inception of the lease, discounts the future rental payments and the estimated residual value of the leased asset at the termination of the lease to an amount equal to the estimated fair value of the leased asset less any investment tax credit retained by the lessor. The leased asset is depreciated over its useful life or the lease term, whichever is shorter. The lease obligation is amortized over the life of the lease. Applying this methodology, the lease payments are treated as payments of both interest and principal.

Exhibit 4 compares the lessee's accounting for a lease as a capital lease and as an operating lease. Since the lease meets the criteria specified in *Statement No. 13,* it would be accounted for as a capital lease. The assumptions of Exhibit 4 are as follows:

1. A $4 million computer is leased for $1,316,938 per year over a four-year term. Rental payments are made at the end of each year.
2. The fair value of the computer at the end of the four-year lease term is estimated to be zero.
3. The implicit interest rate on the capitalized lease, 12 percent, is less than the lessee's incremental borrowing rate.
4. No investment tax credit is available on the leased asset.
5. The lessee uses straight-line depreciation for accounting purposes.

Although total pretax expense under both methods of accounting is the same over the lease term, expenses are higher in the earlier years and lower in the later years of a capital lease as the leasehold obligation is paid down and the interest cost declines. Thus, accounting for a lease as a capital lease rather than an operating lease affects both the balance sheet and the income statement. Furthermore, the leasehold obligation recorded under a capital-lease method must be split into its current and long-term portion, thereby reducing working capital.

From a lessor's standpoint, *Statement No. 13* classifies leases as sales-type, direct-financing, leveraged, or operating leases. Lessors and

EXHIBIT 4
Capital and Operating Leases Contrasted

Capital-Lease Treatment

Year	Minimum Lease Payment	Present Value of Minimum Lease Payments at 12 Percent
1	$1,316,938	$1,175,837
2	1,316,938	1,049,855
3	1,316,938	937,370
4	1,316,938	836,938
	$5,267,752	$4,000,000

	(1)	*(2)*	*(3)*	*(4)*	*(5)*	*(6)*
Year	*Leased Asset at Beginning of Year*	*Depreciation Expense (1) ÷ 4*	*Lease Obligation at Beginning of Year (3) − (4) + (5)*	*Lease Payment*	*Interest Expense (3) × 12%*	*Total Pretax Expense (2) + (5)*
1. . .	$4,000,000	$1,000,000	$4,000,000	$1,316,938	$ 480,000	$1,480,000
2. . .	3,000,000	1,000,000	3,163,062	1,316,938	379,567	1,379,567
3. . .	2,000,000	1,000,000	2,225,691	1,316,938	267,083	1,267,083
4. . .	1,000,000	1,000,000	1,175,836	1,316,938	141,102	1,141,102
		$4,000,000		$5,267,752	$1,267,752	$5,267,752

Operating-Lease Treatment

Year	Rental Expense
1	$1,316,938
2	1,316,938
3	1,316,938
4	1,316,938
	$5,267,752

Comparison of Capital-Lease and Operating-Lease Treatments

Year	Pretax Expense under Capital-Lease Treatment in Excess of (Less than) that under Operating-Lease Treatment
1	$ 163,062
2	62,629
3	(49,855)
4	(175,836)
	$ —

lessees use the same basic criteria in determining whether a lease should be capitalized, but as a practical matter there are often differences between the lessee's and lessor's classification of a lease. This could happen, for example, when the lessee cannot determine the lessor's interest rate implicit in the lease, which is the case when the lessee is unable to determine the lessor's estimate of the residual value of the leased asset at the end of the lease term.

A leveraged lease is essentially a capital lease (more specifically, a direct-financing lease; i.e., a lease which does not give rise to a manufacturer's or dealer's profit or loss) that has the following additional attributes:

1. It involves at least three parties: a lessee, a long-term creditor, and a lessor (equity investor).
2. The debt financing involves substantial leverage and is non-recourse with respect to the general credit of the lessor, although the creditor may have recourse to the leased property and unremitted rental payments.
3. The lessor's net investment in the leased property declines in the early years and rises during the later years of the lease, before its final elimination.

A number of special characteristics of leveraged leases should be noted. First, the lessor's investment in a leveraged lease is recorded on a net basis (i.e., the lessor's nonrecourse debt is netted against its investment in the lease). This is a rare instance in accounting in which it is permissible to offset a liability against an asset. Second, the lessor recognizes income over the life of the lease in a pattern that front-ends much of the income. This is due to the fact that income recognition is a function of the lessor's net aftertax investment; as the net investment declines, less and less income is recognized, and conversely, when the net investment is at its highest in the early years, income will be higher. These two aspects of leveraged leases coupled with the lower overall financing costs to the user of the equipment provide strong incentives for a lessor to finance a transaction through a leveraged lease.

Financial statement presentation

Financial statement disclosures of lease transactions are relatively straightforward. Lessees must disclose the amount of rental expense under operating leases, as well as future minimum lease payments under noncancelable operating leases (net of subleases) in the aggregate and for each of the five subsequent years. A general description of the leased property and the significant lease terms should also be included. For capital leases, the disclosures required for operating leases also apply and in addition the aggregate amount of future minimum lease payments must be stated and reconciled to the lease obligation shown on the balance sheet. The gross amount of leased assets recorded on the balance sheet must also be disclosed.

The preceding discussion is a brief synopsis of *FASB Statement No. 13.* The *Statement,* as amended, contains many rules covering specific types of transactions, such as sale-and-leaseback transactions, leases involving land as well as buildings, leases involving parts of a building, revision or termination of an existing lease, subleasing, and leasing among related parties. The reader should review the applicable sections of the *Statement* when considering any one of these specific types of leasing transactions.

Tax-Benefit-Transfer Leases[1]

General

The changes in the income tax treatment of leases embodied in the Economic Recovery Tax Act of 1981 (ERTA) have led to new types of lease transactions. Briefly, the ERTA allows for transactions which are structured in the form of leases for tax purposes and are, in substance, solely the purchase and sale of tax benefits, that is, deductions under the Accelerated Cost Recovery System (ACRS), investment tax credits (ITC), and energy credits.

A primary purpose of the ERTA is to encourage investment in new plant and equipment by substantially shortening the depreciable lives of most property and equipment and by liberalizing the investment tax credit. Congress was concerned, however, that companies with net operating losses, ITC carry-over tax positions, or large amounts of unused foreign tax credits might not receive current tax benefits from ACRS or the liberalized ITC and therefore might not be encouraged to increase investment in capital assets. The ERTA therefore provides a leasing mechanism which enables companies to sell the ACRS and ITC benefits that they cannot use.

Leasing has been an important means of financing plant and equipment for many years, and leases have often been structured to transfer ITC and depreciation deductions to the party best able to benefit from them. The ERTA, however, will bring about substantially increased leasing by companies that do not need traditional lease financing but wish only to sell tax benefits. That increase will occur for several reasons.

First, the shorter depreciable lives of ACRS and the liberalization of the ITC will place more companies in net operating loss or ITC carry-over positions that will preclude them from using depreciation deductions or ITC currently. The interaction of ACRS with foreign tax credits may put other companies in the position of having large amounts of unused foreign tax credits. For these reasons, more companies should be in a position to benefit from leasing their capital equipment and

---

[1] Portions of this section have been adapted from "The 1981 Tax Act: Accounting for Leases," by Philip R. Peller, John E. Stewart, and Benjamin S. Neuhausen of Arthur Andersen & Co., *Financial Executive*, January 1982.

transferring their ACRS deductions and ITC to lessors that can use them.

Second, the ERTA contains safe harbor rules that make it easier to structure leases that transfer depreciation deductions and ITC from one party to another. Under preexisting tax rules, the lessor had to assume more than nominal risks of ownership of the leased property in order for the lease to be treated as a lease for tax purposes.

Third, at the high interest rates of recent years, a company incurs a significant cost if its tax position results in a delay in realizing depreciation deductions or the ITC.

Finally, under previous tax rules, it was difficult to qualify a lease for special property as a lease for tax purposes because, under those rules, the leased property had to be usable by someone other than the lessee at the end of the lease term. Under the new safe harbor rules, this is no longer a requirement. The residual value of special-purpose property can reside with the user/lessee, thereby making it relatively simple to structure a lease for such property.

The new types of transactions created by the changes in the tax code involve the sale or purchase of ACRS deductions alone or combined with investment tax credits and energy credits. The purchase and sale of tax credits only (the so-called ITC strip-out leases) were not explicitly approved by the Treasury Department's temporary regulations issued in October 1981.

In mid 1982, certain proposals were made in Congress to repeal and/or amend the provisions of the ERTA which allow tax-benefit-transfer leases. Adoption of these proposals could significantly change the economics of these leases.

Accounting treatment

The major accounting question about ERTA leases is whether the transactions should be treated as leases in accordance with *FASB Statement No. 13* or whether they should be accounted for as purchases and sales of tax benefits. Under *Statement No. 13,* the seller of tax benefits would, in effect, record the income from the sale ratably over the term of the lease in the form of lower rental expense (for an operating lease) or lower interest and depreciation expense (for a capital lease). By contrast, if the seller does not sell the ITC benefit, existing accounting standards allow the ITC to be flowed through to income in the year it is generated. If the transaction is to be treated as the sale of tax benefits there is also a question of whether the simultaneous sale of ITC and ACRS deductions should be accounted for separately or as a single unit.

The buyer of tax benefits might have a cumulative cash outflow from the lease before considering the secondary earnings effects from the reinvestment of cash flows resulting from the temporary tax savings.

Statement No. 13 requires a buyer, at the inception of the lease, to record a loss equal to the cumulative cash outflow. Some accountants believe that recording a loss in these circumstances makes little sense from an economic point of view.

In April of 1982, the FASB issued an exposure draft of a proposed statement, "Accounting for the Purchase and Sale of Tax Benefits through Leases." The exposure draft provides that *Statement No. 13* does not apply to tax act leases meeting certain defined criteria. As a basic approach to accounting for the ITC and ACRS deductions, the exposure draft follows a unitary or nonallocation approach. The basic requirements of this exposure draft are as follows:

1. In the period in which the transaction is entered into, the seller records income equal to the total proceeds (for ITC as well as ACRS) received from the sale of tax benefits. The seller provides deferred taxes on the proceeds, as appropriate. This accounting applies regardless of the seller's traditional accounting policy for ITC.
2. The buyer reports a constant rate of return (income) on its unrecovered investment. This is accomplished as follows:
   a. During the initial phase, the buyer records income in an amount equal to its unrecovered net investment multiplied by the lower of its aftertax incremental borrowing or short-term investment rate.
   b. After the buyer has recovered its initial investment, the buyer is effectively "borrowing" from the government. During this period, the buyer records a cost of "borrowing" equal to the sum of (i) the inherent "loss" on the lease, i.e., the excess of the purchase price of the tax benefits over the total estimated tax savings (before considering secondary earnings) and (ii) the net-of-tax earnings recorded in 2(a) above. By the end of the lease term, the "borrowing" will have been repaid in the form of tax payments and the amortization of the "borrowing" cost (using a constant-interest method) will have been completed.

The exposure draft provides that this accounting applies prospectively for transactions entered into after the date that a final statement is issued. Thus, a proliferation of accounting treatments exists for tax lease transactions consummated to date.

An example of accounting by a buyer and seller in accordance with the terms of the exposure draft follows. These assumptions are made:

1. Ajax Company purchases for $100,000 a piece of equipment with a depreciable life of 5 years under the ACRS and a useful life of 10 years.

2. Because of its tax position, Ajax will not be able to utilize the ITC generated by the purchase of the equipment, nor will it be able to use the first year's depreciation deductions under the ACRS.
3. Beta Company, by contrast, has sufficient taxable income to utilize both the ITC and the depreciation deductions on the equipment, and Beta has excess cash for which it is seeking an attractive investment opportunity.
4. Accordingly, Ajax and Beta enter into a sale-and-leaseback agreement with the following provisions:

   a. Ajax sells the equipment to Beta for $100,000 and leases it back for a 10-year term. Beta pays $22,000 to Ajax and gives Ajax a $78,000, 12 percent note for the remainder of the purchase price. The note is payable in equal installments over 10 years, and Ajax's rental payments are exactly equal to Beta's payments on the note.

   b. Ajax and Beta have the right to offset their payments to each other against amounts owed to them by the other party.

   c. Beta will hold legal title to the equipment during the lease term and will claim the ITC and depreciation deductions.

   d. At the end of the lease term, Ajax can buy the equipment from Beta for $1.

5. The lower of Beta's incremental aftertax borrowing rate or short-term investment rate is 8 percent.
6. Ajax's and Beta's tax rates are 50 percent.
7. The investment tax credit rate is 10 percent.

Under the terms of the sale-and-leaseback, Beta pays Ajax $22,000 at inception and Ajax pays Beta $1 after 10 years. No other cash changes hands between the parties during the lease term.

Exhibit 5 illustrates the cash flows of the two companies under the sale-and-leaseback agreement, including income tax effects. Note that Ajax's cash flows ignore the operating cash flows generated by the equipment, which are unaffected if Ajax enters into the sale-and-lease-back agreement. In the early years, Beta receives heavy cash inflows as a result of tax savings from the ACRS depreciation in addition to the ITC; in later years, the tax savings related to depreciation are repaid. Thus, Beta is effectively able to borrow funds interest-free from the Treasury. While the cumulative effect to Beta is a $1,000 cash outflow, that is not the total economic result. The cash inflows in the early years can be invested in Beta's business or in securities, or they can be used to repay short-term debt. The cash inflows are repaid in later years, but Beta retains the benefits obtained from its use of the cash in the inter-

EXHIBIT 5
Illustration of a Tax-Benefit-Transfer Lease

Ajax Company's Cash Flows

		Income Tax Effects				Cash Inflow (Outflow)	
Period	Equipment	Rental Expense	Interest Income	Net Tax Deductions	Related Tax Effect*	Pretax	Aftertax
Inception	$(100,000) 22,000	$ –	$ –	$ –	$ –	$(78,000)	$(78,000)
1	–	13,805	9,360	4,445	2,222	–	2,222
2	–	13,805	8,827	4,978	2,489	–	2,489
3	–	13,805	8,229	5,576	2,788	–	2,788
4	–	13,805	7,560	6,245	3,122	–	3,122
5	–	13,805	6,811	6,994	3,497	–	3,497
6	–	13,805	5,971	7,834	3,917	–	3,917
7	–	13,805	5,031	8,774	4,387	–	4,387
8	–	13,805	3,978	9,827	4,914	–	4,914
9	–	13,805	2,799	11,006	5,503	–	5,503
10	–	13,805	1,484	12,321	6,161	–	6,161
	$ (78,000)	$138,050	$60,050	$78,000	$39,000	$(78,000)	$(39,000)

*The transaction normally makes sense only if Ajax is in a tax loss or ITC carryover position. Hypothetical tax savings, therefore, might not materialize.

Beta Company's Cash Flows

		Income Tax Effects				
Period	Rental Income	Interest Expense	ACRS Depreciation	Net Tax Deductions (Income)	Taxes Saved/ (Paid)*	Cash Inflow (Outflow)
Inception	$ –	$ –	$ –	$ –	$ –	$(22,000)
1	13,805	9,360	15,000	10,555	15,278	15,278
2	13,805	8,827	22,000	17,022	8,511	8,511
3	13,805	8,229	21,000	15,424	7,712	7,712
4	13,805	7,560	21,000	14,755	7,378	7,378
5	13,805	6,811	21,000	14,006	7,003	7,003
6	13,805	5,971	–	(7,834)	(3,917)	(3,917)
7	13,805	5,031	–	(8,774)	(4,387)	(4,387)
8	13,805	3,978	–	(9,827)	(4,914)	(4,914)
9	13,805	2,799	–	(11,006)	(5,503)	(5,503)
10	13,805	1,484	–	(12,321)	(6,161)	(6,161)
	$138,050	$60,050	$100,000	$ 22,000	$21,000	$ (1,000)

*Includes $10,000 of investment tax credit in year 1.

vening years (often referred to as "secondary earnings"). In general, lengthening the lease term will delay Beta's repayment of its cash inflows in the early years, thereby increasing the economic benefit to Beta and also, presumably, the cash down payment that Beta is willing to pay at the inception of the transaction.

Ajax would reflect the $22,000 proceeds, net of applicable deferred taxes, in its income at the inception of the lease. The note receivable from Beta and the rentals payable to Beta would not be recorded on Ajax's balance sheet because the right of offset exists.

Beta has essentially made an investment of $22,000 and would recognize a return on its investment in a systematic and rational manner, as illustrated in Exhibit 6.

OFF-BALANCE SHEET FINANCING METHODS

The existing framework of accounting relies heavily on the legal form of transactions, with the result that form rather than substance often controls the recording of business transactions. As a consequence, although some exceptions exist (e.g., the percentage-of-completion method and leases), the decision on whether assets should be reflected on the balance sheet is frequently based on the concept of legal title (ownership). For liabilities, exceptions are less common, and liabilities are generally recognized when there is a contractual arrangement (either specific or implied). Many accounting commentators believe that a different view, based on the concept of the assumption of the risks and rewards of ownership, should be used to determine what assets and

EXHIBIT 6
Illustration of a Tax-Benefit-Transfer Lease: Beta Company's Net Income Effect

Year	(1) Investment at Beginning of Year (1 – 4 – 5 + 6)	(2) Cash Inflow (Outflow)	(3) Accretion of Income on Unrecovered Investment (1 × 8%)*	(4) Recovery of Investment (2 – 3)	(5) Effective "Borrowing" Activity (2 – 3 – 4)	(6) "Interest Expense" on Borrowing (1 × 3.66%)†	(7) Net Effect on Net Income (3 + 6)
1	$ 22,000	$15,278	$1,760	$13,518	$ –	$ –	$ 1,760
2	8,482	8,511	679	7,832	–	–	679
3	650	7,712	52	650	7,010	–	52
4	(7,010)	7,378	–	–	7,378	(257)	(257)
5	(14,645)	7,003	–	–	7,003	(536)	(536)
6	(22,184)	(3,917)	–	–	(3,917)	(812)	(812)
7	(19,079)	(4,387)	–	–	(4,387)	(698)	(698)
8	(15,390)	(4,914)	–	–	(4,914)	(563)	(563)
9	(11,039)	(5,503)	–	–	(5,503)	(404)	(404)
10	(5,940)	(6,161)	–	–	(6,161)	(221)	(221)
		$21,000	$2,491	$22,000	$(3,491)	$(3,491)	$(1,000)

*An aftertax rate of 8 percent is assumed to approximate the lower of Beta's aftertax incremental borrowing rate or short-term investment rate.

†3.66 percent is the interest rate implicit in the cash flows in Column 5.

liabilities are to be included in the balance sheet. The FASB recognizes the need for a better definition of what consititutes an entity's assets and liabilities and has begun conceptual studies to define the elements and objectives of financial statements.

The current accounting model has had great difficulty in coping with the many complex financing transactions that have arisen over the past decade or two. In fact, many of these transactions are structured in part to achieve a predictable accounting result based on the significant reliance on transaction form. The following transactions are examples of situations in which it has been difficult to ascertain when the assets and related financing should be recorded:

1. Take-or-pay contracts.
2. Throughput agreements.
3. Product financing arrangements.
4. Production payments.
5. Cutting contracts.

During 1981 the FASB demonstrated its continuing interest in certain of these issues through the issuance of *Statement No. 47* and *Statement No. 49.*

In *Statement No. 47,* "Disclosures of Long-Term Obligations," the FASB required that companies disclose certain purch se obligations (e.g., take-or-pay contracts) that a buyer and seller negotiate to help the seller secure financing for facilities to provide contracted goods or services. Companies are required to describe the agreements and to disclose the total payments as well as a breakdown of the payments for each of the next five years. Although the *Statement's* requirements are limited to disclosure, the FASB can be expected to give continuing consideration to the need for reflecting certain obligations in the financial statements.

In *Statement No. 49,* "Accounting for Product Financing Arrangements," the FASB reaffirmed the principles set forth in earlier professional literature and required that a product-financing arrangement be accounted for as a borrowing rather than as a sale. While the *Statement* applies only to arrangements in which one company is in substance the owner of a product and another entity holds the product to facilitate a financing arrangement, it is an indication of the FASB's movement toward the requirement that certain financing arrangements be recorded in financial statements.

The following example illustrates the criteria and characteristics of a transaction that would be considered in determining whether the transaction is to be recorded on the balance sheet or disclosed as an off-balance sheet item.

Basic Case

Excess Timber, an integrated forest products company, has a substantial investment in relatively mature timber and timberland in excess of its current needs. This timberland is being held to meet expected future requirements. Excess Timber's long-term strategic plan is to use the timber from one such tract (tract T-27) during a succeeding growth cycle. As a result of inflation, the current value of the timber on tract T-27 ($50 million) is much higher than its historical cost carrying amount on Excess Timber's balance sheet ($10 million). Excess Timber wants to use these undervalued assets as a source of funds without sacrificing its future supply of timber.

Excess Timber sells the right to the timber now standing on tract T-27 to XYZ Company for $50 million. Excess Timber retains the right of first refusal to buy, at fair market value, any timber cut by XYZ. XYZ assumes the risks and rewards of ownership since it bears the price risk as well as the risk of fire or other damage to the timber.

Excess Timber records $40 million of income at the time of sale since the earning process is completed, as evidenced by the transfer to a third party which has assumed the risks and rewards of ownership and by Excess Timber's lack of continuing obligations with respect to the timber. Excess Timber retains its direct ownership interest in the land and thus maintains the right to reforest for its own account.

Second Case

Assume the same basic facts except that XYZ has the right to put to Excess Timber any timber cut from tract T-27 at fair market value. As in the basic case, XYZ is assuming the risks and rewards of ownership.

Because of its continuing involvement through its obligation to repurchase any cut timber, Excess Timber has not completed the earning process and would not recognize any profit on the sale of the timber to XYZ. The $40 million proceeds received in excess of cost would be reflected as deferred income and would be included in income as the timber is cut and sold to Excess Timber or a third-party purchaser.

Third Case

Assume the same facts as the basic case except that Excess Timber is obligated to pay $12 million per year for the timber for five years, on a take-or-pay basis (i.e., Excess Timber pays even if the timber is not cut or if it cannot be cut due to fire or other damage to the property).

Because Excess Timber retains all the risks and rewards of owner-ship (other than the credit risk), it would record the $50 million received from XYZ as a borrowing.

COMMODITY-BACKED BONDS

Commodity-backed bonds are a relatively recent innovation in the field of corporate finance. These bonds typically have some or all of the following characteristics:

1. They represent rights to fixed amounts of a commodity (e.g., oil, coal, or silver) or to a specified percentage of the appreciation in a specified commodity.
2. They may be convertible into common stock at fixed or determinable amounts.
3. The final settlement price may be solely dependent on the underlying asset's value or on the greater of a minimum amount (usually face value) or the value of the underlying asset.
4. Final settlement may be payable by delivering the required amount of the asset or cash (or some combination of the two).

The basic motivation for issuing these bonds is that they allow debt to be issued without committing the issuer to high cash interest rates on a long-term basis. Alternatively, this can be expressed as a desire to substitute price inflation on a specified asset for the inflation element implicit in the market interest rate. Thus, the bond issuer is able to obtain funds at a below-market interest rate by giving up the right to the "opportunity gain" on the value of the underlying asset.

The accounting literature does not specifically address the accounting for commodity-backed debt issues.

Bonds payable in nonowned noncash assets might be carried at the current fair market value of the related assets. If the creditor has an option to receive either cash or noncash assets, the bonds would be carried at the greater of the cash amount or the current fair market value of the noncash assets. If the option is the debtor's, the lower of the two amounts would be used. Adjustments in carrying amounts would be included in income.

Bonds payable in owned assets might be accounted for as a current sale with future delivery. Applying this logic, the seller (debtor) would carry the bonds at a value equal to the proceeds received on issuance. Subsequent changes in the asset's, and hence the liability's value, would not be reflected in the debtor's financial statements until the bonds are retired.

Bonds whose repayment is to be made in cash that is tied to specific commodity prices might be considered to be a borrowing at a below-market interest rate, as defined in *APB Opinion No. 21*. Applying this approach, the liability would be recorded at a discounted value to reflect an effective rate of interest equal to the "market rate" at the date of issuance. Any difference between the recorded liability, including imputed interest at the "market rate," and the ultimate settlement price would be reflected in income in the year of settlement.

As this discussion shows, the accounting for commodity-backed bonds has not been developed into a set of definitive policies and procedures. There are, in fact, alternative accounting methods that are theoretically supportable. Should these bonds become a significant factor in corporate finance, it is likely that the FASB would issue specific guidelines.

SUMMARY

This chapter has briefly touched upon the accounting and financial reporting aspects of certain methods and techniques used in left hand financing. The discussion has been limited to some of the more frequently used techniques. As previously indicated, the accounting and financial reporting practices discussed in this chapter are subject to change or modification; accordingly, the accounting treatment for a transaction should always be reviewed for current applicability.

CHAPTER 5

Marketing Considerations

JANET G. SPRATLIN
JOHN L. STEFFENS
Merrill Lynch, Pierce, Fenner, and Smith Inc.

Left hand financing enables corporations to finance their operations at lower cost, with greater flexibility, and with different assumptions of risk than would be possible through more traditional financing channels. A thoughtful observer of the process might be inclined to ask, "How can this be? If the business is the same, if the management is the same, if the outlook for the industry is the same, then why would investors be prepared to accept a lower return, less flexibility, and different risks to fund the operation of this business with left hand financing than with more traditional financing? *What's in it for the investor?"* The answer to this question is critical. Deals must be structured and positioned to meet the investors' requirements because if investors see no advantages, left hand financing programs cannot succeed.

SEGMENTING THE MARKET IS THE KEY

In a broad sense, all left hand financing techniques succeed by identifying and appealing to some subgroup of investors whose individual circumstances or points of view lead them to prefer investments with special features that address their particular needs. To obtain such special features, some investors will be prepared to accept a lower guaranteed return than "the market" would demand from the same company were it to use the standard financing instruments. Note: this is *not* a zero-sum game in the sense that any gains to the employer of capital do not necessarily mean losses to the investor. If deals are properly structured, both the corporation and the investor can benefit. Such targeting

85

on the needs of specific groups of clients is referred to by marketing professionals as "segmenting the marketplace," and it underlies most corporate marketing activities today.

What does it mean to segment the financial marketplace? Financial theory tells us that investments can be ranked according to their expected risk and their expected return and that in general, financial markets require higher expected returns for assuming more risk. In practice, however, investors do not all use the same criteria in making decisions, and they do not all reach the same conclusions. At any point in time, the market's evaluation of the riskiness of any investment (and hence its required return) reflects the allocation of investors among all available investments, and to some extent, the resulting rate structure represents an averaging of investment objectives and expectations. This means that when an investor differs significantly from that average—with respect to either investment objectives or expectations about the future—then in a very real sense, existing investment vehicles are failing to satisfy that investor's needs, and there is an opportunity for some new financial instrument to attract the funds of a segment of the investor community.

SEEKING INVESTORS WITH SPECIAL NEEDS

Investors' objectives vary depending on the investors' particular circumstances. Most investors view both risk and return as multidimensional concepts, and at any point in time, certain types of return and certain types of risk are more critical than others. For example, a retired individual who depends on the return from his portfolio to meet his daily living expenses is understandably concerned about the level and regularity of that income stream. In contrast, for a 50-year-old executive or professional with substantial other sources of income, the current income from an investment may be far less important than the investment's ability to shelter noninvestment income from taxes.

Similarly, risk means different things to different investors. Some require a high degree of liquidity; others are prepared to forgo liquidity if they can protect themselves against inflation; still others appear to have a positive preference for ventures with substantial amounts of uncertainty so long as the ventures promise extraordinary gains to the "winners."

Not only do investors' objectives vary depending on their particular circumstances and individual willingness to bear risk, but even among investors with similar investment objectives, divergent expectations about the future will result in a wide range of investment decisions. At any point in time, the returns available on the major financial instruments tend to reflect a consensus about the expected business environment. This includes such factors as inflation, government deficits, government regulation, international trade, and the probability of events such as war, famine, the continued success of the OPEC cartel, etc. But some investors either have expectations that deviate from this consensus or are unusually vulnerable to particular possibilities. This provides opportunities to devise investment vehicles that offer protection or flexibility tailored to their particular situations.

WHOSE NEEDS ARE NOT WELL SERVED BY EXISTING MARKETS?

Some investors are well served by the traditional financial markets. This is probably the case for reasonably risk-averse investors whose demands for steady investment income and/or liquidity are high and whose expectations about the future economic environment do not differ significantly from the consensus. Analysts tend to rate securities by (1) their expected ability to provide investors with a steady stream of interest or dividends, (2) their expected appreciation in value (which can result, for example, from the anticipated reinvestment of profits, and (3) their expected liquidity (which can depend as much on the characteristics of the market in which the security is traded as on the characteristics of the company being financed). External factors, such as inflation, are factored into these analyses, but their impact on returns tends to reflect a consensus.

It is clear that the needs of some investors are *not* well served by the established marketplace, and these are the investors toward whom one would want to target new investment vehicles. It has been our experience that these less well served segments include:

1. Investors with a high need to shelter other income from taxes.
2. Investors with "nonconsensus expectations" of or unusual exposure to inflation risks.
3. Investors who need to protect the purchasing power of a stream of income no matter what rate of inflation eventuates.
4. Investors who wish to protect the principal of their investment if a very high rate of inflation is experienced during the investment period.
5. Investors who are genuine risk takers.

Tax Investments

In the past, a large fraction of the more successful asset-based financing programs could be classified under the rubric of tax shelters or tax investments. These programs appealed primarily to individuals whose marginal tax rates could range as high as 70 percent (prior to the 1981 Economic Recovery Tax Act).

Tax investments tend to fall into two broad categories:

a. Those designed to shelter from taxation income generated by the investment itself. Many real estate deals fall into this category.

b. Those designed to pass through to investors the losses, depletion allowances, or investment tax credits incurred during the early years of the venture. The investors can then use the losses, allowances, or credits to offset taxable income from other sources. This category includes oil and gas partnerships, venture capital partnerships, and the so-called tax-benefit leases.

To the investment banker, the distinctions between these two types of tax shelters are more a matter of degree than of kind, but from a marketing standpoint, the two types would appear to appeal to distinct investor segments.

Investments in real estate, which typically enjoy venture-generated tax deductions that minimize the taxation on the income from the investment itself, appeal to investors with a need for some steady, tax-sheltered income. Our research indicates that these investors tend to be neither extreme risk takers nor are they heavily concentrated in the highest marginal tax brackets. But they do expect to be paying a significant fraction of their income in taxes over a period of several years, and they are seeking to minimize the impact of taxes and inflation on the long-term return to their savings.

In contrast, investments in oil and gas partnerships are highly illiquid and can be expected to generate no cash income during the early years, but they do provide the investor with quite significant write-offs which can be used to shelter other income. Obviously, the value of these write-offs to the investor depends entirely on the existence of substantial taxable income from other sources. If an investor discovers an unexpected need for cash flow or an unexpected reduction in taxable income, such tax shelters can turn out to be very bad investments. Consequently, investors in these "high write-off" tax investments tend to be in very high tax brackets and to be prepared to take significant risks (with at least some fraction of their portfolio). Typically, they foresee no need for cash income from such investments and they anticipate that the timing of their other taxable income will correspond well with the expected stream of tax benefits.

Investors with "Nonconsensus Expectations"

Another group of investors whose needs may not be well served by traditional financial markets comprises those investors whose expectations of the future and/or vulnerability to particular future events cause them to seek flexibilities or guarantees different from those offered by the standard debt or equity investments. For example, current long-term bond rates include a premium which reflects the market view about expected inflation. But the premium is not likely to be adequate for the individuals or institutions that expect inflation to exceed 15 to 20 percent during a significant portion of the next 10 years or that wish to hedge some fraction of their portfolios against this possibility. In exchange for a hedge against high levels of inflation, such investors would be very willing to put some portion of their total portfolios into instruments that offer less guaranteed income today, or greater credit risk, or less liquidity.

As noted above, real estate investors typically trade off liquidity for an inflation hedge. Similarly, leasing deals enable the investor to obtain direct ownership of assets that may appreciate in value with inflation. But the permutations and combinations of inflation hedge vehicles are almost unlimited. For example, many investors who would be uncomfortable owning illiquid assets, such as real estate partnerships or railroad boxcars, would be attracted to such investments as the bonds of Sunshine Mining Company. Issued in 1980, these bonds carried an 8½ percent coupon, which at the time was probably some 500 to 600 basis points below the market for straight bonds and provided Sunshine Mining with a very low cost source of funds. But the principal amount of these bonds was indexed to the average market price of 50 ounces of silver. Although the "conversion value" of $20 an ounce is significantly above current silver prices, if inflation were to push the price of silver back to the levels of January 1980 ($48 an ounce), these would become very lucrative investments indeed. (See pages 34-37, Sunshine Mining Company—Silver-Indexed Bonds for a more complete description.)

Foreign Investors

Only recently has the average U.S. investor come to realize that every investment involves some kind of "bet" on inflation. But many countries have had longer experiences with rapid inflation than the United States, and as a result, foreign investors are frequently more sensitized than U.S. investors to the risks involved, making them an important target for some left hand financing investments.

The investment objectives of foreign investors are somewhat different from those of their American counterparts. For example, since this market segment typically does not incur substantial U.S. tax liabilities, the tax shelter attributes that are key selling points of many left hand financing investments provide little attraction.

On the other hand, many foreign investors are particularly vulnerable to political unrest and foreign exchange risk—factors which are relatively unimportant to the average American investor. Many of these investors view the United States as a capitalist haven in an increasingly socialist world. This, combined with the recent strength of our dollar, has lured significant amounts of foreign investment to U.S. capital markets.

The liquidity and anonymity of U.S. debt and equity markets have traditionally attracted large quantities of foreign investment, and the recycling of "petro dollars" has made foreign investment an even more significant source of funds. In the past, the vast majority of foreign investors preferred highly liquid portfolio investments. But the recent political changes in countries such as France may have pushed into the U.S. capital markets a different kind of foreign investor. Although hard data are difficult to obtain, growing numbers of foreign entrepreneurial investors appear to be considering the United States as a possible permanent residence for themselves and their capital. As a consequence, the foreign interest in less liquid, left hand financing investments has probably grown. Certainly, foreign investors who are resident in countries that are experiencing political and social unrest have a motivation to diversify their investments across national boundaries.

Risk Takers

Risk takers comprise a third segment of the investing public that is not well served by our existing financial markets. What kinds of investments are available to an investor who wants to put $20,000 to $100,000 in a truly risky venture in hopes of making $1 million? New companies are rarely publicly held; information on such firms is not easily available; and the marketplace for this kind of venture capital is informal at best.

Our experience indicates that a wide demand exists for high-quality venture capital investments but that because these deals are so varied and the available information is so diffuse, some investors are justifiably uneasy about assuming what may turn out to be totally unreasonable levels of risk. Marketing would appear to be quite important here. There is clearly a need to provide some substitute for the kind of systematic securities research opinions that support investment decision making in the listed securities area. In the absence of such an information dissemination process, the market will probably remain fragmented.

A key problem here is that in many cases, the necessary information does not exist, the risks are very real, and many investors probably cannot justify this kind of investment. It is critical that customer suitability criteria be developed and enforced. Neither borrowers nor distributors benefit if investors who are not bona fide risk takers lose significant amounts of capital because they are overinvested in highly risky ventures.

Venture capital funds that enable investors to diversify away part of the risk are one approach to making this market accessible to investors who are more risk averse. Alternatively, investment in assets that are leased to new enterprises can offer some of the high rewards normally expected from venture investment while limiting the downside risk.

LEFT HAND FINANCING—A SUBSTITUTE FOR A DIVERSIFIED PORTFOLIO?

Left hand financing deals that limit the downside risk may perform the same function in fragmented markets that portfolio diversification accomplishes in more organized markets. For example, bonds used to be viewed as safer investments than stocks, but in these days of steadily rising prices, it has become clear that there are also significant risks to holding bonds. Many investors follow the standard prescription for minimizing risk and diversify by holding both debt and equity securities in their portfolios. But this strategy typically confines them to publicly listed companies. Some left hand financing investments act like hybrid stock/bond combinations, ensuring a minimum guaranteed income while also providing for some equity-like appreciation. In this sense, they may effectively substitute for diversification and thus should be particularly attractive to investors who wish to limit the risk of investing in smaller, more closely held companies.

This type of arrangement includes retailing leases that pass through to the investors some percentage of revenues. For example, a retailer may be able to lease its facility for a lower guaranteed rate of return if it can at the same time provide investors with some protection from inflation, and it is becoming increasingly common to structure such deals so that when the sales of a store rise above some anticipated level, investors receive some percentage of the gross sales revenues.

MARKET ANALYSIS IN ORDER TO ANTICIPATE CHANGES

A careful analysis of the needs of investors is an important input to the strategic planning of borrowers and their bankers. As was noted above, most of the identifiable investor segments can be classified by their particular circumstances, their willingness to bear risk, and their (nonconsensus) expectations about (or vulnerability to) future high and unpredictable rates of inflation. Examining the sources of these differences more closely may make it possible to anticipate and profit from changes in the marketplace.

For example, some investor needs depend on external but predictable factors, such as taxes. Taxes are external in the sense that investors may have little short-run control over their individual tax liabilities, but they are predictable in that typically tax rates are broadly known in advance. Borrowers or their bankers should be able to forecast the impact of changes in such factors on potential investors and to respond fairly quickly with "new" products.

Investor preferences can also be traced to some external but less predictable factors. These include inflation and its impact on financial markets. If inflation were to decline for an extended period of time, many investors would adjust downward their expectations for future inflation, and the demand for some types of left hand financing would probably decline. But here it is much more difficult to identify which investors will be affected and what their most attractive alternatives might be.

Similarly, many investment decisions are tied closely to the life cycle. Examples were cited earlier: the liquidity and income needs of a retiree living on the returns from his portfolio; the tax-shelter needs of a high-income middle-aged executive. To a very large extent, changes in the age and income distribution of our society are predictable—certainly over the near to medium term. Consequently, bankers should be able to anticipate the impact of demographic changes on investment needs.

Of course, not all of the factors that influence investment can be traced to predictable phenomena. Who knows what makes some people become risk takers while others of the same age, income, and so on, are overly risk averse? Nonetheless, there is enough systematic behavior among investors in our economy to enable employers of capital to profit by targeting their financing methods to meet specific investment characteristics sought by some of the more easily identifiable groups of investors.

CHAPTER 6

Selecting an Investment Banker

RICHARD W. CARRINGTON
American Airlines, Inc.

Investment bankers are the indispensible intermediaries who skillfully and efficiently channel funds from investors to corporations and, in so doing, provide the lifeblood of our free enterprise system. According to the zoological jargon of Wall Street, there are bulls, there are bears, and above all there are pigs; and in good times and bad, through thick and thin, it is reassuring for the corporate client to know that the investment banker will always be there to serve him—as long as he gets his pound of flesh.

Beginning with this well-balanced perspective on investment banking, the corporation, in establishing its financial policies, is confronted with the question of how it is to manage its investment banking relationships. The choice of an investment banker is not a decision to be made without carefully reasoned justification. There is a critical role to be performed in matching the objectives of the corporate issuer with those of the investment community. The investment banker is the middle link in the chain. He must know what his client requires and what the capital markets demand. To quote a recent proposal letter from an investment banker, "American Airlines will achieve financing terms that are significantly more attractive than those which might be ordinarily obtained. At the same time, the investor will benefit substantially as a result of this structure." The skill with which the investment banker brings these two forces together will determine how closely the needs of a corporation are met and how much it must pay for capital.

93

HISTORY AND EVOLUTION

A survey of major corporations by *Fortune* magazine indicated that the two predominant factors in the decision to use a particular investment banker were "personal relationships" and tradition ("our company has always used the underwriter").[1] The survey was conducted in 1967— only 15 years ago, but on the spectrum of financial history, those days represent an ancient and bygone era.

Profound changes have taken place across three dimensions: the corporation and its financial strategy, the structure of the investment banking industry, and the world capital markets. The halcyon days of 1967 were simple and ordered; they didn't seem so back then, but now we have 1982 as the basis for comparison.

The Corporation

Although 1967 was hardly the peak in the stock market, equities could be sold at a fair price—the average price-earnings ratio for the Standard & Poor's 400 was close to 20. Moreover, corporate management was, in general, conservative in its capitalization philosophy, preferring to maintain a low debt-to-equity mix. In fact, much was written in academic journals about optimum capital structures, maximum debt capacities, and inflection points on cost of capital curves. The suggestion was that many companies were ignoring opportunities to take on more debt and create value through leveraged earnings. And debt was cheap then— between 5 percent and 6 percent for most of the year for single-A industrials. Earnings and internal cash flow were high in relation to capital expenditures. (In 1967, even the airlines made money.) When one did have to resort to borrowing, a bank loan could easily be arranged at a prime rate of 6 percent.

The world of the 80s offers the corporate treasurer no such luxuries. The S&P 400 can be bought at a price-earnings ratio of less than 8. Out of necessity as much as a change in philosophy, companies have turned to debt to satiate their massive appetite for capital. Many ingenious methods have been developed to leverage companies to the hilt. The level of capital expenditures has reached exaggerated proportions due to the impact of inflation on replacement costs, the technological transition toward energy efficiency, and nonproductive requirements, such as pollution control equipment. At the same time, cash flow from operations has waned. The widening gap between sources and uses can only be filled by debt capital which, at the time of this writing, costs in excess of 16 percent for a single-A industrial. Commercial banks might lend at the prime rate of 16.5 percent, but since customer loyalty and

---

[1] "A Fortune Survey on Investment Banking Firms," *Fortune*, September 1967.

compensating balances have all but disappeared, this alternative is by no means certain.

At best, the cost of financing now has a material impact on earnings (in the airline industry, interest costs will be several times as great as operating profits even in the best of times); at worst, the required capital may not be available at all, and an important project will have to be abandoned. In the corporate finance function, the difference between a good job and a bad job is too critical to leave totally to outsiders.

With the increased "value added" at the finance function, corporations have built up large professional finance departments. These departments play an active, in-house role in controlling working capital, making resource allocation decisions, financial planning, and external financing. The latter two tasks, which had been previously delegated to investment bankers, are in many cases either being assumed or at least shared by corporate treasury departments staffed with individuals whose academic credentials and professional training are often comparable to those of investment bankers. While there are many ramifications of this organizational development, certainly one of them has been to dispel the awe and mystique of Wall Street and to make corporations more aggressive and self-confident in pursuing their financial activities.

Structure of Investment Banking

Back in 1967, the industry had an orderly structure with the participants' roles clearly defined. There were firms that initiated deals, underwrote them, and orchestrated the marketing effort. There were the brokerage houses led by Merrill Lynch which had their retail networks of sales offices. Then there were trading firms (e.g., Salomon Brothers) with powerful, institutional distribution capabilities. The firms in the first group, which handled the corporate clients and originated the transactions, comprised a private club and experienced little competition either among themselves or from the other firms primarily engaged in distribution. Of course, those were the days when commercial banks practiced commercial banking, insurance companies sold insurance, American Express was in the travel business, and Sears Roebuck was a chain of big stores. The upheaval that has followed—the mergers, acquisitions, bankruptcies, divestitures, and diversifications—has left the investment banking landscape barely recognizable from what it was 15 years ago. And the revolution has only begun. Whereas the first phase witnessed the emergence of the distribution and retail-oriented houses[2] into the upper echelons of the more lucrative investment banking sec-

---

[2] Merrill Lynch, Salomon Brothers, and Goldman Sachs are certainly the most notable. Others in this category who have made significant strides are Dean Witter, E. F. Hutton, Bache Halsey Stuart Shields, and Shearson/American Express.

tor, the second phase is likely to be marked by the invasion of financial conglomerates, such as Prudential, Sears, American Express, and Citicorp.

With the intensity of the new competitive thrusts, there has been considerable piracy of personnel. Moreover, since most of the firms are now publicly held, individuals are no longer handcuffed by their partnership interests. Turnover has been heavy, and articles in *Corporate Financing Week* read like gossip columns in movie magazines explaining who has left whom to go with whatever. For example, on a recent domestic public issue by American Airlines, the lead manager did an exceptional job; yet the three individuals most responsible for it have all left the firm, each going to a separate competitor. Personal relationships can be important assets in this business, but maintaining them can be more difficult than keeping up with a blind date at a wife-swapping party.

The Capital Markets

Any summary comments concerning the transformation of the world capital markets would be an understatement. For the corporate treasurer, the redistribution and recycling of capital has created many diverse pools of funds while leaving others dry. The massive flows of "petro dollars," the explosive growth of the Euromarkets, the burgeoning development of the Asian capital market have all had a profound impact. Domestically, there has been the dominance of the institutional investors, most particularly the pension funds that have accumulated vast concentrations of this country's monetary wealth. The passage of ERISA, the dismantling of currency controls and fixed foreign exchange rates, tax legislation and regulations governing leasing have all fundamentally affected the world of corporate finance. In 1967, the airline industry in the United States was financed almost exclusively by a half dozen insurance companies and a group of eight commercial banks. American Airlines was no exception. Now we have found that our traditional sources are no longer able or willing to adequately meet our needs. In one year alone, American Airlines arranged a leveraged lease with debt being contributed by pension funds, established a project financing for an oil and gas venture, issued Eurobonds with warrants, privately placed a dual currency bond in Switzerland, floated a tax-exempt special facilities bond issue, took down a hedged deutsche mark loan, and negotiated a back-to-back, so-called double-dip lease between several institutions in the United Kingdom and a U.S. equity investor—just to name a few examples! With respect to the financing of our Boeing 767s, we are presently working to put together a syndicate of Japanese financial institutions.

As the sources of capital have become more diverse, the financial instruments themselves have become more complex. Straightforward, "pure vanilla" deals can still be done by AT&T, but from lesser mortals, the investors are demanding more. From the issuer standpoint, such is the competition for capital that companies strive to differentiate their securities by adding special features to attract certain investor interests. What was once disparaged as gimmickry now is extolled as brilliant innovation. *Left hand financings,* zero coupons, stock-for-bond swaps, leveraged preferreds, arcane tax maneuvers, and back-to-back currency transactions are all part of today's scene. There are extendables and retractables, convertibles and reversibles, things that can be accelerated and things that can be deferred. Just recently, there have been several issues of "equity notes" which look like debt but must convert into equity, to be contrasted with dual option warrants which look like equity but under certain conditions revert into debt. Matching the needs of the investor with those of the corporate issuer requires a lot more ingenuity than it used to.

Fit Between Corporation, Investment Banker, and Capital Markets

Out of the maelstrom of change must come a fit among the corporation's financial needs, the qualifications of the investment banker, and the demands of the capital markets. The investment banker is the middle section of the three parts that must be dovetailed together. He must meet his client's objectives and execute the transaction in the marketplace. It is a relationship of dynamic forces. Achieving it in one instance provides no guarantee that the situation will continue because conditions inevitably change. The right investment banker for today's U.S. leveraged lease may be less suited for tomorrow's yen financing. Because of these factors, tradition-bound loyalty to one investment banker is becoming a rarity. If all parts of the equation are in flux, it seems logically inconsistent for the choice of an investment banker to be permanently entrenched.

CRITERIA FOR CHOOSING

There are numerous criteria for selecting a particular investment bank, and to attempt a complete listing would expand the pages of this chapter beyond the covers of the book itself. The first premise is that this selection is an integral part of the corporation's financial decision-making process. It should always be subject to review, and each financing calls for a new decision as to which firm can best represent the company given the circumstances at the time. Past relationships are important to be sure, and a company's choice should naturally be influenced by a firm's performance in prior deals. But the dynamics of the process cannot be ignored, and a firm should earn its commission each time the client has a financing at stake.

The following seven criteria are discussed below:

1. Specific expertise.
2. Creativity.
3. Working relationships in client organization.
4. Human factors.
5. Priority given to client.
6. Effective communication.
7. Price.

The relative importance of each of these factors will vary with the nature of the deal and the corporate client; hence, no inherent ranking is implied. The first three arise out of the evolution previously discussed; that is, the diversity and complexity of financings and the organizational requirements of a company's decision-making process. The second three considerations are time-honored values that continue to be as applicable today as they have been in the past. The final criterion listed—price—has really not been a factor in the past, but it would seem negligent to omit it entirely. Companies can negotiate hard for lower fees or spreads, but rarely is business awarded to a particular firm because it is known that their services are less expensive. There are, however, certain types of transactions created by recent legislation which may provoke price-cutting activity in the future.

Specific Expertise

General information about an investment bank is good to know, but it should never be a deciding factor. One should be generally aware of a firm's standing in the financing "sweepstakes" (calculated annually by *Institutional Investor*), major clients gained or lost, its institutional and retail distribution network, and its capital position. More particularly though, a corporate issuer should focus its attention on a house's demonstrated expertise in the particular area in which it is interested. No house is equally good at everything. Most of those who have gained a significant share of the investment banking market have done so using a specific strength to bring in clients and then have gone on to expand their scope of activities. Conversely, those who have seen established clients turn to other houses to fill a specific need, have been firms who, either by choice or circumstance, have had certain limitations in their product line. This is not to say that a house should attempt to be all things to all people but rather that it should build a coherent strategy around its individual strengths. The point is that the prospective client should recognize these same strengths and weaknesses and act accordingly.

I recently learned of a case of a corporation which had decided to institute a commercial paper program. Rather than select a dealer-manager with whom he was unfamiliar, the chairman chose the company's traditional investment bank to do the job. The trouble was that the investment bank did not have even one dedicated commercial paper salesman nor did it act as dealer for any other clients. Nonetheless, it took on the job. The company, needless to say, was not well served. It was poorly introduced to the market, there was little breadth of distribution, and the company paid premium prices compared to issues of similar quality. Within six months, it appointed a new dealer-manager that had proven its qualifications.

The firm's qualifications should be those specifically directed toward the relevant market and financial instrument under consideration. In the case of commercial paper, a survey of major buyers could produce a list of firms who have a superior market presence. Client lists and volume figures are also available. The number of salesmen, both overall and per client, could serve as an indicator of sales coverage. A firm's performance vis-à-vis other houses in handling split programs can demonstrate certain competitive advantages. Equally informative is news of corporations that have added or replaced certain firms as their dealers. Assistance in structuring a program is another factor. Discussions with several houses will allow a company to evaluate their ideas on setting up a captive finance company, key provisions in an operating agreement, forms of bank support, and the most effective approach to the rating agencies. Other essential qualifications would include the ability to presell the client's name to investors and gain the necessary credit approvals, the market knowledge to offer valuable maturity counseling, and, finally, the willingness to take a position in the client's paper. Once the prospective commercial paper issuer has particularized his needs, he can ask the incisive questions and differentiate among firms along the pertinent dimensions.

As in the example above, one should analyze the capabilities of an investment bank for each type of financing. Its strengths must match the requirements of the deal. Overgeneralizations can be dangerous. The ablest manager for the corporation's common stock issue may be unqualified to put together a left hand financing. By not recognizing this in advance, a company can do itself irreparable damage. In the worst case, the financing could fail to materialize altogether, causing the company to abort a strategic project. More often though, a company will suffer through a poorly managed deal in which it pays too much, capitulates to unnecessarily restrictive terms, or leaves the underwriting group and investors with indelible memories of a failure to be recalled on the next financing the company attempts to do. Such unseen consequences or hypothetical comparisons are sometimes hard to substantiate and easy to ignore, but it can be most constructive to study the outcomes of similar financings and second-guess one's performance for the benefit of future transactions.

Creativity

If necessity has been the mother of Wall Street's inventions, the investment bankers have been active midwives. As the demand for common equity and simple fixed-income securities has dissipated, a number of innovative financing techniques, such as those involved in left hand financing, have been developed to meet the needs of issuers and investors alike. With respect to the former, execution had been the critical factor, but with the new wave of innovations, the emphasis is on creativity. The design and structure must be carefully tailored to a given set of situational variables in order to achieve the borrower's objectives, tap the appropriate segment of the capital markets, and differentiate the financial instrument being sold from others of perhaps higher-quality names which threaten to "crowd it out." Timing and execution are still important, but the environment of the 80s calls for a product orientation. Investment bankers talk of research and development and test marketing in the same way as a product manager might discuss a new line of personal computers. Task forces of financial theorists, securities salesmen and traders, accountants, and tax experts combine their talents to create and apply new ideas for the financial marketplace.

Clearly, the economic rewards for financing in recent years have been achieved through ingenuity in design. Not eighths or quarters but hundreds of basis points have been saved through the creation stage of a financing. The brainstorming, the experimenting, and the embryonic development are the key activities. It is the architects of the left hand financings, as well as zero coupons, leveraged preferreds, equity notes, stock-for-bond swaps, etc. that have created the most value for their clients. Some have been marketed well, others not so well; but all have saved the issuers substantial capital costs when compared to the more standard, traditional alternatives.

Just as brilliant design has produced the major success stories in the financial world of the 80s, faulty design has been the root of some notable debacles. The case of Laker Airways is illustrative. Over the past several years, it purchased a fleet of wide-bodied aircraft financed through 10-year, U.S. dollar-denominated debt totaling some $400 million. This decision had several interesting ramifications. First, it leveraged the company with debt capital, committing it to a heavy, fixed, repayment schedule. Given the volatility of fares and traffic in the airline industry, more permanent equity or equity-related capital would have been more appropriate for a start-up carrier. Second, there was Laker's choice to own its aircraft, ignoring opportunities to enter into some beneficial form of left hand financing, such as leveraged leasing. On the one hand, such an arrangement could have given the airline the flexibility of a short-term lease (so it could elect not to renew if business turned down); on the other hand, a long-term lease for a period of 18 years would have lowered annual debt service and stretched out the repayment schedule. Moreover, there were sizable tax benefits, totally worthless to Laker, that could be utilized by high tax bracket investors. These tax benefits could be worth between 400 and 500 basis points in lower interest costs. Finally, there was the mismatch in currencies. Laker was saddled with a dollar repayment schedule (not to mention its dollar-based fuel bill), but unfortunately, its cash was largely denominated in pounds sterling. The exposure was unnecessary and later proved to be the coup de grace. When the pound plummeted to $1.75, Laker's obligations increased some 40 percent over what was anticipated. On February 5, 1982, Laker Airways declared bankruptcy. This was not a well-designed financing. Nothing was wrong with the execution, the syndicating, or the marketing; the fundamentals at the front end of the financing, the design itself, were ill-conceived.

How can a corporation make sure it can avail itself of the full spectrum of state-of-the-art financing technology? The creative process is stimulated by corporations seeking out new ideas in a competitive environment, and it is nurtured and sustained by the client rewarding firms for their efforts. No investment bank has a monopoly on creativity, nor is it likely to be motivated unless new business can be won. A corporation can best foster creativity by soliciting ideas from multiple banking relationships, maintaining confidentiality and the proprietary nature of those ideas, and being prepared to give its business to a house that offers valuable contributions. In order to not limit the flow of creative ideas and to be sure all the alternatives are assessed, a corporation must be open-minded in considering both new concepts and new investment banking relationships.

Working Relationships

The new approach to financing calls for a multilevel working relationship between a corporation and its investment banks. Relationships that exist solely between a senior partner and the company's chairman will be neither productive nor long-lasting. The final decision of selecting an investment bank will almost always require the chairman's concurrence, but the work of his own financial organization should provide a sound basis for a recommendation. The evolution of financial organizations has already been described. While no corporation can be totally self-sufficient with its in-house financial staff (Exxon has probably gone further than anyone in this regard), more work is being assumed internally. The investment banker's place has shifted away from being a surrogate corporate treasurer to serving as an adjunct who can complement the internal treasury function.

In managing the creative process of designing the optimum financial instrument, a corporation takes on a large amount of the analytical workload. Having first set out the objectives of a financing, it then solicits ideas and proposals from the investment banking community. Then the staff work begins. All alternatives must be evaluated against the stated objectives of the company. Advantages and disadvantages of each one are identified, modifications and refinements are made, certain criteria are quantified over a range of financial scenarios, and various sensitivities are measured. Recently, for example, the American Airlines staff evaluated the following alternatives of financing a group of used aircraft: (1) a Eurobond issue with various innovative features, (2) a Swiss franc private placement, (3) a placement in the Middle East backed by a Letter of Credit, (4) a peppercorn lease in Australia, (5) a convertible debenture sold publicly in the United States, and (6) a floating-rate term loan from a syndicate of commercial banks. These proposals came from four investment banks, each one touting its own forte. In order to thoroughly analyze these alternatives and to develop new derivatives, the corporate financial staff must work closely with the investment bankers at the associate level. Not only the inevitable number crunching but also much of the creative interchange of ideas should take place in the trenches.

Once the alternatives have been narrowed down, questions of judgment and policy may remain to be referred to senior levels. At this point, the relationship between a partner of a firm with the chairman or president of a corporation is very beneficial in giving credibility to an innovative financing concept or reinforcing his firm's commitment to take on a major underwriting. Partners and chairmen are needed for opening doors initially and ultimately closing deals, but the critical work in between must rely on a constructive interface between the investment bank and the client company at all levels.

Human Factors

No criteria in choosing an investment banker should supercede the eternal qualities of honesty and integrity. All deals sound best at the outset; at closing, there is always that apprehensive feeling that something was given away. Understanding that investment bankers are the world's foremost salesmen, the corporate client must be confident that he has been fully apprised of all the risks and uncertainties of a transaction. The investment banker cannot promise everything; there are too many variables outside of his control. To be honest, however, he should point out the pitfalls, estimate an acceptable range of outcomes, and establish a set of reference indices whose behavior can explain changes in the terms of a financing. To illustrate this last point, a warrant to purchase common stock would be expected to derive its value from the exercise premium, the life of the warranty, the volatility of the shares, the investor's borrowing rate, and any foregone common dividends. If the investment banker states that the warrant can be sold for $5, the client must count on realizing approximately that price as long as those critical indices remain unchanged. If the variables in fact improve but the pricing actually deteriorates, then most likely the client has been baited. This happens too frequently. It may be one of the negative consequences of the intense competition for corporate clients. A glittering proposal is made, a mandate is given, and bit by bit the deal begins to move away from its original terms. By that time the hapless client may have foregone other options and be forced to make 11th-hour concessions he would have never considered had they been anticipated in advance. In a profession in which closing deals is the ultimate objective, personal integrity will never be an overrated virtue.

Second, chemistry of personalities should not be overlooked. The interminable monotony of road shows, the exasperating sessions with a room full of lawyers discussing what words mean, and the many hours traveling together on airplanes call for a superhuman threshold of boredom. Much of the strain and pain can be assuaged by compatible personalities. A dose of good humor at the right time can be just the thing to save a financial officer from an early grave.

From my personal experience, I offer three personality tests. The investment bankers must be: (1) discriminating enough not to discuss the marketing strategy of a European bond issue while dining at the Longhorn Barbecue Pit (even for us clients in Texas), (2) enough of a boulevardier that when he offers to take you on a tour of Amsterdam, you don't end up visiting rows of flower shops on Thursday morning, and (3) enough of a connoisseur that he will allow his client to eat and drink his way through 49 percent of his fee on a well-priced deal.

Priority Given to Client

The priority afforded a client is another significant factor in investment banking relationships. A priority status can have several advantages. First, it can give a company ready access to a senior partner who can mobilize the full resources of his firm to the clients cause. Second, a company can enjoy the position of being one of the first who is approached to capitalize on a new idea or unique opportunity. The last issuer of zero coupon bonds, for example, is not going to reap the same benefits as the first. In studying acquisition candidates, most candidates would be more attractive if acquired yesterday. Responsiveness is a third advantage. I remember several years ago working with an investment bank with whom we had done very little business. It had performed a fairly comprehensive analysis on a particular financing alternative, and upon reviewing it, I had suggested that another set of assumptitions might be more realistic. That was on July 3. The following Monday, I received by express mail a reworked 12-page analysis reflecting all the suggested changes. There was no particular urgency (the financing was scheduled for late September), but the firm had obviously worked for the better part of the Fourth of July weekend to produce a very thorough presentation. Naturally, we were impressed with the attention we received. Looking to the future, there would be situations where quick decisions would have to be made, and this kind of responsiveness would be crucial.

Finally, one would expect an investment bank go the extra mile for an important client. There will be circumstances where the firm must make a decision to bend its policies, take on a higher degree of risk, or expose itself to a potentially hostile situation. It is impossible to predict when a crisis might develop, but a client who enjoys a preferred status at its investment bank is better prepared to weather the storm.

Becoming a priority client can be a difficult goal. A Fortune 500 corporation who undertakes several major financings a year will always attract considerable attention from any firm, while a small company with an irregular financing schedule will never be anyone's top priority. A preferred status can be brought about through a company's past relationship with the firm or, more importantly, the prospect for future business. It can also arise from sheer prestige (e.g., IBM), a unique position in an exciting industry (e.g., Genentech, Apple Computer), an exotic geographic location (e.g., China Airlines), a reputation for competitive selection (e.g., Citicorp), or strictly personal ties between the company and the investment bank.

No matter how a company attains a position of priority, there are some practices it should avoid in order not to take on a persona non grata status in the Wall Street community. A company that indiscretely shops deals is unpopular; a company that shops a deal developed by another firm is unethical. Indecisive clients, who simply enjoy liquid lunches and big cigars, are a waste of time. Coy and elusive behavior also provokes a negative reaction. A client who has carefully thought out his financial strategy and has drawn up a clear set of objectives is best advised to disclose the same information to his investment bankers and be prepared to act decisively in awarding the business to the candidate who genuinely deserves it. As in most business dealings, being direct and forthright goes a long way in cultivating valued and enduring relationships.

Effective Communication

The flow of communication between a company and its investment bankers is essential for a productive relationship. The presentation below describes the informational responsibilities of both parties.

Company	*Investment Banker*
1. Long-term financial plan: Capital expenditures Sales, profits Cash flow projections	1. Capital markets outlook: Equity and debt Public and private Domestic and foreign
2. Financial policies: Acceptable price for common stock Debt/equity mix Short-term versus long-term debt Floating versus fixed rates Leasing and equipment residual values Maintenance of cash balances and working capital	2. Short- and long-term outlook for interest rates and other relevant economic indices 3. Expectations on foreign exchange rates 4. Industry research reports
3. Current financing schedule and objectives: One-year schedule of financing Objectives relating to type of financing instrument, cost, term, capital market diversification, etc.	5. Information concerning trading and holdings of company's securities 6. New financing ideas 7. Advice on company's time schedule and financing objectives
4. Tax position: Unused tax carryforwards and investment tax credits Estimated tax position given future outlook for profits and capital expenditures	8. Information regarding legislative developments on pertinent topics: Leasing and tax benefit transfer Tax-exempt bonds Rule 415, etc.
5. Important covenants in loan agreements and indentures	
6. Acquisition policies	

With periodic meetings, conversations, and written exchanges, both the company and its investment bankers can keep themselves abreast of what they need to know to do their jobs efficiently and effectively. A firm can expend much time and effort to no end because it has not elicited the pertinent information from the client. There have been tax saving schemes for clients who in fact pay no taxes, stock offering proposals for clients with a firm policy against dilution, short-term financing techniques when only long-term capital is desired, and floating-rate deals for companies requiring fixed-rate terms. Barraging a client with an avalanche of ill-considered and unsuitable proposals does not engender a constructive relationship. Time is the most precious resource in this business. The client wants to be able to rely on the investment banker's judgment, and he needs to be assured that the company's financial position, corporate policies, and specific objectives are well understood.

Trust is the all-important quality in a banker-client relationship. It is derived from the banker's personal integrity and his professional skills, as discussed earlier. Yet in addition to these characteristics, trust is derived from an empathy for the client's concerns, a sharing of values, and a commonality of purpose. This is the essence of effective communication.

Price

In the area of corporate finance, the price of an investment banker's services has been rarely a criterion used for differentiating one house from the other. However, there have been changes over the past year which are likely to introduce price competition with respect to certain transactions.

On a public offering, the gross spread becomes a fairly standard requirement to enable the issue to be sold. The other variable in the equation, of course, is the issuance price of the security, and here the company should press for everything it can get (the underwriters will know where to stop). Yet going into a transaction prior to the price being set, there is really no opportunity to comparison shop.

In seeking to arrange a privately placed deal, price shopping is again not appropriate. Having decided the best house for the deal, it would be unwise to then move it to a second or third choice for a small difference in fee. The success of the deal is of primary importance to the corporation, and any action which threatened to detract from that objective would be "pound foolish." A company should select the investment banker optimally suited for the job and then negotiate a "reasonable" fee. (It should be reasonable relative to the value added or reasonable relative to fees charged by others, but similar to the world of entertainers and professional athletes, it definitely will not be reasonable relative to what any human being has a right to earn for an honest day's work.)

Recently, situations have developed where there can be constructive price competition in which the success of a deal is not jeopardized or compromised in any way. The so-called Rule 415, which enables companies to tap the public markets instantaneously with shelf-registered issues, will make possible principal bids, bought deals, and small, nonsyndicated underwritings. A deal can be initiated and consummated in a matter of hours. No time for the client to ponder, ruminate, and anguish over the choice of an investment banker. The deal is the deal here and now, and either the price warrants an affirmative response or it doesn't. Go/no go and it all depends on the numbers. Radical changes are likely to occur in situations in which Rule 415 is invoked. For companies who can take advantage of the new regulatory reform, there will be definite cost efficiencies in entering the public marketplace.

In August 1981, another financial instrument was created by the Economic Recovery Tax Act. Wash leases or tax benefit transfers (TBTs) involved the selling of tax benefits for capital equipment. Notwithstanding some complications, they were essentially commodity-type deals. There was little to differentiate one transaction from the other. The only question was the price. Investment banks were in a position to make a market in TBTs, and they charged clients fees ranging from ¼ percent to 3 percent. Since there was no precedent for pricing, no one knew what was fair. In deals where the only differentiating characteristic is price, a corporation is best served by soliciting competitive bids.

CONCLUSION

Stability is a word not often mentioned in describing today's world of corporate finance and the capital markets; nor is the term likely to characterize investment banking relationships. The diversity of the sources of capital and the complexities of financings call for special expertise and creativity on the part of the investment banking community. Traditional ties between certain houses and corporate clients have given way to a performance orientation. Financing costs have had a measurable impact on bottom-line earnings, and corporations have reacted by building professional financial staffs of their own. The stakes are too high to passively accept turn-key services from their investment bank. The in-house staffs have given the corporations a sense of confidence in aggressively pursuing new financing techniques and new investment banking relationships.

In spite of this independence and emphasis on performance, corporations must be careful not to sacrifice other cherished values in the process. Personal integrity, effective communication, and a priority status are enduring qualities not to be foresaken. Trade-offs among the seven criteria are inevitable at times. In some situations, the specialized expertise of a particular firm will justify a more prominent weighting;

in other cases, personal integrity would be the key ingredient. As in many kinds of decisions, one has a general set of principles which he has to apply differently in different situations. Finally, there may be circumstances in which the only criterion will be price. If there is no other distinguishing aspect to the deal, it should go to the winning bidder.

For the corporate financial officer, managing investment banking relationships, at a time when the firms themselves are undergoing upheaval in their industry, promises to be a most challenging task. The comfortable relationships of the past will be tested in an environment of intensifying competition. Scarce capital, volatile markets, and high financial stakes will put considerable pressure on the results achieved by the corporate treasurer and his chosen investment bankers. There will still be good wines and sumptuous meals to be devoured at Lutece, but for the most part, the 80s will be sober times for the lean and hungry.

PART 3

Specialty Financing—
The Roots of Left Hand
Financing

CHAPTER 7

An Overview of Lease Financing

PETER K. NEVITT
BankAmeriLease Group

FRANK J. FABOZZI
Fordham University

As explained in Chapter 1, *left hand financing* is any financing that furnishes resources to a corporation if the financing (*a*) draws its investment characteristics from the left hand side of the balance sheet and (*b*) avoids the need or lowers the cost of expanding the capitalization of the corporation. Leasing is a financing vehicle for left hand financing since it draws its investment characteristics from the asset side of the balance sheet and it provides the opportunity to avoid expanding the capitalization and to obtain a lower cost of funds.

Several types of leasing arrangements are discussed in Part 3. In this chapter, we will provide an overview of lease financing.[1]

TYPES OF LEASE FINANCING

Many types of financing transactions are termed "leases." In order to appraise why lease financing is a vehicle for left hand financing, the dif-

---

[1] In contrast to lease financing transactions, an *operating* or *service* lease typically has a term shorter than the life of the asset, can be canceled at the convenience of the lessee, and is a gross lease. The lease payments from one lessee are usually insufficient for the lessor to recoup the entire investment. Instead, the lessor expects to benefit from the tax benefits associated with ownership, from additional lease payments when the asset is subsequently leased to other parties, and from the proceeds from the disposal of the asset. Operating leases are true leases. Chapter 8 discusses operating leases.

ference between a true lease, a conditional sales agreement, and a "safe harbor lease" must be understood.

Lease transactions, by definition, have a lot to do with ownership rights. It would be appropriate, therefore, to discuss the concept of ownership in the effort to better understand the various types of lease financing transactions and how they affect the prospective lessee.

There are three categories of lessor ownership: *true ownership, nominal ownership,* and *no ownership.*

True Leases

The distinction between *true* and *nominal* ownership relates to how ownership is viewed for tax and legal purposes. The very terminology of lease financing connotes ownership by the lessor. If, at the end of the lease term, the lessee has the option to purchase the asset at the then existing fair market value, then the lessor's ownership is true. In this situation, ownership for tax purposes rests with the lessor, who is entitled to benefit from accelerated cost recovery allowances and the investment tax credit. Since the lessor enjoys these tax advantages, it is in a position to offer a reduced financing cost to the lessee. This is one of the principal advantages of leasing from both the lessor's and the lessee's points of view. It presupposes, however, that the lessor has a significant tax base while the lessee, conversely, has a minimal tax appetite.

This type of transaction is also considered to be and referred to as a true lease for legal purposes. That is, the lessor is considered to be the true owner under state security laws, such as the Uniform Commercial Code.

There are two general categories of true leases—single-investor or direct leases and leveraged leases.

A *single-investor* or *direct lease* is a lease in which the owner/lessor is "at risk" for the entire cost of the leased property; that is, the owner/lessor provides the funds to purchase the property. The single investor may be a single entity or a partnership or syndication.

A *leveraged lease* is quite similar to a single-investor or direct lease, but it is more complex in terms of size, number of parties, documentation, legal involvement, and the unique advantages to all parties. In a leveraged lease, at least three parties are involved: a lessee, a lessor, and a long-term lender. The lessor becomes owner of the leased property by providing only a percentage (20 to 50 percent) of the funds necessary to buy the property. The remainder of the funds is borrowed from institutional investors on a nonrecourse basis to the lessor. Thus, the lessor is not at risk for the borrowed funds. The loan is secured by a first lien on the property, an assignment of the lease, and an assignment of the lease payments. The legal expenses and administrative costs associated with a leveraged lease confine its use to financing projects requiring large amounts of capital.

Nominal Ownership

Nominal ownership essentially occurs with an installment sale or a conditional sale, whereby the "lessee" is buying the asset over time. The IRS considers this a form of purchase since it permits the "lessee" to build an equity interest in the property. Nominal ownership can result in two types of financial arrangements. One exists when, at the end of the "lease" term, the "lessee" has the option to purchase the asset for a nominal fixed dollar amount (usually $1). This is known as a financial lease. A second form of nominal ownership occurs when the client has the right to use the asset as long as the conditions of the contract are met and receives title to the equipment automatically when all of the conditions (i.e., final payment) have been satisfied. Until all of the conditions have been met, the "lessor" has nominal ownership and the "lessee" has true ownership for tax purposes.

No Ownership

Transactions in this category have no suggestion whatsoever of any ownership on the part of the lender. Examples would be chattel mortgages and other straight financing methods. What usually happens in no-ownership arrangements is that the lender receives a mortgage (lien) on the asset as security against the performance of the mortgagor, who is the owner of the asset.

Safe Harbor Leases

If the safe harbor rules of the Economic Recovery Tax Act (ERTA) of 1981 are satisfied, the tax benefits associated with ownership may be transferred under a safe harbor lease to a corporate entity. Such transactions may take the form of a true lease or a nominal lease. "No-ownership financing" may be used by the "lessee" in a sale-and-leaseback to provide financing to fund a safe harbor lease. The safe harbor rules are discussed in the next section.

FEDERAL INCOME TAX GUIDELINES FOR TRUE AND SAFE HARBOR LEASES

The guidelines and requirements for a safe harbor lease are compared with those for a true lease in Exhibit 1. The rules for a true lease con-

EXHIBIT 1
Comparison between a True Lease and a Safe Harbor Lease

Under IRS guidelines, a transaction which does not meet the safe harbor requirements of Section 168 must meet the following requirements and may have the following characteristics to qualify as a true lease in which the lessor is to be able to claim the tax benefits associated with equipment ownership:

1. No affirmative election to treat the lessor as owner of the property is necessary.

2. The tax benefits are passed from the lessor to the lessee as a reduction in rents.

3. The lessor, at all times during the lease and at the time the equipment is first placed in service, must have a minimum at-risk investment in the equipment of at least 20 percent of the adjusted basis of the property.

4. The remaining useful life of the equipment at the end of the lease term must be the greater of one year or 20 percent of its originally estimated useful life.

5. The lessor must be able to show that the transaction is entered into for profit, apart from the transaction's tax benefits (i.e., without consideration of the tax deductions, allowances, credits, and other tax attributes arising from the transaction).

6. The lessor must own the new leased property at the time it is placed in service in order to claim ITC and tax depreciation applicable to the new property.

7. The lessee must not have a contractual right to purchase the property at less than its fair market value, and the lessor may not have a contractual right to cause any party to purchase the asset.

8. The lessee cannot furnish any part of the purchase price of the asset or loan or guarantee any indebtedness created in connection with the acquisition of the property by the lessor.

9. Limited use property (valuable only to the lessee) may not be leased.

Under ERTA, the lessor in a lease of new Section 38 property which meets the following guidelines or has the following characteristics will be treated as the owner for federal tax purposes:

1. Both the lessor and the lessee must affirmatively elect to treat the lessor as the owner of the property.

2. The tax benefits may be passed from the lessor to a lessee in either a lump-sum payment or as a reduction in rents.

3. The lessor must have a minimum at-risk investment of not less than 10 percent of the adjusted basis of the property.

4. The term of the lease cannot exceed the greater of 90 percent of the useful life of the equipment or 150 percent of the class life of such property.

5. The fact that deriving a profit or cash flow from the transaction depends on tax benefits or ownership is not relevant.

6. A lessor must own the leased property within three months of its being placed in service in order for the transaction to qualify as a safe harbor lease.

7. At the end of the lease, the lessee may have a purchase option at a fixed price and the lessor may have a put to the lessee at a fixed price, and such purchase option or put may be at more or less than the fair market value.

8. The lessee or a related party may provide financing or guarantee financing for the transaction. Presumably, such debt could include a share of residual value warrants, stock rights, or conversion to equity features. (Equity rights may result in other tax consequences.)

9. Limited use property will qualify for a true lease.

EXHIBIT 1 *(concluded)*

10. It is not clear that a lessor may lease a percentage of a piece of equipment (where, for example, a lessee holds property as tenants in common).

10. A lessor may lease a percentage of the property.

11. Recapture of ITC and tax depreciation will result from the bankruptcy of the lessee and disposition of the equipment prior to the time such benefits are vested.

11. No recapture of ITC and tax depreciation will result in the event of bankruptcy and disposition of the equipment, provided appropriate notices are given to the trustee, the transferee, and the IRS.

12. The lessee must pay rents to the lessor or its assignee. In the case of a leveraged lease, the lessor must pay debt service to the leveraged debt holder. The obligations of the lessee and lessor must be evidenced by formal documentation.

12. Rents may be offset against leveraged debt. No actual payment of rent by the lessee or debt by the lessor has to actually occur. The obligations of the lessee and lessor can all be spelled out in a single document. (This type of safe harbor lease is called a TBT lease, wash lease, nominal lease, swap lease, offset lease, or phantom lease.)

13. New and used personal property can be leased under a true lease.

13. Only new personal property which qualifies as Section 38 property can be leased under a safe harbor lease. (As noted above, the lessor can acquire ownership of the property within three months of its being placed in service.)

14. Personal property located outside the United States can be leased under a true lease.

14. Most equipment located outside the United States does not qualify as Section 38 property. (Only new personal property which qualifies as Section 38 property can be leased under a safe harbor lease.) Under certain conditions, aircraft and ships used outside the United States will qualify as Section 38 property.

15. There are no formal IRS reporting requirements.

15. After the enactment of ERTA, Congress imposed stringent reporting requirements on lessees and lessors under safe harbor leases. Failure to comply with these requirements can result in loss of the protection of the safe harbor.

tinue to be important as a fallback position where some question exists as to whether a particular transaction qualifies as a safe harbor lease. Also, true leases will continue to be written for transactions which clearly do not qualify as safe harbor leases, such as leases of used equipment and real property or leases of equipment located outside the United States.

116

EXHIBIT 2
Schematic Presentation of True Leases, Safe Harbor Leases, and TBT Leases

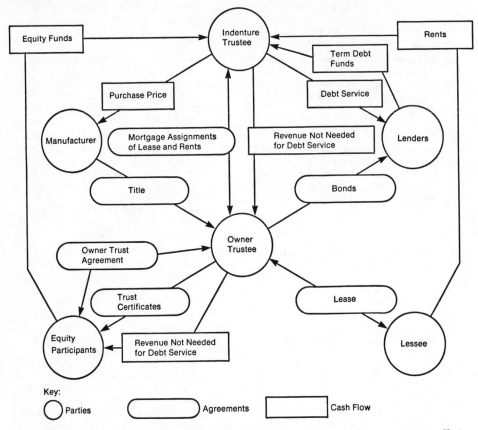

Key:

◯ Parties   ⬭ Agreements   ▭ Cash Flow

*Tax benefit-transfer leases. Also known as wash leases, nominal leases, swap leases, offset leases, and phantom leases.

Exhibit 2 may be helpful in distinguishing between true leases and safe harbor leases. Notice that while safe harbor leases generally have different characteristics than true leases, in some instances a true lease may also be a safe harbor lease. (The TBT leases in Exhibit 2 will be discussed in the next section.)

In order to qualify for the safe harbor rules, the lessor must be a corporation other than a Subchapter S corporation or a personal holding company, a partnership in which all the partners are qualifying corporations, or a grantor trust whose grantor and beneficiaries are all either qualified corporations or qualified partnerships.

A summary of the regulations issued by the Treasury dealing with leasing under ERTA is appended.

IMPLICATIONS OF SAFE HARBOR LEASES FOR LESSEES

Following are some of the major implications of safe harbor rules for lessees. (However, the reader is cautioned that Congress is considering changes in the safe harbor rules which may adversely affect their economics and attractiveness for lessees.)

1. The new safe harbor rules have given rise to a new type of lease transaction which is in substance a sale of a tax shelter. The transaction is structured as a leveraged lease in which the lessee provides the leveraged debt and the lease rental payments exactly equal the payments required for debt service. They offset each other. No payments are actually made. The equity investment by the "lessor" is actually the amount being paid to the lessee for the tax benefits. This type of transaction is called a *tax-benefit-transfer* lease (TBT lease), *wash* lease, *nominal* lease, *swap* lease, *offset* lease, or *phantom* lease. As shown in Exhibit 2, TBT leases are always safe harbor leases and never true leases. Further, not all safe harbor leases are TBT leases.

To illustrate a TBT lease, suppose that Company B owns equipment costing $10 million which it purchased on December 1, 1982. Company B recognizes that it cannot realize the tax benefits (ITC and depreciation) associated with the ownership of the equipment; however, it does locate Corporation A, a qualified lessor, which can use these benefits. On December 15, 1982, Company B agrees to lease the equipment *from* Corporation A under a lease agreement calling for a five-year lease term and a nominal option purchase price of $1 at the end of the fifth year. Both Corporation A and Company B affirmatively agree to have the lease agreement treated as a safe harbor lease. Corporation A agrees to buy the equipment from Company B for $10 million with a 15 percent down payment (A's investment) and financing from Company B for the balance, $8.5 million, payable over five years in equal installments. (The minimum investment for a lease agreement to qualify for safe harbor treatment is 10 percent.) The annual rental payment and the loan repayment schedule (interest and amortization) are constructed so as to be equal and offset. For example, if the interest rate on the loan is set at 15 percent, the annual rental and installment payment on the loan would be $2,535,682. Furthermore, Company B agrees to pay all costs normally associated with ownership of the equipment, including insurance, property taxes, and maintenance. (No rental or loan payments are actually made because of the offset.)

Exhibit 3 shows the annual tax effect on Corporation A of this hypothetical TBT lease.

2. The safe harbor rules introduce the nominal lessor, a new kind of investor in leveraged leases. (In the nominal lease illustration above, Corporation A is the nominal lessor.) The entry of nominal lessors (which provide 15-40 percent of the cost of the equipment) will ex-

EXHIBIT 3
Corporation A's Annual Tax Effect for Hypothetical TBT Lease

Year	Revenue*	Depre-ciation†	Interest‡	Taxable Income	Tax Saving at 46 Percent
1982 . . . . . $ −	$ 1,500,000	$ −	$(1,500,000)	$(1,690,000)§
1983 2,535,682	2,200,000	1,275,000	(939,318)	(432,086)
1984 2,535,682	2,100,000	1,086,000	(650,318)	(299,146)
1985 2,535,682	2,100,000	868,430	(432,748)	(199,064)
1986 2,535,682	2,100,000	618,342	(182,660)	(84,024)
1987 2,535,682	−	330,638	2,205,044	1,014,320
Total . . . $12,678,410	$10,000,000	$4,178,410	$(1,500,000)	$(1,690,000)

*Annual rental payment.
†Based on Treasury-prescribed cost recovery rates.
‡Computed by multiplying 15 percent times balance at beginning of year (rounded).
§Includes $1 million investment tax credit.

pand the availability of equity capital, raising debt for 60-85 percent of the cost of the equipment at rates and on terms which a lessee can afford to pay. This will present new problems for some lessees. Such features as residual sharing, floating rate debt, collared floating rate debt, warrants, stock rights, and equity conversion rights may be necessary to raise debt and keep the debt service within the lessee's ability to pay.

3. Lessees can now negotiate for fixed-price bargain purchase options at the end of a lease. Until now, lessees in tax-oriented leases had to rationalize the loss of the residual except at fair market value at the end of the lease. However, the right of a lessee to acquire the leased equipment at a fixed-price nominal purchase option at the end of a lease will raise the level of rents a lessor will expect to receive during the lease to compensate for the loss of the expected residual.

4. Lessors providing funding for leases will tend to seek floating rental rates to offset the loss of residual value which served as an inflation hedge against rising funding costs.

5. Lessees will realize ordinary income in excess of basis when they sell equipment acquired under a nominal purchase option.

6. Lessees will not be able to report leases with puts or bargain purchase options as operating leases for financial accounting purposes. (A bargain purchase option is at a price which is sufficiently lower than the expected fair value at the exercise date so that eventual exercise of the option is reasonably assured at the inception of the lease.)

7. Tax-oriented leases contain provisions requiring the lessee to indemnify the lessor against partial or total loss of the lessor's anticipated tax benefits arising from the transaction. The circumstances under which the lessee is responsible for indemnifying the lessor's anticipated

tax benefits, the procedure for determining the loss, and the method of compensation must also be specified. The relative bargaining power of the parties determines the extent of the indemnification and the precipitating circumstances.

Since leasing will resemble lending more closely than in the past, lessors will insist on indemnification from loss of tax benefits due to future changes in the corporate income tax rate. The more a lease resembles an outright sale of tax benefits, the more a lessor will insist on complete tax indemnification. In England, where nominal leases have been used for a number of years, lessees provide lessors with broad indemnities.

8. In the past, equipment which was valuable only to a particular lessee could not be leased under a lease in which the lessor claimed the income tax benefits associated with equipment ownership. This excluded many items of equipment from being financed under true leases, such as pollution control equipment, equipment which was part of a production facility, and equipment difficult to transport. The new legislation permits such limited use equipment to be leased under a tax-oriented lease.

9. Under the old law, an army of tax lawyers was engaged in providing tax advice to lessors and lessees. The tax, legal, and printing costs of a large leveraged lease often amounted to hundreds of thousands of dollars. A great deal of time was spent in drafting qualified tax indemnities which lessees should now feel more comfortable in granting. Since the new law is relatively simple and straightforward, such costs should eventually be substantially reduced.

IMPLICATIONS OF THE SAFE HARBOR RULES FOR SPECIFIC INDUSTRIES

Airlines and Railroads

Airlines and railroads were very supportive of the new legislation providing for fixed-price purchase options. They understandably were not pleased with losing or being required to purchase valuable equipment at fair market value at the conclusion of a tax-oriented lease. Strong airline and rail credits will now be able to obtain tax-oriented leases with fixed-price purchase options. However, airline and railroad transportation companies with less than Baa- or BBB-rated debt will find few lessors willing to take a subordinated position to leveraged debt without an equity kicker or a high or fair market value purchase option.

An aircraft leased to a foreign airline must be new Section 38 property in the hands of both the lessee and the lessor in order to qualify under the safe harbor rules which permit a fixed-price purchase option.

Utilities

Utilities have substantial capital spending programs under way to meet the energy needs of the nation. While utilities have been utilizing leasing to finance some of their projects, they have been reluctant to lease in the past because only fair market value purchase options or renewal options were available at the end of the lease term. Since nominal purchase options are now permitted, utilities will find leasing a much more attractive method of financing plant and equipment.

The provisions permitting leases of limited use property and a percentage interest in equipment will create more leasing opportunities for utilities.

Leasing will be especially attractive to utilities since most utilities do not currently have federal income tax liability. Furthermore, energy tax credits available on many utility projects may also be claimed by a lessor.

Shipping

The new legislation opens up some new opportunities for the leasing of ships. In the past, many U.S. flagships have been leased because leases of 20 to 25 years were possible through use of debt guaranteed by MARAD. Ship lessees were not concerned about loss of residual value after 20 to 25 years. However, very few foreign-built ships were leased because long-term, 20-25-year debt was not readily available and because foreign shipyard debt generally did not exceed 8 years and did not match the equity investment requirements for a leveraged lease.

Under the new legislation, foreign-built ships which are registered in the United States can be leased under leveraged leases for terms which match available foreign shipyard financing and which contain nominal purchase options at the conclusion of the lease term. Such leases might be structured with balloon payments at the conclusion of the construction yard financing which could be triggered by a put or call by the lessor or lessee. A ship must qualify as new Section 38 property in the hands of both the lessee and the lessor under the safe harbor rules which permit fixed-price purchase options.

Foreign flagships or ships owned by a foreign corporation which is not a U.S. taxpayer do not qualify as Section 38 property and are not protected by the safe harbor rules permitting fixed-price nominal purchase options.

Agriculture

Farmers have generally preferred to purchase rather than lease their farm equipment because of the high residual value of such equipment.

The new legislation cures this problem in leasing agricultural equipment. Since many farmers are not in a position to use ITC and tax depreciation as efficiently as a lessor, most farm equipment will probably be leased in the future under leases with nominal purchase options. This will have the effect of an across-the-board equivalent of 15-20 percent savings in the purchase price of farm equipment.

LEVERAGED LEASES

Leveraged lease transactions not structured as TBT leases are structured as true leases for tax purposes.

The concept of the leveraged lease is quite similar to that of a nonleveraged or direct lease but is more complex in terms of size, number of parties, documentation, legal involvement, and the unique advantages to all parties. In a leveraged lease, the lessee selects the equipment and negotiates the lease in the same manner as for a nonleveraged lease. The terms of both leveraged and nonleveraged leases are similar as to rentals, options, and responsibility for taxes, insurance, and maintenance.

However, a leveraged lease involves at least three parties: a lessee, a lessor (equity participant), and a long-term lender. In a nonleveraged lease (or direct lease) the lessor provides 100 percent of the capital necessary to acquire the asset from its own funds, while in a leveraged lease, the lessor becomes the owner of the equipment by providing only a percentage (20-50 percent) of the required amount. The remainder of the capital in a leveraged lease is borrowed from institutional lenders on a nonrecourse basis to the equity participant. The lenders agree to look for repayment solely to the proceeds available for distribution under the lease, together with the collateral. The equity participant is specifically relieved of any personal obligation to retire the long-term debt in the event of a default by the lessee. This loan is secured by a first lien on the equipment, an assignment of the lease, and an assignment of the lease rental payments. The interest cost of the nonrecourse borrowing is a function of the credit standing of the lessee and is reflected in the lease rate.

The equity participant can claim all of the tax benefits incidental to ownership of the leased asset even though the equity participant provides only 20 percent to 50 percent of the capital needed to purchase the asset.

The "leverage" created by the nonrecourse debt in a leveraged lease magnifies the effect of tax shelter relative to the lessor's equity investment, and thus the lease payments can be lower than might be the case in a nonleveraged lease. However, the leverage with respect to the benefits in a transaction creates a magnified risk exposure to the extent that the benefits are not realized. Thus, leverage is a two-edged sword for the lessor. While it magnifies tax benefits, it also magnifies risk!

The leveraged form of true lease is the ultimate form of lease financing. It was developed over the past few years to satisfy a need for lease financing of especially large capital equipment projects with economic lives of up to 30 or more years, although it is sometimes used in instances where the useful life of the equipment is considerably shorter. The leveraged lease can be a most advantageous financing device when used for the right kinds of projects and structured properly by reputable professionals.

Parties

Leveraged leases are complex from a legal and tax standpoint. A number of parties are involved. Their functions and characteristics are as follows.

The *lessee* selects, uses, operates, and receives all revenue from the asset. The lessee makes rental payments.

The *equity participants* provide the equity contribution (20 to 50 percent of the purchase price) to purchase the asset. They also receive rents after payment of debt service and trustee fees, if any. They claim the tax benefits incidental to the ownership of the leased asset. The equity participants are referred to as the lessors. Actually, in most cases, they are the beneficial owners by way of an owner trust which is the lessor. Equity participants are also sometimes referred to as equity investors, owner participants, or trustors.

The *lenders* (debt holders) are typically banks, insurance companies, trusts, pension funds, and foundations. The funds provided by the lenders, together with the equity contributions, make up the full purchase price of the asset to be leased. The lenders provide 50 to 80 percent of the purchase price on a nonrecourse basis to the equity participants, and they receive debt service from the indenture trustee.

The *owner trustee* holds title to the leased asset for the benefit of the equity participants subject to a mortgage to the indenture trustee. The owner trustee issues trust certificates to the equity holders evidencing their beneficial interest as owners of the assets of the trust, issues bonds to debt holders, grants to the indenture trustee the security interests which secure repayment of the bonds (i.e., lease, lease rentals, first mortgage on the leased asset), receives distributions from the indenture trustee, and distributes earnings to the equity participants. Additional practical reasons for having an owner trustee from the standpoint of the equity participants are: insulating liability on the bonds, avoiding liabilities on the balance sheet, and avoiding regulatory considerations involved in the issuance of certain securities.

The *indenture trustee* receives funds from lenders and equity holders, pays to the manufacturer the purchase price of the equipment to be leased, holds the security interest in the leased equipment for the benefit of lenders, and receives rents and other sums due under the lease from the lessee. The indenture trustee also services debt upon receipt of the rental payment and distributes revenues not needed for debt service to the owner trustee. In the event of default, the indenture trustee can foreclose on the asset.

The *manufacturer* or supplier of equipment receives the purchase price and delivers the equipment.

The *packager* is the leasing company arranging the transaction. From the standpoint of the lessee, it is desirable that the packager also be an equity participant, as is often the case. The packager may, in fact, be the sole equity participant.

Structure

A leveraged lease transaction is structured as follows where a third-party leasing company arranges the transaction.

The leasing company arranging the lease, "the packager," enters into a commitment letter with the prospective lessee which outlines the terms for the lease of the equipment, including the timing and amount of rental payments. The commitment letter also sets forth the amount of equity investment to be committed to the transaction by the packager. Since the exact rental payment cannot be determined until the debt is sold, rents are agreed upon based on certain variables, including several assumed debt rates.

After the commitment letter is signed, the packager may contact other equity participants and arrange for firm equity commitments from them if and to the extent that the packager does not intend to provide the total amount of the required equity funds from its own resources. The packager also arranges the debt either directly or in conjunction with the corporate finance department of a bank or an investment banker. If the equipment is not delivered for a considerable period of time, the debt arrangements may be deferred until delivery.

If an owner trust is utilized, a bank or trust company mutually agreeable to the equity participants and the lessee is selected to act as owner trustee.

Again, if utilized, another bank or trust company acceptable to the debt holders is selected to act as indenture trustee. On small transactions, a single trustee may act as both owner trustee and indenture trustee. (Such an arrangement, however, may result in a conflict of interest between the owners and the security holders and should be avoided if possible.)

Exhibit 4 illustrates the cash flows and agreements between the parties.

EXHIBIT 4
Leveraged Lease Cash Flows and Agreements

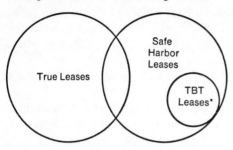

If a leveraged lease to a project is arranged by an industrial sponsor of the project that wants to be the lessor, the structure and procedure are essentially the same as a leveraged lease by a third-party lessor. In such a situation, the sponsor is the equity investor.

When an industrial sponsor is the equity investor, care should be taken because Internal Revenue Service guidelines for tax rulings do not permit leases in which the equity participant/lessor and the lessee are "related parties."

When the parties to the leveraged lease transaction are identified, all except the indenture trustee enter into a financing agreement or a participation agreement which spells out in detail the various undertakings, obligations, indemnities, and responsibilities of the parties with respect to providing funds and purchasing, leasing, and mortgaging the equipment.

When the transaction is about to close, the equity participants pay the amount of their equity investments to the indenture trustee. The debt holders also pay the amount they are lending on the transaction to the indenture trustee. The owner trustee then issues equity participation certificates to the equity holders and bonds or debt certificates to the debt holders.

In the meantime, a lease agreement for the equipment has been signed by the owner trustee (as lessor) and the lessee. The indenture trustee has recorded a security interest or mortgage on the equipment to be leased. The lease agreement and the right to receive rents under it are assigned, and a mortgage is granted to the indenture trustee as security for the debt holders under the security agreement between the owner trustee and the indenture trustee.

At the closing of the purchase of the equipment, the lessee signifies its acceptance of the equipment by signing an acceptance certificate. The indenture trustee pays the purchase price for the equipment to the manufacturer and any construction lenders using funds collected from the debt holders and the equity participants. Title is then conveyed to the owner trustee, subject to the previously recorded security agreement and mortgage. The equipment is delivered to the lessee, and the lease commences.

The lessee pays periodic rents to the indenture trustee, who uses such funds to pay currently due principal and interest payments to the debt holders. The balance of the rent payments is paid to the owner trustee. After payment of any trustee fees and any other expenses, the remainder of the rent payment is paid to the equity participants.

The lease agreement usually requires the lessee to furnish the owner trustee and the indenture trustee with financial statements, covenant compliance data, evidence of insurance, and other similar information. The trustees distribute this information to all parties to the transaction.

Certain capital equipment produced especially for the lessee may take a period of time for the manufacturer to produce. Consequently, the manufacturer may require that progress payments be made during the production period. Under such circumstances, a separate interim loan agreement must be entered into by the lessee, owner trustee, and lenders. The agreement will usually require the lessee to directly or indirectly guarantee the interim loan but subsequently eliminate any lessee guarantees on or before delivery of the equipment. Eliminating lessee guarantees of the owner's debt obligations is necessary in order to receive a favorable advance tax ruling.

POTENTIAL COST ADVANTAGES IN LEASE FINANCING

The principal advantage of using a tax-oriented lease to obtain the services of an asset is the economic benefit which comes from the indirect realization of tax benefits otherwise lost. If the lessee is unable to fully utilize the tax benefits associated with ownership for tax purposes, the effective cost of owning property will be higher. Under these conditions, leasing may be a less costly alternative, as the lessor utilizes the tax benefits and may either pass on most of these benefits to the lessee through a lower lease payment or purchase the tax benefits for cash in a safe harbor lease. In a leveraged lease, as noted above, the "leverage" created by the nonrecourse debt magnifies the effect of the tax benefits relative to the lessor's equity investment, and thus the lease payments can be lower than might be the case in a nonleveraged lease.

The cost of a tax-oriented lease depends on (1) the creditworthiness of the seller of the tax benefits, (2) the availability of the ITC and energy tax credit and whether it is taken by the lessee or the lessor, (3) whether the lessee or the lessor has the right to the residual value, (4) whether the lease is a single-investor lease or a leveraged lease, (5) the timing of the tax benefits to be received by the lessor (for example, tax benefits closer to the time that the lessor must pay its quarterly tax bill will be more valuable than tax benefits acquired soon after the quarterly filing), (6) the discount rate used by the lessor to obtain the present value of the future tax benefits, and (7) the legal costs of documentation and closing.

AVOIDING CAPITALIZATION

Prior to 1973, financial reporting standards did not mandate the disclosure of lease obligations. Thus, leasing was commonly referred to as "off-balance sheet financing." As explained in Chapter 4, current reporting standards for leases require that lease obligations classified as capital leases be capitalized as a liability on the balance sheet. According to *FASB Statement No. 13,* the principle for classifying a lease as a capital lease for financial reporting purposes is as follows:

> [A] lease that transfers substantially all of the benefits and risks incident to ownership of property should be accounted for as the acquisition of an asset and the incurrence of an obligation by the lessee.

FASB Statement No. 13 specifies four criteria for classifying a lease as a capital lease. Leases not classified as capital leases are considered operating leases. Unlike a capital lease, an operating lease is not capitalized. Instead, certain information regarding such leases must be disclosed in a footnote to the financial statement.

There is a belief shared by chief financial officers that avoiding capitalization of a lease will enhance the corporation's financial image. There is generally ample room for designing lease arrangements so as to avoid having a lease classified as a capital lease, and CFOs demand that lease agreements be structured accordingly. However, is there any empirical evidence to support or refute the concern of CFOs that capitalization of leases influences the evaluation of financial analysts, lenders, and bond-rating agencies? Two behavioral studies can shed some light on this question.

In a 1979 study sponsored by the National Association of Accountants and the Society of Management Accountants of Canada, the investigators interviewed two bond raters.[2] They asked the raters whether the FASB requirement produced lower bond ratings if a firm now had to capitalize its lease whereas it did not have to prior to *Statement No. 13.* The raters' response was that because they had already given effect to the capitalization of leases prior to *Statement No. 13* in determining the bond rating of an issuer, the requirement did not produce lower

---

[2] William L. Ferrara, James B. Thies, and Mark W. Dirsmith, *The Lease-Purchase Decision* (National Association of Accountants and the Society of Management Accountants of Canada, 1980), pp. 23-24.

bond ratings. In fact, one of the rating agencies indicated that not only had it capitalized leases now covered by *Statement No. 13* but that it had also been capitalizing lease obligations not covered by *Statement No. 13* and take-or-pay contracts. According to this bond rater, the real question is "whether the facility or asset involved is essential to the ongoing business operation, e.g., warehousing (we need it) or a retail store (we need it). Regardless of legal term, it must be renewed to keep the business going."[3] Based on this study, there is some doubt that the judgment of bond-rating agencies is affected by having long-term, noncancelable leases classified as operating leases.

In an FASB-sponsored study dealing with the impact on lessees of *Statement No. 13*, "Accounting for Leases," the researchers found the following:

> The majority of analysts and bankers responding to the straightforward survey questions claimed that there are not substantive grounds for the assertion that they changed their evaluation of the companies affected by capitalization of leases. However, that response was not validated when analysts and bankers were asked to respond to a similar question indirectly. The indirect approach consisted of a request (as part of the survey) to evaluate two (economically) identical companies that differed only in the method of accounting for leases. The condensed financial statements of the two companies were produced side by side and respondents *were told that they "are almost identical (the difference lies in their method of accounting for leases)."* The results were quite a surprise: Over 40 percent of the responding financial analysts and commercial bank loan officers considered the company that did not capitalize the 20-year noncancelable lease more profitable, whereas only about 8 percent considered the other company more profitable, and about 50 percent considered them equally profitable. Since, by design, the two companies were identical in real terms, respondents who favored one over the other did so based on the numbers shown on the face of the financial statements.[4]

Moreover, more than 25 percent of the analysts and bankers responding to the survey indicated that the company that kept leases off the balance sheet had a better debt-paying ability. The researchers concluded:

> It is evident from these results that what responding users *say* they do and what they *actually* do may be substantially different. Note that the indirect question resembled a financial analyst's task more closely than the direct one. Taken by itself, that evidence is not unequivocal. However, it tends to support the concern that some preparers of financial statements have indicated, namely that the evaluation of their success indicators by users is quite often influenced by cosmetic accounting changes.[5]

---

[3] Ibid.

[4] A. Rashad Abdel-khalik et al., *The Economic Effects on Lessees of FASB Statement No. 13, Accounting for Leases* (Stamford, Conn.: Financial Accounting Standards Board, 1981), pp. 23-24.

[5] Ibid.

LEASE PROGRAMS

Lessors can structure lease transactions to suit the needs of most companies. The various lease programs available are described below.

A *standard lease* provides 100 percent long-term financing with level payments over the term of the lease. Standard documentation facilitates quick handling and closing of the lease transaction. Installation costs, delivery charges, transportation expense, and taxes applicable to the purchase of the equipment may be included as part of the lease financing package.

A *custom lease* contains special provisions designed to meet particular needs of a lessee. It may, for example, schedule lease payments to fit cash flow. Such a lease can be particularly helpful to a seasonal business.

A *master lease* is an agreement that allows the lessee to acquire during a fixed period assets as needed without having to renegotiate a new lease contract for each item. With this arrangement, the lessee agrees to the fixed terms and conditions that will apply for a specified period, usually one year. At any time within that period, the lessee can add fixed assets to the lease up to an agreed maximum, knowing in advance the rate to be paid and leasing conditions.

Designed as a sales tool for equipment manufacturers or distributors, a *vendor lease* program permits suppliers to offer financing in the form of true or conditional sale leases. After the lessee's credit is approved and standard documents are completed, the equipment is delivered to the lessee and accepted. Vendor lease programs are discussed in Chapter 12.

An *offshore lease* is an agreement to lease equipment to be used outside the United States. Offshore lease programs offer leases calling for payments in U.S. dollars or local currencies for equipment used abroad. Both true leases and conditional sale leases can be arranged for firms requiring capital equipment in overseas operations.

A transaction that converts fixed assets owned by the company into cash is a *sale-and-leaseback* arrangement. The asset is purchased by the lessor and then leased back to the seller.

An entire facility—a plant and its equipment—can be leased. Under this arrangement, known as *turnkey facility financing,* a lessor provides construction financing for a facility. Interest costs during construction can often be capitalized into the lease. The lease contract goes into effect when the completed facility has been accepted by the lessee.

Where the costs of a plant exceed the dollar limits of industrial revenue bonds, a lease can often finance the equipment portion of the project to keep those costs within limits. Leases can be structured using industrial revenue bonds or pollution control bonds as leveraged debt. Corporate-related municipal finance is discussed in Chapter 11.

Lease agreements designed for specific assets are also available. For example, *computer leases* that permit additions of memory core, upgrades, and special features during the course of the initial lease can be arranged. *Ship leases* utilizing a leveraged lease and Title XI can be arranged.

SUMMARY

Lease financing is a vehicle for left hand financing because it provides the corporation with the opportunity to procure funds without increasing capitalization and/or at a cost of capital lower than that of traditional financing. Although lease financing was a popular vehicle for left hand financing prior to the new tax legislation, there are now greater opportunities for utilizing this vehicle because of the safe harbor rules. It bears repeating, however, that safe harbor leases are available only under prescribed circumstances. Therefore, lease financing involving used equipment and real property has to satisfy the requirements for a true lease that existed prior to the new legislation.[6]

APPENDIX

Summary of Treasury Department Regulations on Safe Harbor Leases

The Treasury issued regulations to provide guidance to taxpayers executing agreements under the safe harbor election. The regulations are intended to discourage potentially abusive transactions that may be undertaken by taxpayers. For example, rules are prescribed that would prevent the parties from *creating* tax credits and ACRS deductions that would otherwise be unavailable. Rules are also prescribed to prevent "front loading" deductions. Moreover, the regulations permit the parties to an agreement to disclaim it as a lease for purposes other than federal income tax purposes, but specify that since the lessor receives all the tax benefits (except in the case when the ITC is passed through), the lessor will bear the entire burden of any recapture rules should they come into play.

Election to characterize the transaction as a lease

(1) For an agreement to be treated as a lease:

1. The lease agreement must be executed not later than three months after the property was placed in service.

---

[6] Although property placed in service for three months is used property, it still qualifies for safe harbor election.

2. The agreement must be in writing and must state that *all parties* to the agreement consent to characterize it as a lease for purposes of federal income taxation and elect to have the provisions apply to the transaction.
3. The agreement must also name the party that will be treated as the lessor and the party that will be treated as the lessee.

(2) Information return concerning the election

The lessor and lessee must file information returns concerning their election. Each information return must be filed by the lessor and lessee. Failure by the *lessor* to file the information return shall be a "disqualifying event." This will result in the agreement not being treated as a lease under the safe harbor rules.

The information return by the *lessee* shall include:

— The name, address, and taxpayer identification number of the lessor and lessee.
— The district director's office with which the income tax returns of the lessor and lessee are filed.
— A description of each property with respect to which the election is made.
— The date on which the lessee places the property in service.
— The "recovery property class" of the leased property.
— Such other information as required by the return or its instructions.

The information return must be filed by each party with its income tax return for its taxable year during which the lease term begins.

(3) The election is irrevocable

A safe harbor election once made is irrevocable.

(4) Disposition by lessee

Except in bankruptcy, liquidation, receivership, court-supervised foreclosure, or in any similar proceeding, the agreement will cease to be treated as a lease if the lessee (or any subsequent transferee of the lessee's interest) sells or assigns its interest in the lease or the property unless (*a*) the transferee furnishes to the lessor within 60 days following the transfer the transferee's written consent to take the property subject to the lease, *and* (*b*) the transferee and lessor file a statement with their income tax return for the taxable year in which the transfer occurs containing information prescribed in the temporary regulations. The characterization of an agreement as a lease will terminate as of the time of the sale or assignment, *not* as of the date of the election.

An implication of this rule is that a sophisticated lessor will require tax indemnification to protect against disqualification of the agreement as a lease as a result of disposition of the leased property by a lessee.

(5) Disposition of lessee's interest in bankruptcy, etc., or similar proceeding

Prior to the issuance of the temporary regulations, ailing companies such as Chrysler began lining up buyers for tax benefits. However, the temporary regulations included a provision that made the acquisition of tax benefits from a financially weak company too risky for a potential buyer should the lessee's interest be disposed of in bankruptcy or similar proceeding. As a result, companies such as Chrysler could not find buyers of their tax benefits even after discounting these benefits substantially. To preserve the intent of the ERTA with respect to transferring tax benefits, especially for ailing companies, the Treasury on November 10, 1981 amended the temporary regulations so that the acquisition of tax benefits would be less sensitive to the creditworthiness of the lessee. More specifically, whereas the original temporary regulations stipulated that the agreement would cease to be characterized as a lease if a bankruptcy trustee, receiver, or similar person appointed by a court refused to honor the lease agreement, the amendment stipulates that the agreement will continue to be characterized as a lease and the purchaser or assignee shall take the property subject to the lease if:

a. Before the consummation of the sale or assignment, the lessor gives written notice of its federal income tax ownership to the judicial or administrative body having jurisdiction over the proceeding and to the debtor in possession of the interest, or, if at such time a trustee, receiver, or similar person has been appointed by the court, to the person appointed.

b. The lessor files a statement with its timely federal income tax return for the taxable year in which the sale or assignment occurs that includes the prescribed information.

c. Before the consummation of the sale or assignment, all secured lenders of the lessee with interests in the property, which interests arose not later than the time the lessee first used the property under the lease, specifically exclude or release in writing the federal income tax ownership of the property from their interests.

The new regulation will help ailing firms in selling tax benefits associated with property that can be easily identified, such as aircraft or railroad cars, but will be of less value when the tax benefits arise from a variety of qualified equipment sold in a single transaction. It is difficult to assess at this time how much less buyers will pay for tax benefits of companies of lower credit standing, especially for the tax benefits of nonpublic companies in which timely financial information is unavailable. For what it is worth, lessors will probably include a provision in the leasing agreement that requires the lessee to notify the lessor in the case of bankruptcy or similar proceeding.

Requirements for lessor

The new law requires that a lessor be a "qualified lessor" in order to satisfy the safe harbor rules. If at any time during the term of the agreement the lessor fails to be a qualified lessor, the agreement will no longer be treated as a lease under the safe harbor rules *as of the date of the event causing such disqualification.*

The lessee should *not* allow the lessor to include a tax indemnification provision protecting the lessor against disqualification of the lease due to the failure of the lessor to qualify under the safe harbor rules. Instead, the lessee should seek tax indemnification provisions that will protect the lessee as a result of unfavorable tax consequences due to the lessor's inability to qualify.

The temporary regulations specify that with respect to the leased property only one person may be a qualified lessor under the safe harbor election. Therefore, the property may not be subleased under an agreement for which another safe harbor election is made. Moreover, once property is leased under a safe harbor election, the leased property can never again qualify as property that can be leased under the safe harbor election. The implication of this rule is important for lessees. Make sure that the first agreement in which a safe harbor election is made is with a reputable lessor so that the agreement is not disqualified at a later date, because you cannot lease the same property again and make a safe harbor election.

As discussed later in this appendix, if a lessor sells or assigns in a taxable transaction its interest in property in which a safe harbor election is made, the agreement will cease to qualify as a lease under the safe harbor election. The property can never again be used as leased property in a safe harbor election. However, lease brokers may prepare *executory* contracts with the lessee whereby the lease broker's assignee may execute a lease as lessor. If all other rules are satisfied, the lease will qualify for the safe harbor election. For example, suppose Corporation Z enters into a contract with a lease broker in which the latter agrees to buy equipment needed by Corporation Z and Z agrees to execute a safe harbor election in which it is treated as a lessee with a third-party assignee of the lease broker's interest in the property. If the lease broker assigns the equipment to Corporation T within the prescribed time period and all other conditions for a safe harbor election are satisfied, the agreement between Z and T will be characterized as a lease for federal income tax purposes.

Term of the lease

The ERTA specifies the maximum term of a safe harbor lease. The regulations define the minimum term. The term of the lease must at least equal the recovery property class of the leased property.

The rationale for this rule is that it prevents the front loading of deductions. For example, suppose Corporation T purchases equipment for $1 million and the equipment has a five-year recovery period. Corporation T would write off the equipment over five years. Instead, suppose that Corporation T sells the equipment to Corporation V and leases the equipment back in an agreement that specifies a two-year lease term. For illustration purposes, suppose that the annual lease payment is $500,000. Since Corporation T is the lessee, it would be entitled to write off the lease payment in the year the payment is made. Hence, it would effectively be writing off the equipment in two rather than five years.

Qualified leased property

The property must be "qualified leased property." Qualified leased property must be new Section 38 property at the beginning of the lease and must continue to be so in the hands of the lessor *and* lessee throughout the lease term. The fact that the lessee used the property within the three-month period in which it was deciding whether to enter a sale-and-leaseback arrangement or before entering into a lease agreement for which a safe harbor election is made, will not disqualify the property from being treated as new Section 38 property of the lessee.

The regulations define when leased property is considered as placed in service as follows:

1. At the time the property is placed in a condition or state of readiness and availability for a specifically assigned function. If an entire facility is leased under one lease, property which is part of the facility will not be considered placed in service under this rule until the entire facility is placed in service.
2. For purposes other than determining whether property is qualified leased property, property subject to a lease will be deemed to have been placed in service not earlier than the date such property is used under the lease.

Loss of safe harbor protection

The following events will cause an agreement to be disqualified as a lease as of the date of the "disqualifying event."

1. The lessor sells or assigns its interest in the lease or in the leased property in a taxable transaction.
2. The lessor fails to file the required information return.
3. The lessee (or any transferee of the lessee's interest) sells or assigns its interest in the lease or in the qualified property in a transaction not resulting from a bankruptcy or similar proceeding, and the transferee fails to execute the consent agreement explained earlier.
4. The lessor ceases to be a "qualified lessor."

5. The property ceases to be Section 38 property in the hands of the lessor *or* lessee.
6. The minimum investment required by the lessor becomes less than the 10 percent specified in the new law.
7. The lease terminates.
8. The property becomes subject to more than one lease for which a safe harbor election is made.
9. The property is transferred in a bankruptcy or similar proceeding, and the lessor fails either (*a*) to furnish the appropriate notification or (*b*) to file the prescribed statement with its income tax return.
10. The property is transferred in a bankruptcy or similar proceeding, and not all lenders with perfected and timely interests in the property specifically exclude or release the federal income tax ownership of the property.
11. The property is transferred subsequent to a bankruptcy or similar proceeding, and the lessor fails to furnish notice to the transferee prior to the transfer or fails to file a statement with its income tax return, and either the lessor fails to obtain the consent of the transferee or the transferee or the lessor fail to file the prescribed statements with their returns.

If there is a "disqualifying event," the lessor will bear the full brunt of the burden if recapture provisions should come into play.

Should an event occur that disqualifies an agreement from being characterized as a lease, the characterization of the lessor and lessee will be determined without regard to the safe harbor election. If the lessee would be the owner of the property without regard to the election, the disqualifying event will be deemed a sale of the qualified leased property by the lessor to the lessee. The lessor will be treated as having realized, as a result of the sale, the outstanding amount (if any) of the lessor's debt on the property plus the sum of any other consideration received by the lessor. The following two examples illustrate the foregoing provision.

Suppose that Corporation R owns property and determines that it would be beneficial to arrange a sale-and-leaseback transaction with a qualified lessor, say Corporation W. All parties elect to have the agreement treated as a lease, and all other requirements are satisfied for the agreement to be characterized as a lease for federal income tax purposes. For all other purposes, however, R (the lessee for tax purposes) is still the owner of the leased property. The election is made on December 2, 1981. On August 24, 1983, before the termination of the agreement, an event occurs that disqualifies the agreement from being characterized as a lease for tax purposes. Since R is the owner for all other purposes, W is deemed to have sold the leased property to R on

August 24, 1983 (the time of the disqualifying event), for the amount of the purchase-money debt on the property then outstanding and W's gain is then measured by the difference between this amount and his tax basis in the property (undepreciated cost). Subsequently, R's tax basis for the property will be equal to the amount of the outstanding obligation and R will use this amount for cost recovery purposes. Remember that R cannot use the leased property in an agreement with another party to make a safe harbor election.

In the second example, let us consider the case when the lease terminates. Suppose that Corporation G and Corporation F enter into an agreement characterized as a lease pursuant to a safe harbor election wherein G is treated as the lessor and F as the lessee. The term of the agreement is seven years. At the end of the seventh year, suppose F has no option to renew the lease or to purchase the property. For all other purposes, F is considered the owner of the leased property. At the end of the seventh year (the termination of the agreement), the property will be deemed to be sold by G to F for the amount of the purchase-money debt outstanding with respect to the leased property. Assuming that the debt is self-liquidating, at the end of the lease term there are no "sales proceeds" and consequently there is no gain or loss to be recognized.

CHAPTER 8

Operating Leases

LESTER SCHOENFELD
CAROLYN G. HUBSCH
Merrill Lynch Leasing Inc.

Leasing is currently the predominant form of *left hand financing* for equipment. When leasing is mentioned, leveraged leases, single-investor leases, and tax-benefit transfers are the forms that first come to mind to those within the corporate financial community. This is natural in view of the tremendous growth in leveraged and single-investor leases during the 1970s and the great public attention drawn to leasing by the provisions of the Economic Recovery Tax Act (ERTA) of 1981 relating to "safe harbor" leases. These provisions allow a company to sell the tax benefits of an asset while retaining control of the asset for its full economic life. The last 20 years, however, have brought the development and blossoming of the operating lease as an alternative form of asset acquisition, and as offshoots of the operating lease, various "nonlease" methods of asset acquisition have developed with surprisingly little publicity or notoriety. This chapter traces briefly the supply of and demand for these types of financings and then treats in some detail the more interesting technical features and the risks and benefits of the various types of operating leases and the related financing methods from the viewpoints of both the user and the supplier of funds.

BACKGROUND

There are two basic types of leases: operating leases and financing leases. The definition of each type depends on whether you are analyzing the lease from an accounting, tax, or business point of view. For accounting purposes, if a lease meets the following standards, it is treated as an operating lease and therefore not recorded on the balance sheet of the company acquiring the use of the asset.

1. The lease term is less than 75 percent of the economic life of the leased property.
2. The present value of the minimum lease payments is less than 90 percent of the fair market value of the leased property minus any investment tax credit retained by the lessor (where the discount rate used by the lessee is its incremental borrowing rate).
3. The lease contains no bargain purchase option.
4. The lessor retains title to the property at the end of the lease term.

For many years, corporate treasurers have sought financing methods that would be treated as "off-balance sheet" obligations for accounting purposes. The corporation's primary objective has been to increase its borrowing capacity to a level greater than would be acceptable if all its obligations were on the balance sheet. How often have investment bankers and corporate treasurers attempted to structure leveraged leases, operating leases, take-or-pay contracts, throughput agreements, or the like, principally or even solely to achieve that accounting result! This fixation on accounting treatment stemmed from the belief that creative accounting could increase the real borrowing capacity of the firm, notwithstanding the insidious decline in financial strength hidden from all but the most sophisticated readers of balance sheet footnotes.

When leasing as a financing method first developed, the applicable accounting rules did not impose significant requirements or guidance as to how leases were to be treated for accounting purposes. Essentially, each company had substantial latitude to decide how it would record a lease. The accounting profession took particular note of the abuses arising from the flexible accounting for leasing transactions and from the inconsistencies in the accounting treatment among companies. After years of consideration, the Financial Accounting Standards Board issued *Statement No. 13*, which, among other things, provided rules (summarized above) for the classification of leases. While *Statement No. 13* addressed many of the accounting inconsistencies of leasing, it did not require symmetry in accounting between the lessee and the lessor, and it did not properly take into account the full benefit of the investment tax credit to the lessor. In establishing a cutoff point for operating lease treatment by allowing the deduction of the aftertax value of the investment tax credit from the present value of the pretax rental payments, the accounting profession was making it easier for the lessee to treat a lease as an operating lease. As a consequence, under *Statement No. 13*, many long-term leveraged leases that are, in fact, very much the equivalent of financial leases or term loans are not required to be shown on the lessee's balance sheet.

However, corporate treasurers did not obtain off-balance sheet financing without penalty. The lessee cannot control the asset for its full economic life and cannot control the residual value of the property at the end of the lease term. Also, the Internal Revenue Service rulings guidelines for a "true lease" require that the lessor assume the full risks and rewards of property ownership.[1] The more important of the requirements are:

1. At the inception of the lease, the parties must be able to demonstrate that at the end of the lease term (including any renewals or extensions at less than fair market value) the remaining useful life of the equipment will be the greater of one year or 20 percent of the original useful life.
2. At the end of the lease term (including any renewals or extensions at less than fair market value), the value of the equipment will (without giving effect to inflation) be at least 20 percent of its original value.
3. The lessee does not have the right to purchase the leased equipment at less than its fair market value.

The failure of a "lease" to qualify as such means that the "lessor" is not entitled to the tax benefits of ownership, that the "lessee" may be required to make tax indemnification payments under the "lease," and, at a minimum, that the "lease" rental payments will not be an expense deductible for tax purposes (rather, the lease rental would be treated as being partly a payment of interest, which would be deductible as an expense, and partly a repayment of principal, which would not be deductible). Even more to the point, if lessors are not completely confident that the tax benefits of ownership will accrue to them, they will be unwilling to provide lease rates low enough to enable lessees to meet *Statement No. 13* tests.

With the passage of the ERTA, a new form of tax lease has been created—the safe harbor lease. The significant feature of the safe harbor lease is that the lessee is allowed to control the asset for its entire economic life through the use of a fixed or even nominal price purchase option.[2] Even though the lessor has no real risks of ownership, it is allowed to reap the tax benefits of ownership.

---

[1] The rulings guidelines are not substantive law and are not binding on the courts. However, many revenue agents treat rulings guidelines as if they were law, and rulings guidelines do indicate the views of the National Office.

[2] The safe harbor lease created by the ERTA is available in a wide variety of situations. However, the most widely reported use of the safe harbor lease—the so-called tax-benefit transfer—is actually a sale of tax benefits (even though it is structured as a lease) and, under most circumstances, will be treated as such for accounting purposes.

Contrast the ease with which corporations are permitted to obtain the benefits of ownership under the ERTA with the ownership risks individuals are required to assume in order to be entitled to the same benefits. Individuals are excluded from participating in safe harbor leases. In addition, an individual can claim investment tax credit on equipment subject to lease only if the lease is treated as an operating lease for federal income tax purposes.

For federal income tax purposes, a lease is classified as an operating lease only if (*a*) the length of the lease is shorter than half the midpoint (the class life) of the Asset Depreciation Range (ADR) for the asset type under lease and (*b*) during the first 12 months after the equipment is delivered to the lessee, the ordinary operating expenses (other than taxes, interest, or depreciation) paid by the lessor are more than 15 percent of the gross rentals.[3] Under the ADR system, assets were assigned class lives or years over which they could be depreciated without challenge by the IRS of the life utilized. For example, railcars have a class life of 15 years; vessels, 18 years; and commercial aircraft, 12 years. Any lease including periods of renewal at the option of either the lessor or the lessee, even if at fair market value must be one day shorter than half the class life. For this reason, from the viewpoint of both the lessor (whether a corporation or an individual) and the lessee/user, short-term operating leases are dramatically different from leveraged leases treated as operating leases for accounting purposes.

Some observers believe that short operating leases are not a financing technique at all but rather elements or components of a business strategy. Indeed, the word *operating* implies business operations and not accounting treatment; and in view of the shortness of the contract period relative to the probable economic life of the asset, decisions to acquire the use of assets with this technique have not historically been decisions of the corporate treasurer. The decision to use assets subject to short leases has typically been within the authority of line or operating management subject to the operating budget approval process rather than the financing approval process.[4]

---

[3] Whether or not under *Statement No. 13* a lease would be treated as an operating lease for accounting purposes is not relevant to whether it is an operating lease for tax purposes.

Prior to the ERTA, the standard was half the depreciable life used for tax purposes, which could be 20 percent higher than the midpoint life or even longer if "facts and circumstances" were used.

[4] Corporations have not satisfactorily distinguished short-term operating leases from financing leases treated as operating leases for accounting purposes. While the acquisition of an asset with a short lease could be the decision of line management, the financing terms should not be. Line management will normally choose a lease with investment tax credit retained by the lessor rather than a lease with investment tax credit retained by the lessee (regardless of whether the corporation as a whole could utilize the investment tax credit) because the rental in the former structure is lower and the benefit of the investment tax credit tends not to be allocated to the operating unit for profit center performance purposes. Because the operating unit will make the decision that has the most favorable effect on its own performance standards, .. may make financing decisions that are improper for the corporation as a whole.

DEMAND FOR SHORTER-TERM, OPERATING LEASES

In order to effectively utilize the operating lease as an asset acquisition technique, it is important to understand the benefits to the lessee associated with this type of lease.

The operating lease has many of the same aspects as the leveraged lease, the single-investor lease, or the safe harbor lease in that it provides a method of obtaining 100 percent financing for the asset. It also provides a means of reducing overall financing costs by allowing an entity which can effectively utilize the tax benefits to do so and in turn to pass back at least a portion of this benefit to the lessee in the form of lower rental payments.

For those concerned with accounting treatment, the operating lease is not carried on the balance sheet. Also, if structured properly, the expense of the lease rental payment will usually have less of an impact on book earnings than will the depreciation and interest payments associated with the purchase of the same asset. This has a positive effect on a company's return on assets for reporting purposes.

Financing by means of a lease, whether an operating, single-investor, leveraged, or safe harbor lease, allows a company access to an alternative source of capital. This reduces the company's reliance on traditional sources of capital, which often impose a costly penalty on overly frequent users. While a lease contains provisions regarding rental payment, insurance, and maintenance of the asset, it generally does not contain the restrictive financial covenants traditionally found in debt indentures.

While all types of leasing have many similar benefits, the operating lease offers one benefit that is not available from the longer-term lease—flexibility. The shorter operating lease permits the lessee to add to or reduce its "capital base" more in line with business trends by adding leased assets or by not renewing leases upon their expiration. This is valuable for a company whose business is subject to cyclical swings. In addition, in an industry where technology is in a state of flux, a shorter-term lease permits companies to switch to more advanced technology as it becomes available.

A good example of demand creating a market for asset leasing is the 100-year-old tank car leasing industry. Since tank cars were viewed initially by the railroads as special-purpose, limited-use cars which might be subject to rapid technological obsolescence, the railroads would not expend the capital to acquire them. A void was thus created, and third parties, such as Union Tank Car and General American Transportation, purchased tank cars and leased them to the railroads. As time went on, these third parties began to lease tank cars directly to the shippers that transported their goods in the cars. Due to the cyclical nature of the shippers' business, the leases in this industry often tend to be shorter-term, operating leases.

The spot chartering of tankers is another example. The integrated petroleum companies have often sought to own their key manufacturing, transportation, and marketing facilities. However, in recognition of the cyclical nature of this business, most integrated petroleum companies "spot" or time charter (the equivalent of operating leases, though the lengths of the charters can extend from one trip to 25 years and the terms of the charters can vary substantially) a portion of their tanker fleets, giving them flexibility to reduce their capital exposure during periods of weak demand.

The 1960s saw the development of intermodal transportation: the movement of goods by more than one means of transportation (rail, truck, water, or air) while in the same container. One type of container commonly used in intermodal transportation is the maritime container. The major shipping companies were simply too short of capital and too weak financially to provide both the container vessels and the containers. For the most part, they opted to control the vessels, and as a result, the container leasing industry was born. The growth of this industry in the short span of 20 years has been astounding. In this industry, worldwide logistics have played a crucial role. Trade imbalances, customer requirements, and cyclical demand created a need for flexible asset management. Flexibility has been provided through the "master lease" arrangement, under which the shipping company/lessee agrees to pay a rental for a stated minimum number of containers (regardless of whether all of that minimum are fully used during the lease term) and is assured access to additional containers as needed; rental for the additional containers is charged only for actual use.

In fact, there are numerous examples to illustrate the demand for operating leases. For a variety of reasons, including limited capital and cyclical needs, the shorter-term operating lease method of financing the acquisition of assets has grown into a substantial business in its own right.

SUPPLY OF EQUITY FUNDS

Banks have been a traditional source of capital for the leasing companies, either through direct loans or through the purchase of the stream of lease rental payments at a discount on either a nonrecourse or a recourse basis. It was then a logical step for banks to take an equity position in leases. In order to limit the operating risk exposure of banks in leasing transactions, the Board of Governors of the Federal Reserve System imposed Regulation Y, which requires that, in a leasing transaction in which a bank invests equity, the net present value of the nonterminable lease rental payments must be equal to or greater than 75 percent of the cost of the asset. This "full payout" requirement limits the amount of business risk that the bank, as lessor, is permitted to assume in developing its pricing practices by limiting the risk that the bank is permitted to assume with respect to the re-leasing or sale of the asset. This limit converts the principal risk of a lease from an operating risk to a credit risk related to the lessee's ability to make lease rental payments. The other major corporate equity participant, the credit company, has a similar preference for credit risks rather than operating risks and, thus, for longer-term financing leases.

The individual equity market existed to a very limited extent during the late 1950s and early 1960s and began to expand and develop in the early 1970s. Ironically, during that period and continuing to the present, the tax laws applicable to equipment leasing have grown increasingly burdensome to individual investors.

Prior to 1969, the maximum tax on an individual's income, whether earned or unearned, was 70 percent. Accordingly, individuals in higher income tax brackets had a substantial incentive to seek a means of sheltering their income. At that time, most of the tax laws applicable to equipment leasing did not distinguish between corporate and non-corporate investors. As a result of the differential in tax rates, the return to individual investors from equipment leasing transactions was potentially higher than the return to corporations.

In 1969 and the early 1970s, there were several changes in the tax laws.

First, Congress created a new tax, the "minimum" tax on "items of tax preference," which was intended to ensure that taxpayers who enjoyed certain tax benefits still paid at least a minimum income tax. In the case of individuals, that tax was 10 percent of the amount by which the taxpayer's tax preference items in any year exceeded the sum of (a) $30,000, (b) the taxpayer's regular income tax liability for the year (other than certain specified taxes), and (c) in some cases, some or all of the taxpayer's regular income tax liability for the seven preceding years. Among the tax preference items for individuals was the excess of accelerated depreciation over straight-line depreciation claimed with respect to personal property subject to a net lease.

Second, Congress limited to 50 percent the income tax on an individual taxpayer's "earned income" (generally, wages, salaries, professional fees, and compensation for personal services), even though the applicable marginal rate is higher. However, the amount of an individual taxpayer's income in any year that would be treated as "earned taxable income" and therefore would be subject to taxation at not more than the 50 percent maximum rate was reduced by the amount the taxpayer's tax preferences for that year exceeded $30,000.

Finally, the investment tax credit provisions of the Internal Revenue Code were amended to provide that individual taxpayers (or partnerships or Subchapter S corporations comprised of individuals) could claim the investment tax credit with respect to leased property only if the lease were an operating lease (described in the text above and in the "Investment Tax Credit" section below).

In practice, the minimum tax was applicable only to taxpayers with very substantial amounts of tax preferences. Similarly, only taxpayers with substantial amounts of tax preferences suffered any significant loss of the benefits of the maximum tax on earned income. However, the provision that investment tax credit with respect to a lease of personal property was available to individual investors only if the lease was an operating lease did affect returns from equipment leasing transactions.

Due to the limited risk associated with full-payout lease transactions and the individual's ability to assess the true tax savings from a net lease transaction, investors often chose to forgo the investment tax credit and to enter into full-payout, limited-risk tax-shelter transactions. Even without the benefit of the investment tax credit, individuals were able to compete with commercial banks and other corporate equity sources (a) because the tax losses were more valuable to individual investors with substantial income, at least so long as a portion of that income was not earned income (since individuals were subject to a marginal tax rate of up to 70 percent versus the 48 percent marginal tax rate for corporations), and (b) by assuming a greater residual value risk than would be assumed by a bank or other corporate equity source.

The amendments to the Internal Revenue Code adopted by Congress in the 1976 Tax Reform Act significantly changed the economics of leasing as a means of sheltering an individual's income. The 1976 Act amended the minimum tax on tax preference items (a) by increasing the tax rate to 15 percent and (b) by subjecting to the minimum tax the amount by which the taxpayer's tax preferences for the year exceeded $10,000 or, in the case of individuals, one half of the taxpayer's regular income tax (less certain credits) for the year, whichever was greater. Under the 1976 Act, the excess of accelerated depreciation over straight-line depreciation on all leased personal property (rather than merely net-leased personal property) became a tax preference item. In addition, the 1976 Act revised the maximum tax on earned income (which was renamed "personal service income") by providing that the amount of personal service income treated as "personal service taxable income" and eligible for the maximum rate limitation would be reduced dollar for dollar by the taxpayer's tax preference items. By providing that tax preferences would reduce personal service taxable income dollar for dollar, the 1976 Act reduced the value of the initial tax losses to the individual investor while maintaining the level of the tax liability in the later years of investment.

The 1976 Act also provided that noncorporate taxpayers (and Subchapter S and certain closely held corporate taxpayers) could claim tax losses currently only to the extent that they were "at risk" in the transaction. In general, as described in greater detail under "Evaluation of Return" and "Effect of Leverage," the effect of the at-risk rules is to reduce the economic benefit to individual investors of highly leveraged equipment purchases which take advantage of nonrecourse financing.

The importance of this tax law change is evident when one considers its effect on the aftertax benefits from two identical leasing transactions, one of which was completed before the tax law changes effected by the 1976 act and one after. Because of the lower aftertax value of the tax losses in the latter transaction, that transaction could realize the same overall return (and be priced to be competitive with the former transaction) only if the residual value of the leased property were substantially higher than had been assumed in pricing the former transaction. In one case, the residual value assumption went from 5 percent to 40 percent.

In 1978, Congress expanded the at-risk rules to provide for "recapture" of "negative at risk." This provision further reduced both the present value of depreciation deductions and the economic benefit of highly leveraged lease transactions.

With a marginal rate closer to that of the corporation and without the benefit of the investment tax credit or the full economic benefit of leverage, in order to be competitive in the leasing market, the individual had to assume a higher residual value in order to overcome the effects of the lower tax rate.[5]

The effects of the 1976 Act and the amendments adopted in 1978 were continued and magnified by the ERTA. Among other things, the ERTA reduced the marginal tax rate on all taxable income of individuals to 50 percent, thereby reducing further the value of tax losses to individuals compared to corporations. In addition, by reducing the depreciable lives of most assets, the ERTA heightened the impact of the at-risk rules on individual investors.

During this same period, inflation was starting to become a source of concern for investors, and as a result, they began to seek investments that provided protection against inflation as well as a means of sheltering income. The difficulty in determining the effect of tax preferences (a problem not faced by corporate investors), combined with the higher residual risk that an individual investor had to assume, made it hard for individuals to compete with corporate investors for the full-payout, longer-term leases. Therefore, individuals began investing in long-lived assets subject to operating leases.

---

[5] It should be noted that this law had a different effect on different individuals, depending on each individual's particular tax situation. As an example, an individual with substantial unearned income but no personal service income could still shelter income taxed at 70 percent advantageously since the maximum tax of 50 percent on earned income was of no value to him or her. However, the at-risk rules still operated to reduce the economic benefit of a high degree of leverage to a 70 percent taxpayer.

The individual investor found that there were several benefits to such an investment. First, the operating lease structure enabled the individual investor to qualify for the investment tax credit, which helped to mitigate the effect of the business risk related to the re-leasing of the asset. Also, because the leases were subject to renewal, inflation was likely to cause an increase in the rental rate upon renewal, thus creating the possibility for increased cash flow from the transaction (a feature missing in a full-payout lease). Particularly with long-lived assets, the residual value also provided a means of hedging against inflation. Finally, while the transaction did involve operating risks, it also provided a means of sheltering income.

ECONOMICS OF INVESTING IN OPERATING LEASE TRANSACTIONS

Elements of Return

There are three primary components to the return from a leasing transaction: cash flow, tax benefits (including investment tax credit and tax deferrals from depreciation), and residual value. Because of the varied nature of the assets and the varying duration of the investment, the relative importance of these components may vary.

Take, for example, two assets, both qualifying for investment tax credit and both having a five-year depreciable life under the ERTA. Assume, however, that one asset has a 15-year economic life and that the other has a 30-year economic life. At the end of 10 years, only one third of the expected economic life of the first asset remains, while two thirds of the economic life of the second asset remains. It is logical, then, to assume that at the end of 10 years, the residual value for one asset would be considerably less than that for the other. Therefore, in order to achieve the same return over the same time period, the asset with the lower residual value would have to have a higher cash flow relative to its value than would the asset with the higher residual value.

For two assets with similar cash flow and depreciable lives, of which one qualifies for the investment tax credit and the other does not, a higher residual value is needed to compensate for the lack of investment tax credit. If the cash flow from the transaction without the investment tax credit were increased sufficiently, a comparable return could be achieved without assuming incremental residual risk.

Another potential benefit, though one difficult to quantify and accurately forecast, is the greater ability of the operating lease to keep pace with inflation. Because most operating leases will be renewed during the term of the investment, the lease rental payment should reflect, at least to some extent, the pace of inflation. There is always the chance that the renewal rates will reflect weak demand or technological change.

However, there is a real possibility of increasing cash flow as a result of inflation.

Evaluation of Return

There are numerous methods for determining what the "return" from a leasing transaction is and for gauging whether that return is appropriate. No one method is suitable for all investors, because each investor will have particular investment objectives and must select a return measure appropriate for those objectives.

Although this is not a recommended method of analysis, an investor seeking a means to shelter income may be concerned only with the "write-offs" from the transactions. Therefore, that investor might look only to the investment tax credit and tax losses (generated primarily from depreciation, intangible drilling costs, and other noncash tax-deductible expenses). In such a case, the return might be stated as a ratio of the write-offs to the investment (e.g., 2-to-1 write-offs).

Another investor might be interested in a transaction that provided cash flow and therefore might quote the return as cash flow generated relative to cash invested. For this investor, a 10 percent "cash-on-cash return" might be a relevant measure. Since leasing transactions tend to be tax sensitive, an investor may miss an attractive investment by not determining its aftertax benefits.

A third investor might be interested in the aftertax return over the period of the investment. This investor would determine the cost and benefits from the transaction, including the cash investment, cash flow, residual value, investment tax credit, debt service payments, tax losses generated (as well as whether effective use could be made of the losses), and tax liabilities. An investor could then select a "hurdle rate" for the investment which reflected that investor's perception of the aftertax risk inherent in the transaction and could discount the aftertax benefits and liabilities of the transaction to determine whether the net present value is positive. Another method would be to solve for the internal rate of return (that rate which when used to discount the aftertax benefits and liabilities of the transaction results in a net present value equal to the investment) and then decide whether that return is attractive, given the risks of the investment.

One comparison that any investor will make is with the returns available from alternative investments. A write-off investor would compare the write-offs available in other transactions. A cash-on-cash investor might look to the equity market to compare the yield on common stock. An investor interested in the aftertax return might look to the municipal bond market to compare aftertax yields. The investor in an operating lease transaction will probably be some combination of the three investors described above and will make these comparisons as well as others and thus determine whether the investment is appropriate and attractive.

Effect of Leverage

One way to improve the return on investment is to finance a portion of the purchase price with debt. This reduces the investor's out-of pocket expenditure and the amount of investment on which the return is calculated, assuming that the debt is nonrecourse. In theory, as long as the aftertax cost of the debt financing is less than the aftertax return on the investment, incremental leverage will improve the return on the investment.

However, with the benefit of an improved return comes additional risk. In most cases, a portion, if not the entire amount, of debt service is fixed, and it becomes an incremental expense that must be covered by the cash from the transaction. If the amount of rental income or level of expenses can vary, with debt outstanding there is the possibility that no cash will be available to the investor, or worse, that the investor will be unable to meet debt service obligations and the lender will foreclose on the asset. The investor would then be subject to recapture of depreciation and possibly of investment tax credit and might not obtain full value on the sale of the asset.

In addition, recent capital market gyrations emphasize the desirability of fixed-rate financing. Unless the business operation of the borrower will produce revenue that fluctuates with the cost of money, it may not be wise to finance long-term assets with floating-rate borrowings, which are in essence short-term money. And as a general rule, operating businesses/lessors throughout the country have not been able to pass through increased financing costs to the user of the asset if it was previously acquired equipment. In fact, in 1981 it was difficult for lessors to pass through to lessees the financing costs of newly ordered equipment because of the dramatic rise in interest rates and the competitive edge of used equipment. Due to the short-term nature of operating leases, a contraction of economic activity will be felt in the operating lease business. Therefore, to the extent possible, financing costs should be established when lease rates are committed to by an investor.

A loan with a maturity longer than the fixed term of the underlying operating lease creates what is called an "uncovered balloon." As a consequence, the lender will require a collateral package sufficient to amortize the remaining loan balance. Normally, this is achieved through a large equity investment at the inception, so that throughout the term of the loan, the outstanding loan balance will be relatively low compared to the anticipated market value of the asset. This thereby reduces the risk that, in case of default, the value of the collateral would be insufficient to retire the then outstanding amount of the loan. Of course, this design could be frustrated by market conditions because the probable reason for a default would be the imbalance of supply and demand with a corresponding decline in value of the collateral. Therefore, the lender may require additional collateral, such as cash reserves for individual investors or, for partnerships, restrictive covenants limiting or preventing cash distributions to partners.

Another factor that should be considered when determining the appropriate amount of leverage is the effect that the amount of leverage will have on the individual investor's at-risk position. Under the at-risk rules added to the Internal Revenue Code in 1976 and amended in 1978, for purposes of investment in property other than real estate, an individual investor may deduct losses only to the extent that the investor is at risk, and if the investor has a negative at-risk balance, previously claimed losses must be recaptured. The investor's amount at risk initially is the amount of equity invested plus the amount of recourse debt for which the investor is personally liable. Then the amount is periodically adjusted. It is reduced by the amount of losses claimed and any cash distributed to or on behalf of the investor, and it is increased by the amount of taxable income earned. If claiming a tax loss would cause the at-risk amount to be reduced below zero, that amount of the loss is deferred. If a cash distribution is made and that distribution causes the amount at risk to fall below zero, losses previously taken are "recaptured." This is done by deeming such cash, which would otherwise not be taxed, to be income and by requiring that taxes be paid on that portion. The losses deferred and the cash taxed as income are carried forward and can be used as a deduction against taxable income in the future, thus sheltering income that would otherwise be taxable.

The effect of the at-risk rules is to change the timing (and to the extent that sufficient income is not generated, the amount) of the after-tax benefits in a transaction (principally those arising from depreciation). While these tax benefits are not lost, the deferral of recognition can reduce the present value of the depreciation deductions substantially. This timing question should be considered when determining the appropriate amount of leverage for a transaction and whether the leverage should be recourse or nonrecourse.[6] These considerations have be-

---

[6] The appropriate amount of leverage in a transaction, which will determine when, if at all, the investors cease to be at risk and future tax losses are suspended, will depend on a variety of factors, including the amount of the initial equity investment, the depreciable life of the asset, the method of depreciation, the profitability of the lease transaction, and the amount of cash distributed to or for the account of the investors.

Limited partners are, by the nature of the limited partnership structure, not liable for financing incurred at the partnership level, regardless of whether the debt is recourse or nonrecourse. If a limited partner wishes to include a portion of the partnership's recourse financing

come more important now that the ERTA has significantly shortened the depreciable lives of most personal property, which results in greater losses in the early years of a transaction. An individual investor who leverages the investment with nonrecourse debt is now more likely to encounter the at-risk limitations.

This is not meant to be an argument against the use of nonrecourse debt but rather notice of another factor that the individual should consider when including leverage in a leasing transaction.

INVESTMENT TAX CREDIT

The rules relating to the investment tax credit are significant in their implications and often affect dramatically the structure of an investment. As a consequence, some discussion of the rules regarding the investment tax credit is necessary to fully understand the risk profile and basic design of operating lease investments.

The Internal Revenue Code states that investment tax credit will be available to noncorporate taxpayers with respect to equipment which is subject to a lease only if:

1. The term of the lease (including options to renew, whether at fair market value or not) is less than half the equipment's ADR midpoint life.
2. During the first 12 months of the lease, the sum of the ordinary and necessary operating expenses deductible solely under Section 162 of the Code (that is, excluding expenses such as taxes, interest, or depreciation, which are deductible under other code sections) with respect to the leased property exceeds 15 percent of the gross rental income produced by the property.

Also, the Economic Recovery Tax Act of 1981 has imposed an at-risk limitation for the purpose of determining the amount of an individual taxpayer's basis in leased property which is eligible for investment tax credit. Under this new at-risk limitation, the amount with respect to which an individual taxpayer may claim the investment tax credit may not exceed the amount at risk with respect to such property as of the close of the taxable year in which the property is placed in service.

Amounts borrowed on a nonrecourse basis are generally not con-

---

in his or her amount at risk, that investor would have to actually sign the note, thereby accepting personal liability. This can only be done in a private placement because Regulation T of the Securities and Exchange Commission and the Board of Governors of the Federal Reserve System prohibits an underwriter or selling agent from arranging or providing financing to an investor in a registered public offering of partnership interests.

sidered at-risk. However, the ERTA provides a special exception whereby certain amounts borrowed on a nonrecourse basis no later than the tax year the property is placed in service will be considered at risk, provided the following requirements are met.

1. At all times, the taxpayer must maintain a 20 percent at-risk investment with respect to the property.
2. The property must not be acquired from a "related person."
3. The amount must be borrowed from a "qualified person" (which is, in general, pension trusts, regulated lenders such as banks, insurance companies, and other persons actively and regularly engaged in the business of lending money) who is not (a) a person related to the taxpayer, (b) the seller of the property, (c) a person who will receive a fee with respect to the taxpayer's investment in the property, or (d) a person related to any of such persons.
4. The amount borrowed must not be convertible into equity.

While, in most cases, these limitations on the ability of individuals to claim the investment tax credit do not present insurmountable problems, they do require additional care and thought in structuring the leasing transactions in which individuals will invest.

FORMS OF INVESTMENT

For a company seeking access to the individual equity market for capital, whether that company is the end user or an intermediary such as a leasing company, an understanding of the Internal Revenue Code provisions which restrict individuals' investment in leasing transactions is essential. It is also important to understand the motivations of the individuals who will invest in these transactions. Within this framework, it it possible to use a number of different investment structures in raising equity from individuals. To a certain extent the form of investment may be a matter of personal preference, but it is often dictated by the nature of the asset or of the industry or of the risks involved.

Individual Investment

Individuals investing in leasing transactions tend to be passive investors in that they will not be actively involved in the management or operation of the asset. For an asset manager to establish a system for managing a small number of assets may be economically impractical. Therefore, an individual who arranges for the lease of only his or her assets will be more likely to invest in longer-term, net leases where the lessee is responsible for the operation of the asset. In addition, the assets purchased are likely to be smaller, lower-valued assets: that is, a railcar for $50,000 rather than a tuna boat for $10 million.

Limited Partnership Structure

A form of investment that has been used effectively has been the limited partnership. The partnership raises funds through an investment bank or other selling agent, and the partnership, rather than the individual, purchases the asset or assets. The investor owns a percentage interest in the partnership and receives a pro rata share of all cash from operation or sale of the assets and a pro rata share of all tax benefits (including the investment tax credit and depreciation) or liabilities.

Often, the seller or manager of the partnership's assets forms the partnership and acts as the general partner. In many cases, however, the general partner of the partnership is a company, active in the equipment leasing market, which not only supervises the partnership's equipment acquisitions but also arranges for the actual management of the partnership's assets by lessees or other managers.

One of the major benefits of the limited partnership form is its limitation on the potential liability of the investor. Insurance can go a long way toward reducing the risks of an investment, but, if nothing else, these is a psychological benefit in knowing that an investor's liability is limited to the amount invested.

The partnership is able to purchase either an asset of higher value or a larger number of assets than could any one investor. Therefore, through a partnership, investors can purchase assets that would otherwise be beyond their means, or they can reduce the risks associated with operating the assets by spreading the risks over a larger number of assets and investors. This larger number of assets can justify the cost of a manager for them, thus enabling investors to invest in assets subject to shorter-term leases, which require someone to arrange for renewal, and/or subject to "gross" leases, under which the lessor is responsible for arranging for such things as maintenance. Risk is further diversified in those partnerships that acquire a large number of assets managed or leased by different managers or by users in different industries.

Assuming that the partnership has purchased a number of assets, another benefit from ownership at the partnership level rather than the individual level is the sharing of expenditures for such items as major repairs, improvements, or modifications. In addition to the substantial actual cost of these items, the assets are usually out of service while the work is being performed. For an individual, owning these assets, repairs, improvements, or modifications, in addition to requiring an incremental investment, could entail a significant loss of revenues (which might require further investment in order to pay carrying costs and debt service while the assets are out of service). For a partnership, it is possible to use the revenues generated by other assets, either from operation or sale, to cover the cost of such repairs, improvements, or modifications. It is unlikely that all of the partnership's assets would be out of service at the same time and while revenues might be reduced if some assets were out of service for repairs, improvements, or modifications, they would not be interrupted (and the partnership generally could continue to pay operating expenses, carrying costs, and debt service without any additional investment).

Debt financing for the purchase of assets can be arranged by the partnership so that an investor can, in effect, purchase more assets for the same investment. If the investors are individuals, the at-risk rules will still affect the appropriate degree of partnership leverage. However, arranging leverage at the partnership level saves the investor from having to arrange his or her own financing, and the partnership is often able to arrange debt financing on more favorable terms than would be available to the individual investor. While it is unlikely that many individuals could, without personal liability or recourse to any personal assets, obtain a loan secured only by an asset, nonrecourse financing can often be arranged at the partnership level[7] because, while there may be numerous instances when a particular asset is not generating revenue, it is less likely that all the assets in the partnership's pool of assets would not be generating revenue. Therefore, there is less likely to be a payment default, and the loan is more secure.

Under the limited partnership structure, limited partners must be essentially passive investors: a limited partner has limited liability only so long as he or she does not participate in the management of the partnership. The method of depreciation is selected by the general partner at the partnership level. A particular investor might wish to take advantage of a different depreciation method, but in a partnership, that is not within the individual investor's discretion. In addition to surrendering substantial managerial control, limited partners lose some degree of liquidity. In order to preserve the favorable tax treatment afforded partnerships, most limited partnership agreements impose substantial limitations on a limited partner's freedom to transfer his or her limited

---

[7] At times, a lender may require that the general partner be personally liable for a loan to a limited partnership. Prior to the imposition of the at-risk rules in 1976, this would have had a substantial adverse tax effect on the limited partners. As a result of the at-risk rules, it probably does not have a direct adverse effect on the limited partners in most cases, but it may, by creating uncertainties as to the true interests of the parties, create tax risks which investors would find unacceptable. In any event, most general partners with substantial assets and/or other ongoing business interests would be unwilling to accept the business risk of liability (since their liability on the loan would extend to any deficiency, while their interest in the partnership is limited).

partnership interest. In addition, the federal securities laws and state blue-sky laws may impose limits on transferability. Even in those cases where neither the partnership agreement nor federal or state law restrict transferability, because there is only a limited trading market, if any, for limited partnership interests, these interests tend to be illiquid.

Management Program Structure

A combination of the individual ownership of assets and the partnership is the management program. In this type of program, the individual investors each own their own assets but contribute the use of the assets to an operating pool. The operating revenues and expenses are combined and then allocated pro rata to the members of the pool. As in the partnership format, this structure enables investors to spread the operating risk over a larger number of assets and to have an operating base large enough to justify the cost of hiring a manager for the assets. Therefore, investors can also invest in shorter-term leases or in gross leases.

While there are no absolute rules or guidelines, management programs are best suited to the acquisition and management of assets if (*a*) the cost of the assets is low enough to permit them to be purchased by a large number of individuals, (*b*) the assets are "fungible" (that is, their costs, uses, operating characteristics, revenue-producing potential, and anticipated resale values are sufficiently similar to avoid conflict of interest between separate investors in either the acquisition or the management of their assets), and (*c*) the assets do not entail a significant risk of liability to the owner.

As indicated above, for the acquisition of costly assets a partnership, with its potential for the aggregation of capital, may be a more appropriate investment vehicle. Similarly, a limited partnership may be a more appropriate vehicle for the ownership and operation of assets which entail some risk of liability. Also, a partnership may be a better investment vehicle for the ownership of assets which, because of technological or market changes, may require major capital additions or improvements since a partnership facilitates the creation and management of reserves and may facilitate the spreading of the costs over time and over the revenues from the pool of assets.

Since the individual investors own their own assets directly, they have the opportunity to adopt the tax strategies best suited to their individual circumstances and to maximize the tax benefits available to them individually.

1. The individual investor can elect both the depreciable life and the method of depreciation with respect to his or her asset. The Economic Recovery Tax Act of 1981 has limited the alternatives available to tax-

payers, and although this factor was more significant prior to the enactment of the ERTA than it is today, individual investors still have different investment objectives and strategies and even today may wish to elect different methods of depreciation.[8]

2. An investor who is in the trade or business of owning and using assets can claim a full year's depreciation with respect to an asset for the year in which the asset is acquired and placed in service. In contrast, it would appear that a partnership can claim depreciation only for that period of the year commencing with the month in which its assets are acquired and placed in service. Therefore, the individual who, by virtue of his or her business or by virtue of prior investments in assets (including assets owned and used in a management program), can be considered to be in the trade or business of owning and using assets can increase the depreciation deduction available in the year in which the investment is made.

3. The individual investors can take advantage of the ERTA provision permitting a taxpayer to deduct as a current expense in any year up to $5,000 of the capital cost of personal property acquired in that year (the so-called 179 expense). This expense replaces "bonus depreciation," which was eliminated by the ERTA. The limitation on the amount of the 179 expense is measured at the partnership level as well as the partner level. If the investors had acquired interests in a partnership which owned the assets, the investors would have been entitled to deduct only their respective partnership shares of the partnership's $5,000 179 expense (which, for any individual investor, might be an insignificant benefit).

4. Individual investors can claim investment tax credit with respect to up to $125,000 of used equipment which meets certain tests. If used equipment were acquired by a partnership, the $125,000 limitation would be measured at the partnership level. Thus, if used assets were acquired by a partnership, each investor would be entitled to claim only his or her share of the investment tax credit with respect to $125,000 of the used equipment acquired by the partnership.

5. Since the individual purchases the actual asset and then pools it

---

[8] Prior to the ERTA, accelerated depreciation in excess of straight-line depreciation converted personal service income into "unearned" income taxable at the maximum marginal rate. For investors with substantial amounts of personal service income, but without substantial amounts of unearned income, the conversion could have had a significant adverse effect. However, only the individual involved could determine the exact effect and the most suitable tax strategy to minimize that effect. The management program, by affording the investor the opportunity to make his or her own tax elections, permitted individual investors to adopt the tax strategy most suitable to them individually. The ERTA, by reducing the maximum marginal rate on all taxable income to 50 percent and by eliminating the maximum tax on personal service income, has substantially reduced, but not eliminated, the significance of the election of depreciation methods.

with other assets for operating purposes, all or a portion of any selling commission paid in connection with raising funds to purchase the assets for a management program might be considered part of the cost of acquiring the asset. As such, the selling commission could be added to the basis of the asset for purposes of calculating depreciation and the investment tax credit. If the form of ownership were a partnership, the selling commission would be considered part of the cost of purchasing a security and would be added to the capital basis of the security. There would not be any tax benefit associated with this security acquisition cost until the security was sold, at which time the cost would reduce the gain on the sale or be written off as a long-term capital loss.

Unlike partners in a partnership, owners of assets in a management program can determine when it is appropriate to sell their own assets. Therefore, an investor in a management program may be better able to control the timing of the recognition of any gain or loss on sale of the asset. While this may be a benefit to those who sell, it could have a detrimental effect on those remaining in the program. In a partnership, the effectiveness of risk sharing is unimpaired by a particular investor's desire to liquidate his or her investment. The partnership owns the same amount of assets before and after the sale of a partnership interest. The sale of an asset operated in a management agreement usually terminates the management agreement with respect to that asset, and the asset is withdrawn from the pool. The sale of any significant number of assets could dramatically alter the risk profile associated with the remaining assets.

Availability of Financing

The selection of a form of investment can have a significant effect on the type and amount of debt available for financing for these investments. For an individual financing on his or her own, the local bank (the logical source for the debt financing) is likely to insist that the loan be with recourse to the investor's personal assets. As mentioned earlier, a partnership would be better able to arrange nonrecourse financing. A partnership, depending on its size and on the sponsor's reputation and creditworthiness, would be likely to have access to the banks at the larger money centers or to institutional lenders, which tend to have more funds available on terms favorable to investors.

At the time management programs were first being structured, it was believed that it would be attractive to investors if the choice of whether to leverage and of how much to leverage were left to the individual investor. In that way, each investor could evaluate his or her investment objectives and risk preferences and obtain the appropriate amount of debt, if any. Experience has demonstrated that this feature of management programs is actually a major disadvantage.

Investors generally prefer to leverage investment in assets to be operated in a management program and often seek assistance in finding a lender other than their customary banks, using this opportunity to expand credit availability. Knowing that the availability of centralized credit will improve the marketability of a program, the sponsor is faced with a real dilemma. Should the sponsor attempt to arrange a centralized lending source and incur the associated administrative problems, or should the debt financing arrangements be left entirely in the hands of the individual investor?

Many problems are associated with centralized credit, not the least of which is the natural conflict between the marketing organization seeking a sale and the lending organization seeking a good credit borrower. Technical problems that have to be overcome include the various state usury laws and, if the borrower and lender are located in different states, the conflicts of laws regarding which state's usury law would apply.

In addition, the mere logistics of arranging loans with a central lender can be time-consuming, at best. The distribution of forms by the central lender, the return and review of these forms with appropriate financial information from the investor, the credit approval process of the lender, the retransmission of the loan documents, and the final submission of the signed loan and related security agreements (as well as other agreements and documents) require careful monitoring and considerable administrative support.

Loans (whether to a limited partnership, an individual limited partner, or an individual acquiring assets that are to be operated in a management program) to finance the acquisition of equipment that will be leased under an operating lease or operated as a business may be "risky" loans from a lender's point of view. Among other things, protection for the lender can come in the form of a relatively longer-term lease to a creditworthy lessee, of an asset manager with a proven reputation for marketing, or of an asset which has a long life and a wide user market and is not subject to rapid physical deterioration or technological obsolescence. In addition, various mechanisms have been utilized to reduce the risk to the lenders and/or increase the return in order to improve the risk/reward trade-off and thereby broaden the universe of lenders interested in making loans to these borrowers. These devices include (a) an undertaking by a sponsor to advance money on a periodic basis, in the event of cash shortfalls, for the benefit of a senior lender and to take back a loan subordinated to the senior lender and possibly to a priority distribution to the investors; (b) an equity participation ("kicker") for the senior lender in either the periodic cash flows or the residual (though the equity kicker can create questions as to whether the debt will be treated as debt or equity); (c) residual value insurance purchased by the lender (it would appear that any at-risk problems would be avoided if this insurance were purchased by the lender instead of having the lender named as a beneficiary of a policy purchased by a partnership or individual); (d) manufacturer support (or subordination) through a first-loss guarantee or rental makeup agreement; and (e) letters of credit.

In the final analysis, excluding the associated tax benefits, an institutional lender which is considering a loan in connection with an investor-related program will perform a risk analysis very similar to that undertaken by the individual investor who will be supplying the equity.

Liquidity

It appears that a hard asset, even if under lease or subject to a noncancelable management agreement, is more liquid than a limited partnership interest since (a) assets can be sold to users of assets as well as other investors: (b) assets are rarely subject to significant restrictions on transferability, while partnership interests customarily have restricted transferability; (c) the market value of assets is more readily determined or fixed by appraisal than is the value of partnership interest; and (d) assets are financed more readily than partnership interests, thus broadening the market for assets.

Also, upon the sale of an asset, depreciable basis can be reestablished and if the asset was originally purchased after December 31, 1980, or if the owner and the user change at the time of sale, the new owner can use the ACRS method of depreciation (usually over a five-year life) and may claim investment tax credit on up to $125,000 of the purchase price. Because of the difficulties involved in the sale of a partnership interest, partnerships have, with few exceptions, refused to adjust the depreciable basis allocable to the new partner even when the new partner had paid a market price in excess of the previous partner's depreciable basis. In addition, no investment tax credit is available in connection with the sale of partnership interests.

The sale of an asset free of the management agreement is not considered to be the sale of a security and is therefore exempt from the regulations of the state securities commissions and from the securities law.

In the sale of an asset, it is possible to establish, and therefore transfer, clear title to the property. Ownership of partnership interests is more difficult to verify, and while the certificate of limited partnership on file with the appropriate state authority is evidence of ownership at some point in time, it is not necessarily proof of current ownership. This inability to establish positive proof of ownership is one of the factors that has limited the liquidity of partnership interests.

A new device designed to improve liquidity by eliminating the problem of verifiable ownership is the depositary receipt. This is a receipt issued by an independent third party, such as a bank or transfer agent. A partner wishing to obtain a depositary receipt must deposit with the agent evidence of his or her ownership of an interest in the partnership (which can be in the form of a certificate issued by the general partner), and upon such deposit and, in some cases, verification by the partnership of the depositing partner's interest in the partnership, the agent will issue a depositary receipt to the partner. The underlying evidences of ownership of a partnership interest cannot be traded or sold. Upon any sale of the depositary receipt, the agent will reissue the receipt in the new owner's name, just as would be done in the sale of common stock. Therefore, possession of the depositary receipt is proof of ownership, and new owners can be assured that they are purchasing from the true owner.[9]

Other than for frequently traded assets, the problem of valuing an asset, a partnership interest, or a depositary receipt will continue to limit the liquidity of these types of investments. There is no established secondary market for these investments, and even with the added benefits of the depositary receipt, it is unlikely that such a market will have the volume associated with short term trading.

Fundamentals

There are many factors that an individual must weigh when making this type of investment. The most fundamental consideration is the asset and the industry in which it is used. Normal lines of inquiry include whether the asset is a single-purpose asset or has alternative uses or users; whether the asset is subject to rapid physical deterioration or technological obsolesence; what point the asset has reached in its life cycle; the extent of cyclicality in the industry in which the asset is to be used; whether the market is regional or national; the identity and nature of the asset's users; the pricing for the asset; the nature of competition in the market; and the ease of entry into the market. A less than favorable response to any of these inquiries should not

---

[9] The depositary receipt for a partnership interest is analogous to the better-known American Depositary Receipt (ADR), under which securities (generally common stock) of non-U.S. companies, whose securities are not readily negotiable in the United States (because of foreign currency denomination, size and number of security holdings, restrictions of transferability, or other reasons), are deposited with a depositary agent against the issuance of ADRs, which are readily transferable in the United States.

automatically rule out an investment in the asset or the industry if the potential negatives or risks are compensated for by an anticipated favorable return from the investment.

In a partnership, management program, or similar form of investment, the capability of the manager or general partner is of primary importance. Clearly, a crucial factor in any investment where leasing or re-leasing is a continuing risk is the marketing effectiveness of the general partner or manager. Does the manager have sufficient marketing capability to access users? Is the manager resourceful and flexible? What has the manager's track record been? While it may be desirable to have a substantial general partner, the apparent safety derived from size may be counterbalanced by the aggressiveness of a small entrepreneurial company.

Many companies that have the market penetration and capability desired also have substantial investments in their own like assets, which would compete with investor assets for opportunities in the market. Efforts to contract away this conflict through first-in, first-out provisions, geographic priorities, and customer preference provisions may prove adequate. Another method that has developed is the joint venture of partnership assets with like type and aged properties of the general partner or manager. The results of owned and managed assets are pooled, and each group pays its proportionate share of expenses and earns its share of revenues based on some predetermined method, such as percentage of original cost or relative number of units.

Notwithstanding the selection of a quality manager or general partner, it is of the utmost importance to ensure incentive in the transaction for these parties. It is unlikely that a manager that is paid a fixed fee will be as motivated as a manager with an incentive fee. Another form of motivation is the possibility of removal. For instance, if utilization or revenue fall below a certain level or if a stipulated percentage of the assets is not leased for a period of time, the partnership or management agreement could permit the investors to remove or replace the general partner or manager.

There are an endless number of provisions in partnership agreements or management contracts where the interests of the general partner or manager diverge from those of the investors. Often, these provisions deal with the level and purpose of fees and the allocation of benefits. In this regard, the investment banking firm or other selling agent offering the investment has a duty to the investing public to negotiate the provisions of such contracts so that there is a fair and reasonable fee structure and benefit allocation, having due regard for the creativity, efforts, and costs of the sponsor, on the one hand, and the risks and rewards to the investors, on the other.

It should be noted that state securities laws provide for a review process prior to the sale of a security within a state. Certain states require compliance with the securities laws with respect to full and fair disclosure. In other states, commissions actively review the terms of the transactions, giving special attention to the payment of fees and the allocation of benefits based on the subjective standard of what is fair, just, and equitable. Commissions have, at times, required that the terms of transactions be restructured prior to granting permission to sell within a state. The likely requirements of these state commissions should be kept in mind by the sponsoring corporation as well as the investment bank or other selling agent.

THE CORPORATE SPONSOR

A company may seek an opportunity to expand its market share through the addition of assets. However, because the company may be unable to generate sufficient funds internally or unwilling or unable to assume additional debt, it may be unable to purchase the assets. Also, because the company may be unable to effectively utilize the tax benefits associated with owning the assets, it may be unwilling to purchase the assets (even if it could). For such a company, the methods of left hand financing described in this chapter can be an attractive alternative. They provide the company with 100 percent financing while allowing it to control the use of the assets for marketing purposes.

Since the company, as manager or general partner, will be deciding how an asset should be used and how to market and price the asset's use, the company can become a more significant factor in the market without committing an increment of capital and without incurring additional financing liabilities. In addition, the company can become more economically competitive by reducing its cost per asset in service (owned or under management), through the effective utilization of the asset's tax benefits and a reduction in overall financing costs.

The company using a management program or partnership structure can significantly reduce, to the point of almost eliminating, the additional balance sheet support that is associated with owning and operating assets. There would be no accounts receivable from customers, no accounts payable to suppliers, and no deferred taxes associated with these assets. For the general partner or the participant in a joint venture, the extent of participation is likely to be so small that the program could be carried merely as an investment.

As a final plus, the manager, general partner, or joint venture participant would also earn a return from the asset. This could be in the form of a management fee, pro rata cash and tax benefits, or a residual incentive.

These methods of financing are not without their costs. Many management agreements contain clauses that allow the investor to remove the manager under certain circumstances, including poor performance. In addition, the management program must incorporate, as a test for true individual ownership (so that the management program is not deemed to be a partnership), a provision allowing the individual owners to decide when to sell their own assets. Management agreements generally cancel upon sale. In both instances, assets can be withdrawn from the control of the manager.

In a partnership structure, the sponsoring company is unlikely to lose control of the assets since, as general partner, it will be making the decisions regarding the timing of their sale. It is extremely unlikely that a general partner would be removed without cause, given the difficulty and expense involved in finding a new general partner. However, many state securities commissioners require that the partners be able to vote to remove the general partner (even though in many states the Uniform Limited Partnership Act appears not to grant that right to the limited partners).

The individual investors are passive investors. They do not control their investments, because the use is controlled by the manager or general partner, and the investments themselves tend to be illiquid. Therefore, communications with investors are extremely important. This means that any company contemplating the use of one of these structures must be prepared and able to institute and maintain the internal systems necessary for the sponsor not only to adequately manage the assets and maintain the appropriate books and records but also to communicate with the investors on a periodic basis.

These programs require considerable management time to structure and to operate. The programs often have significant front-end costs, such as legal bills and internal start-up costs. However, a well-structured and properly planned left hand financing can be very beneficial to the sponsoring company while providing a very attractive investment for the individual investor.

CHAPTER 9

Joint Venture Financing

JOHN M. NIEHUSS
Merrill Lynch White Weld Capital Markets Group

INTRODUCTORY

The phrase "joint venture financing" covers a broad range of potential financial structures. In the most general terms, it is any financing in which two or more parties share costs, risks, or liabilities associated with raising funds for a project. By participating in a joint venture financing, borrowers can spread risks, minimize credit exposure, and often share in asset ownership.

In the traditional form of joint venture financing, each coventurer raises its share of the funds on the basis of its own direct credit and/or its ownership interest in project assets. In a joint venture *project* financing, the financing for the venture is raised primarily on the revenue stream and/or assets of the project entity and not on the basis of the sponsors' *direct* credit.[1]

This chapter concentrates on traditional joint venture financing, in which funds are raised on each sponsor's direct credit. The next chapter contains a detailed description of project financing. Obviously, many of the points made in this chapter are also applicable to project financing, and much of the discussion in the next chapter is also relevant to traditional joint venture financing.

Because a joint venture financing can take so many different forms,

---

[1] See Chapter 10 for a more detailed discussion of the concept of project financing and how it differs from traditional joint venture financing.

162

generalization is difficult. What is important in one project may be unimportant in another. For each project, the primary factors determining financial structure will be the needs and interests of the coventurers. However, the nature of the industry and the tax and regulatory environment in which the industry operates will also influence the way the venture is structured and financed. Thus, the purpose of this chapter is to identify several of the key factors that financial officers should consider in deciding whether to participate in a joint venture financing. The chapter also briefly comments on the choice of partners and identifies several potential problem areas.

KEY CONSIDERATIONS IN ANY JOINT VENTURE FINANCING

Management needs to review a number of critical areas when considering participation in a joint venture. These areas are discussed below.

Basic Objectives

A potential venturer's basic objectives will determine, in large part, the way management approaches and evaluates a joint venture financing opportunity. Therefore, management should identify at the outset a set of priority objectives that it would like to achieve by participating in the venture. There are, of course, many reasons for participating in a joint venture, including marketing and technical factors as well as financial factors. Among the more common reasons are:

1. To share risk (e.g., financial, technical, and marketing) with others.
2. To increase the leverage associated with financing a project by increasing the amount of debt raised for the project.
3. To obtain off-balance sheet financing for the debt raised for a project.
4. To maximize the tax benefits associated with a project (e.g., ITC, depreciation, interest deductions, and write-off of losses).
5. To comply with indenture provisions or other financial covenants applicable to the company.
6. To obtain capital, know-how, or marketing and other skills from joint venture partners.
7. To protect a market position or to enter a new market as part of a diversification policy.
8. To obtain control over a portion of a particular resource.
9. To obtain control over a portion of the output from a project.

Basic Credit and Rating Agency Considerations

One of the threshold questions that needs to be addressed in any joint venture is whether the proposed participants, either individually or collectively, are creditworthy enough to provide or raise the funds needed. Even if the answer to this question is positive, the participants may not all be willing to actually commit their credit to the joint venture in question. Thus, the key question is whether the coventurers are all able *and willing* to provide enough collective credit support to make the project possible.

Even though a venture may be financeable, it may seriously prejudice the sponsors' ability to carry out other needed projects in the future, and it may have a negative effect on the sponsors' debt ratings. Rating agencies and credit analysts are not bound by the accounting or regulatory treatment of a particular transaction. Even if a transaction is off-balance sheet for accounting purposes, the rating agencies could capitalize the obligation for the purpose of their ratio and coverage analysis. For example, in the case of utilities, the rating agencies generally assume that the lease of a generating facility creates a long-term fixed obligation, and they include the interest portion of the lease obligation in their ratio analysis. Thus, every potential participant in a joint venture must consider the venture's implications on its ratings both for debt associated with the venture and for its other debt issues.

Credit Support Available from the Coventurers

For the reasons noted in the previous section, before any joint venture is undertaken, each potential participant should assess the credit support it is able and willing to provide. Such support could be provided in a number of ways including:

1. Helping to finance the feasibility and/or the licensing and permitting stage.
2. Providing equity and/or debt to the project.
3. Purchasing tax benefits under a "safe harbor lease" or becoming an equity investor under a traditional leveraged lease.[2]
4. Supporting construction period finance through a guarantee, take-out agreement, deficiency commitment, or completion agreement or by arranging for (and paying the costs of) a letter of credit associated with a construction trust financing.
5. Providing a completion guarantee.

---

[2] See Chapter 7 for an explanation of safe harbor leases and traditional leveraged leases.

6. Agreeing to help fund cost overruns.
7. Entering into a take-or-pay contract for project output.
8. Leasing the project facilities and supporting the debt through its lease payments.
9. Entering into a deficiency agreement.
10. Guaranteeing debt for the project.
11. Making advance payments for project output.

Only after the direct funding and/or credit support available from each coventurer has been assessed can a decision be made as to whether the project is financeable.

Legal Form

A joint venture may take many legal forms. For example, it can be a corporation, a partnership, a trust, an undivided-interest arrangement in which the coventurers act as tenants in common, or some combination of these. Tax and accounting considerations, management and control issues, and the need to limit liabilities are the factors which most commonly influence the legal form chosen for a joint venture.

A joint venture may involve equity participation in a project entity by some or all of the coventurers, or it may be a contractual joint venture involving the licensing of technology or a management or construction contract. In addition, the various forms of coproduction and compensation trade arrangements common in East-West and China trade are also types of joint ventures.

Management and Control

Each coventurer will have specific management and control objectives with respect to a project. These objectives range from the complete control of management and operation to merely passive participation and a share in the project's output. However, the desire for control may not always coincide with the ability to make financial contributions, and this may require some adjustment in the specific legal form chosen for the project.

Taxation

Tax considerations are frequently the key to deciding whether to participate in a joint venture and are almost always a critical factor in determining the precise legal form of the venture. A detailed tax analysis of joint venture financing is beyond the scope of this book. However, a number of basic areas are generally reviewed in connection with the structuring of a joint venture financing. These include: (1) ability to utilize losses; (2) ability to use the investment tax credit, depreciation, and interest deductions; and (3) effect on the foreign tax credit in the case of international ventures.

Accounting Considerations

Accounting considerations, like tax issues, have a major influence on the decision to proceed with a joint venture and, in particular, on the form of the venture. Joint ventures are often used by the participants to keep project assets and the related debt off their balance sheets or to minimize the disclosure of contractual obligations under credit-support arrangements, such as take-or-pay contracts and deficiency agreements.

Among the key accounting considerations are the following:

1. When should an interest in a joint venture be consolidated?
2. What method of accounting may be used to reflect the coventurers' interest in the venture?
3. Will the assets and liabilities associated with the project be reflected on the balance sheet?
4. How should contractual obligations under take-or-pay contracts, deficiency agreements, and other credit-support arrangements be disclosed?
5. What sort of accounting treatment is possible for specialized financing arrangements, such as leasing and construction trusts?[3]

Regulatory Factors

For regulated companies, the regulatory and rate-making treatment afforded a joint venture can have a major impact on its structure. For example, in the case of a utility, the financial structure chosen may affect the rate-making process by influencing (1) the size of the rate base, (2) the allowable rate of return, and (3) the allowable operating expenses. These factors, in turn, influence the amount of "required revenue" and "actual revenue," which determines the amount of funds that need to be obtained through rate increases. Specialized joint venture financing (e.g., a joint venture involving leasing) may create special

---

[3] For a further discussion, see Chapter 4.

problems for regulatory agencies. For example, these agencies must decide whether the leased facilities may be included in the rate base or whether the lease costs should be recovered as operating expenses.

Dispute Settlement

No participant enters into a joint venture believing that it will fail or that there will be major disputes among the coventurers. Unfortunately, projects do fail, and differences of opinion do arise among the participants. Thus, any management considering participation in a joint venture must be comfortable with the mechanism that is established for winding up the project and settling disputes. A number of methods are commonly used, ranging from reliance on the normal judicial process to commercial arbitration. More complicated questions regarding choice of forum, applicable law, and enforcement of judgment and arbitral awards arise in the case of cross-border joint ventures involving parties with different legal systems. Before undertaking a joint venture, management should make sure that its lawyers have reviewed the dispute settlement procedures and have found them acceptable.

Conclusion

Any properly structured joint venture must balance the coventurers' interests in some or all of the above areas. In many cases, these interests may be in conflict. Furthermore, the treatment permitted or required for the venture in one area (e.g., accounting) may conflict with the way in which the venture is treated in another area (e.g., taxation or rate making). As a result, considerable negotiation and legal ingenuity are required to structure a venture in a way that meets every participant's needs. Thus, before any joint venture is undertaken, a potential participant must determine its basic objectives and its minimum needs and must meet with its tax, legal, accounting, and financial experts to determine whether these objectives and needs can be satisfied by the venture.

CHOICE OF JOINT VENTURE PARTNERS

General Approach

Any firm considering a joint venture must take the time to ensure that it chooses the right partner (or partners). Obviously, there should be mutuality of interest, and in most cases, the relationship should be complementary rather than supplementary. In short, the partner should add something of value to the venture. An effort should be made at an early stage to identify possible areas of conflict and to reach an understanding with the prospective partner on how these conflicts should be dealt with if they arise. One way to recognize possible areas of conflict is to review the activities of the potential partner *outside the immediate project*. This will help in determining the potential partner's broader goals and objectives, in assessing how the immediate project fits into the potential partner's overall plan, and thus in identifying possible areas of conflict as well as possible additional areas of future cooperation.

In addition, any constraints that may influence the potential partner's attitude toward the structure and operations of the venture should be identified. Four such constraints are given below.

1. Tax and/or accounting considerations may affect the form of the legal entity that the potential partner uses to participate in the venture, the nature of the potential partner's capital contribution, and the form in which the potential partner receives its return on invested resources.
2. Antitrust laws may restrict the potential partner's ability to enter into the venture and may affect the terms and conditions of any licensing arrangements that are entered into with it.
3. Loan agreement and indentures relating to previous borrowings may place restrictions on the potential partner.
4. The potential partner's lawyers may insist on certain choice of law, arbitration, and dispute settlement clauses.

Specific Factors to Consider

The specific factors that are most important in choosing a partner will vary from project to project. Some of the more important factors are set forth below.

1. *Finance.* Does the potential partner have the financial capacity and creditworthiness to provide or attract funds for the joint venture? What is the potential partner's credit rating, and will the presence of that credit rating strengthen or weaken the overall credit of the venture?
2. *Technology and know-how.* Does the potential partner have a patent, know-how, or a process that is essential to the venture?
3. *Skills.* Does the potential partner bring special skills and technical expertise to the project which are essential for its construction or operation?
4. *Marketing.* Does the potential partner have a marketing organization that will facilitate sales from the joint venture?
5. *Management.* What kind of management philosophy does the

potential partner have? Does the potential partner have a centralized decision-making system (which could lead to problems), or does it delegate substantial decision making to the local levels?

6. *General quality and reputation.* Does the potential partner have a high-quality reputation? (The potential partner does not have to be a large, well-known company, as there are many high-quality medium- and small-sized firms.)

7. *Experience in joint ventures.* Is the potential partner experienced in joint ventures, or is this the first one that it has attempted?

POTENTIAL PROBLEM AREAS IN ANY JOINT VENTURE

Given the diversity of interests among participants, which is a common feature of joint ventures, it is not surprising that problems frequently arise in joint venture financings. As noted earlier, an effort should be made to identify potential problem areas and to deal with them before a joint venture gets under way. Some of the more common problem areas are summarized in this section.

Relative Contribution of the Partners

One of the most frequently encountered trouble spots concerns the partners' relative contributions to the joint venture. The partners must agree on:

1. The absolute ratios of contribution.
2. The form of the contributions (i.e., will the contributions be in cash or in kind via equipment, technology, know-how, licenses, lease rights, etc.?).
3. The relative supply of raw materials and other inputs to the venture.
4. The supply of personnel.
5. The sequence of each participant's contribution (the first partner to make a contribution has somewhat more risk than the other partners if the project aborts).

Valuation of the Contributions

There are a number of potential problems relating to the valuation of the partners' contributions. For example, in joint ventures with participants from different countries, what currency is used to value each partner's contribution? Also, how are in-kind contributions, such as licenses and permits, patents, and know-how, to be valued?

Division of Responsibility for Financing the Project

A critical area concerns the extent to which each partner's credit is used for the project. For example, will participants with strong credit be willing to finance a greater proportion of the project? Will they be willing to enter into joint obligations or guarantees requiring them to make up shortfalls left by participants with weaker credit? Will the relative financial support from the participants be in the same proportion as the shares of output from the project?

Control over the Venture

In international joint ventures, legislation in the host country often determines who controls the venture. In other cases, this determination is left to negotiation among the respective parties. The precise mechanism for reflecting decisions on control may vary from project to project. For example, control may be based solely on equity participation, or legislation (e.g., host country legislation concerning foreign investment or host country corporation or partnership law) may specify the control mechanisms. Basic organic documents (e.g., the articles of incorporation, bylaws, or partnership agreement) of the joint venture may grant special rights to certain parties. In addition, special voting mechanisms (e.g., different classes of stock) are sometimes established for decision making in specific situations of special importance to one or more of the partners. Finally, management or licensing contracts may affect control (e.g., a management contract that may be withdrawn at will).

Accounting Problems

Differences in accounting systems often create difficult problems—especially in international projects, whose participants may have very different accounting standards. Differences in accounting systems can create problems in such basic areas as the following:

1. How assets (e.g., land, building, technology, and know-how) are valued.
2. What items are included in calculating cost of production, return on capital, and reporting of profits for tax purposes.
3. How assets are revalued in inflationary periods.
4. What depreciation policies are permitted.

5. What items are included in determining the profits of the venture.

Calculating and Dividing Profits

Problems often arise in this critical area because of differences in accounting systems in international projects and because of the participants' failure to focus in advance on precisely how profits should be calculated. In advance of signing a joint venture agreement, the parties should focus on several key issues:

1. What items are included in determining profits?
2. What is the basis for dividing profits? In other words, will profits be divided in proportion to equity contributions or invested resources, or will they be divided on some other basis?
3. How are various special items treated for the purpose of dividing profits? For example, how are sales by one of the partners to the venture treated? How are sales and purchase commissions treated if one of the partners does all of the marketing or purchasing for the venture? Finally, how are construction contract fees and licensing and management fees paid to coventures treated for profit allocation purposes?

Payout and Reinvestment Policies

Partners often have differing views on how much should be left in the venture for working capital, reserves, or expansion and how much should be paid out to the participants. Such differences may arise because of tax considerations, variations in need for output from the project, and divergent levels of commitment to the venture (i.e., whether the particular participant has an active or passive role in the operation of the project).

Expansion of the Venture

Coventurers frequently have trouble agreeing on when and under what circumstances a joint venture should be expanded. Furthermore, even if they agree on these matters, they often have differing views on how expansion should be financed. Should funds generated by the venture be ploughed back, or should new financing be sought from outside sources? In international projects, what mix of local and foreign funding should be used to finance the expansion?

Other Common Problems

Problems often occur in a number of other areas in joint venture financing. These areas include:

1. Allocation of regional or global production in international projects. A foreign joint venture partner may decide to reallocate production and supply some markets from a plant in another location.
2. Pricing policy for sales to, and purchases from, the venture by the partners.
3. Transfer of the interest of the partners to third persons (e.g., the terms of "first refusal" and "buy-out" clauses).
4. Differences in basic management and business practices (e.g., accounting procedures, labor relations, choice of suppliers, and attitude toward payoffs and political contributions).
5. Approach to marketing (e.g., does the partner concentrate on one product rather than several, thus creating a tendency toward more centralized marketing, production, and decision making?).
6. Dispute settlement (e.g., the applicable law and forum) and buy-out provisions if a dispute cannot be settled.

CONCLUDING COMMENTS

This chapter has summarized various factors that management should consider in determining whether to participate in a joint venture financing. The chapter has concentrated on traditional joint venture financing, in which each participant provides its portion of the financing on the basis of its own direct credit. Most of the factors discussed are equally applicable to project financing, a more specialized form of financing treated in the next chapter. Similarly, much of the discussion in the project financing chapter relates to joint venture financing (e.g., the sections on project planning and sources of finance). Thus, the two chapters should be read together, as each contains information relevant to the financing of any major project.

APPENDIX

Checklist of Items in Joint Venture Agreements

The following checklist of items frequently included in joint venture agreements is included to illustrate the complexity and diversity of the issues that may arise in a joint venture financing.

1. Preamble identifying parties and setting forth the purpose of the venture.
2. Legal nature of the venture.
3. Provisions on amount and type of each party's investment.
4. Design, construction, and commissioning of the plant.
5. Licensing of technology and know-how.
6. Plant site, infrastructure, and utilities.
7. Training of local personnel.
8. Supply and purchase of raw materials.
9. Technical assistance.
10. Marketing arrangements.
11. Pricing of inputs supplied by the partners.
12. Pricing of the project's output.
13. Planning and decision making for expansion or alteration of the project.
14. Control of the venture.
15. Management of the venture.
16. Currency clauses dealing with changes in exchange rates and exchange controls.
17. Accounting procedures to mesh differing systems for purposes of the venture (especially in international projects).
18. Choice of law and effects of subsequent changes in law.
19. Arbitration and dispute settlement.
20. Force majeure clause.
21. Transfer or assignment of interest.
22. Termination.
23. Financing package arrangements.

CHAPTER 10

Project Financing*

JOHN M. NIEHUSS
Merrill Lynch White Weld Capital Markets Group

INTRODUCTION

It is becoming increasingly difficult for corporations and governments to arrange financing for major new projects. Inflation has escalated estimated costs; construction risks have increased; new technology has increased the capital intensity of projects; the need to secure sources of supply (including energy) has made backward integration advisable; exchange-rate movements have become more volatile; regulatory and environmental uncertainties have made planning more difficult; and unpredictable capital markets have reduced access to traditional sources of funding on reasonable terms.

Potential project sponsors are, therefore, increasing their reliance on *left hand financing* techniques to fund needed projects. They use joint ventures to spread risks, share in asset ownership, and reduce financing costs. In addition, they often adopt innovative capital-raising techniques, generally known as "project financing." As noted below, project financing avoids the need to expand the capitalization of the company undertaking a major project and uses the project's assets as security and/or to generate a revenue stream which serves as the primary basis for raising funds.

*Contributions to this chapter were made by W. Joseph Wilson, Malcolm Binks, and Bruce Matlock, all members of Merrill Lynch White Weld Capital Markets Group.

THE CONCEPT OF PROJECT FINANCING
AND ITS ADVANTAGES

The Concept

In its pure form, project financing is a method of borrowing funds for a project in which the lender's security for the loan is based on (1) the expectation that revenues generated by the project will be sufficient to service debt incurred for the project; and/or (2) a mortgage on the assets of the project entity. Project financing differs from the traditional method of raising funds for projects where the borrower raises money on the basis of its own direct credit and not on the basis of project revenues. In the traditional method, lenders look to the overall creditworthiness of the borrower and all of the borrower's assets as security for their loan and not the assets or revenue from a single project. In the case of a traditional financing for a project, the lender's security would be provided by the basic assets and financial strength of the project's sponsors. In a project financing, lenders would not have direct recourse to the sponsor's assets or revenue but would rely on the economics of the project, project assets, and the revenue stream generated by the project for their security. This is the basic difference between traditional financing and project financing.

In the highly simplified example shown in Exhibit 1, it can be seen that, under the traditional financing method, funds for the project facilities are provided by loans made directly to the project sponsors. Under this method, repayment of the loans would be a direct liability of each of the project sponsors, which would then have to rely for payment on the joint venture that owns the project or on revenues from their other business operations. In this case, the sponsors have at risk not only their equity investment but also the amount of project debt for which they are liable. Under the project financing shown in the exhibit, funds are provided through loans made directly to the joint venture owning the project, and direct liability for this debt would remain with the joint venture, which would rely for its payment on the cash flow or revenue stream generated by the project. In this case, the sponsors are risking only their investment in the joint venture.

In essence, Exhibit 1 illustrates the prime difference between project financing and the traditional financing of major projects. There can, of course, be many qualifications to this simple illustration. However, the basic principle underlying project financing is clear—it is used to shift the burden of direct debt liabilities from the sponsors of a project to the project itself.

It should, however, be noted that pure project financings based solely on a project's assets or revenue stream are extremely rare. Lenders are reluctant to rely solely on revenues generated by the project to

EXHIBIT 1
Comparison of the Traditional Method of Financing a Project with Project Financing

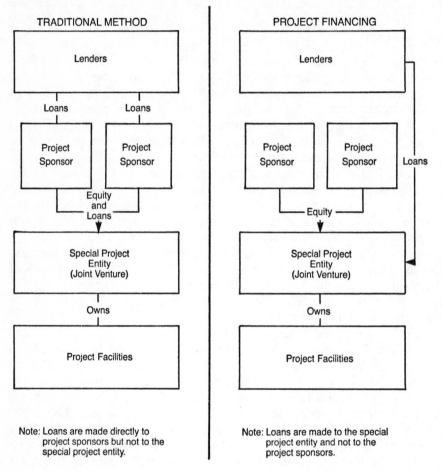

service their debt. Therefore, they generally insist on backup credit support from a project's sponsors, other project participants, or third parties interested in the success of the project. This support is commonly provided through guarantees, contractual obligations, deficiency agreements, or other similar arrangements that are designed to ensure that debt will be serviced by some creditworthy party if the cash flow from project revenues is inadequate or interrupted. Thus, finance plans for most major projects combine elements of "pure" project financing with elements of traditional financing. Commonly, finance plans for a project financing rely *primarily* on project revenues for credit support but also incorporate backup or *secondary* means of support based on the credit of the sponsors, other project participants, or third parties that share some of the project's risks.

The Advantages

A properly structured project financing enables sponsors to shift the burden of direct debt liabilities and to share the risks inherent in large, costly projects with other project participants or interested third parties. By spreading the risk, expenses, and managerial responsibilities among several parties, sponsors are often able to undertake projects that would be too complex, costly, or risky if all the risks were borne by the sponsors themselves.

In addition to enabling the sponsors to proceed with major projects that might not otherwise be undertaken, a properly structured project financing may provide several other benefits. These include:

Preservation of borrowing capacity and creditworthiness

The fact that debt raised for the project is not a direct obligation of the sponsors will help preserve the borrowing capacity and creditworthiness of government sponsors and will keep the debt off the balance sheet of corporate sponsors. The fact that project borrowings are not a direct liability on the sponsor's balance sheet may enable the sponsor to (1) avoid indenture restrictions on issuing additional debt, (2) minimize any dilution of interest coverage ratios, and (3) otherwise avoid impairment of its balance sheet.

Improved debt ratings

In rating project entity debt, the rating agencies look at project economics and/or the credit of those entities that provide the basic credit support for the project (e.g., purchasers under minimum payment contracts, guarantors, obligors under deficiency agreements, and parties to a throughput agreement). In the case of joint and several guarantees or joint and several throughput obligations, the project debt rating is generally equal to that of the highest credit rating of the obligors. Thus, one advantage of project financing for sponsors with lower ratings is the opportunity to bring in stronger credits to improve the rating on project debt.

It should, however, be noted that a project financing may have an impact on the quality of a sponsor's own debt and that the rating agencies generally run supplemental ratios and interest coverage tests which take into account a sponsor's obligations under project finance arrangements. Thus, assumption of large obligations under completion guarantees or take-or-pay contracts might have an adverse impact on the rating assigned to the sponsor's direct debt. This possibility, however, is mitigated by the fact that the rating agency also considers the benefits of the project (e.g., an assured source of supply at a favorable price or increased revenues from project-related sales) on the financial condition of the sponsor.

Broaden the institutional investor market

The legal investment laws of many U.S. states prohibit investment by certain institutions in securities unless the issuer meets specified interest coverage tests or unless the debt is "adequately secured." Some sponsors, and most newly created project entities, fail to meet the interest coverage tests. However, a take-or-pay contract or other project financing technique is often considered "adequate security." This means that insurance companies and other institutional investors may invest in project entity debt even though the normal coverage tests are not met.

Ownership flexibility

Large projects, especially energy and natural resource projects, have very long lead times. During this period, a sponsor's estimate of its need for the output of the project may change. A properly constructed project financing can give a sponsor the flexibility to increase or decrease its share of a project during the planning and construction period. As their own need for the project output changes, participants can shift their ownership interests in a way that might not be possible if they financed the project directly.

BASIC PROJECT RISKS

The risks inherent in most major projects concern the providers of equity and debt funds alike. Although equity investors are theoretically rewarded for assuming risks, they are usually interested in minimizing excessive risk. Lenders to major projects tend to be reluctant to assume what they perceive to be major risks. As a result, in a traditional, on-balance sheet financing, such lenders insist on extensive covenants, debt issuance tests, and maintenance ratios to help ensure the continuing creditworthiness of the borrowing company.

In project financing, investors are especially concerned with any development that might prevent the completion of a project or reduce the revenue generated by the project. Thus, in order to attract funds to a project, special arrangements may have to be made to ensure protection against cost overruns and noncompletion during the construction phase. Further, once a project has been completed and begun operation, there must be sufficient revenues to meet debt service at all times, even when the project is producing below capacity or not at all. This section summarizes key project risks during both the construction and operational phases of a project.

___

Construction Phase

Certain risks associated with the construction phase of any project are of special concern. These are (1) cost overruns, (2) delays in completion, and (3) noncompletion. These risks are commonly dealt with in a project financing in the following manner.

Cost overruns

It is possible that actual project costs will exceed estimated costs for a variety of reasons, including construction problems, inflation, environmental or technical problems, government regulation, and currency fluctuations. To satisfy lenders, every plan for a project financing must contain some mechanism which assures the ultimate funding of cost overruns so that the project is not abandoned prior to completion because of lack of funds.

Overrun funding can be provided from a variety of sources. For example, it is often provided by (1) the project sponsors if they are financially able to enter into overrun funding commitments; (2) the lenders to the project, which agree to provide some additional funding up to a fixed amount; (3) a group of banks, which opens a standby line of credit to cover overruns; (4) the purchasers of output from the project; or (5) governments interested in having the project completed.

In a major project, it is often desirable to arrange for all of the necessary funds required for construction of the project and any interest incurred during construction to be "precommitted." This means that commitments are made with sponsors, lenders, and other third parties prior to the commencement of construction to supply equity and debt to the project on an agreed basis during the construction period. This is done to assure all the participants that funds sufficient to complete the project will be available and to reduce the risks that financial markets will be unable to supply funds on acceptable terms.

Delays in completion

Any delay in the commencement of a project tends to increase the possibility of cost overruns and to create cash flow imbalances for sponsors because of postponement of the receipt of revenues from the project. Therefore, lenders often seek assurances that a project will be completed by a specific date. Such assurance is, of course, difficult to provide. The best way to ensure completion on schedule is to devote adequate time and money to project planning and to use high-quality engineers and contractors. Good engineers and contractors may be more expensive, but the extra cost for their services generally far outweighs the costs of project delay.

Noncompletion

Even if capital is available to fund completion, there may be some technical, political, or economic development which prevents a project from being completed. In the event of noncompletion, the cash flow lenders rely on for debt service will not be forthcoming. To protect against this contingency, lenders generally require some assurance that the funds they have advanced for a project will be repaid even if the project is not completed. While noncompletion is generally a remote risk, it is often difficult to protect against because the contingent liabilities are so large. The risk of noncompletion for any individual sponsor is reduced to the extent that the group of sponsors is enlarged. Sponsors sometimes have sufficient resources to give adequate assurances of debt repayment to lenders, but in larger projects, the purchasers of project output or other clearly creditworthy parties are often asked to assume part or all of the noncompletion risk.

Until recently, it was assumed that any finance plan for a major project funded on a limited recourse basis had to provide some mechanism to protect lenders against noncompletion. However, there has been a trend toward restriction of the scope of the completion guarantees required by lenders. In some recent projects, lenders have accepted partial completion guarantees and assumed reserve risks, market risks, and even political risks during the construction period.

Operational Phase

Once a project has been completed, the interest and principal payments on loans made to construct the project are paid out of the revenues created by the project. Debt must be repaid out of the "revenue stream" from the project as lenders do not rely solely on the general creditworthiness of the project sponsors as security for repayment of their loans. The way in which the revenue stream is created will vary for different types of projects. The most common methods are through payments by the purchasers of output from the project or by the users of the project facilities.

Lenders are always concerned about the possibility of a sustained interruption in project service which will reduce the revenue stream. Such an interruption could result from a number of factors, including (1) a change in the market for the project's output; (2) overestimation of recoverable reserves in the case of a natural resource project; (3) inadequate sources of power, raw materials, or other inputs for the project; (4) change in government regulation; (5) technical failure; (6) environmental problems; and (7) political risks. Lenders' specific concerns in these key areas and some of the methods of dealing with those concerns are summarized in Exhibit 2 and discussed at greater depth later in this chapter.

EXHIBIT 2
Summary of Project Risks and Methods of Protecting against These Risks

Risk Area	Types of Project Risks	Types of Risk Protection for Lenders
Resource	Size and nature of reserves. Continued availability of the reserve or resource. Fluctuations in availability of renewable energy sources, such as water, sun, and wind.	Independent evaluation by more than one geological consulting firm. Dedication of the reserves to the project. Supply-or-pay contract. Producer agrees to make up any shortfall from another source. Careful analysis of meteorological and hydrological data.
Market	Inaccurate demand estimates. Overcapacity emerges (e.g., too many similar projects are being built worldwide). New technology lowers the price of the product from other sources. The price at which the output must be sold is not economic.	Independent market survey. Various types of contractual arrangements, such as long-term purchase contract at fixed price, minimum payments contract, or a deficiency agreement.
Political	Relationship between borrower and lender's country changes. Basic stability of borrower.	Political risk insurance. Multilateral consortia. World Bank cofinancing. Advance exchange control approval. Trust arrangements which segregate revenue stream outside borrowing country until debt service has been paid. The borrower has large stake in success of project. Joint venture with local sponsors or host government.
Government approvals	Government approval of any critical element of the project is not received in form satisfactory to lenders. Government authorities withdraw (or alter) initial approval after project is under way.	Careful advance planning. Sensitivity to concerns of government authorities.
Regulatory, tax, and legislative	Changes in regulatory or tax treatment. Legislature repeals or alters law on which project based.	Monitoring of prospective changes affecting the project. Availability of alternative financial structures.

EXHIBIT 2 *(continued)*

Risk Area	Types of Project Risks	Types of Risk Protection for Lenders
Environmental	Environmental opposition to the project delays construction or forces shutdown or alteration in project. Environmental or safety conditions attached to project approval cause large cost increases.	Careful advance planning. Sensitivity to environmental concerns. Use competent, qualified experts.
Technical	Unexpected difficult production problems. New technology is used and has start-up problems. Technology becomes obsolete.	Independent analysis of technology being used. Guaranty of technology by supplier or operator. Commercial insurance.
Currency	Debt service obligation is in one currency, and revenues are in other currencies which depreciate against the currency in which repayment is to be made.	Careful matching of currency of revenue with currency of debt service. Hedging in futures market. (Note: There are practical limitations due to relatively short maturity of the market.) Currency swapping and other exchange-financing techniques.
Legal	Long-term contracts are often made between parties with different legal systems, resulting in inadequate security for lenders. Sovereign immunity.	Obtain high-quality legal advice. Recognize that disputes inevitably arise, and devise workable dispute settlement mechanism (e.g., specify third-party arbitration in advance).
Transportation	Inadequate transport for the project. Transport bottlenecks develop.	Careful analysis of adequacy of transport.
Managerial	Remote location makes it difficult to attract and retain the types of technicians and managers needed to run project. Size and nature of project requires specialized management skills.	Work force from joint venture partner assigned to the job. Expatriate managers help operate the project in early stages until local work force can be trained.
Construction phase	Cost overruns due to factors such as inflation, poor cost estimates, construction delay caused by technical, environmental, or regulatory problems, or poor contractor. Overruns can create funding problems or make the project uneconomic. Insufficient funds to meet cost overruns can create problems by increasing delay and forcing noncompletion. Noncompletion and abandonment.	*Cost overruns* Fixed-price contract. Turnkey contract. Independent expert check on cost estimates and technology. Financing plan "overfinance" (e.g., plan covers 20 percent over cost estimate). Forward currency contracts (limited use). Overrun funding agreement or other form of standby financial arrangement.

EXHIBIT 2 *(concluded)*

Risk Area	Types of Project Risks	Types of Risk Protection for Lenders
		Completion of project Draw down equity first. Performance bonds from contractor. Tough "completion test." Completion and guaranty agreement (i.e., fund completion or repay outstanding debt).
Operational phase	Interruption or diminution of supply from the project due to the various risks noted above and plant failure, malfunction, extended maintenance and repair, and natural disaster.	*Interruption of the revenue stream* Minimum payments contracts with supplier, user, or purchaser. Deficiency agreement. Alternative source arrangements for key inputs. Insurance. *Abandonment* Contractual relationship where debt service is assumed by supplier, user, or purchaser. Debt guarantee. Insurance.

TECHNIQUES OF PROVIDING BACKUP CREDIT SUPPORT

Many project risks can be covered by insurance, bonding, and contractor or supplier warranties. However, because of the lender's concerns about construction period risks and the possibility of a sustained interruption in service once a project is operational, special techniques have been developed to provide backup credit support and to ensure that the lender's debt will be repaid even if the project is never completed or if it is not producing at the anticipated levels. Project financing techniques can also be used to allocate project risks to those who can bear them, to provide access to different sources of financing, and, in some cases, to reduce the cost of financing. The most common techniques are (1) minimum payment contracts and (2) deficiency payments agreements.

Minimum Payment Contracts (see Exhibit 3)

In a contract-based project financing, lenders advance funds to the project on the basis of a contractual commitment by creditworthy parties

184

EXHIBIT 3
Minimum Payment Contracts

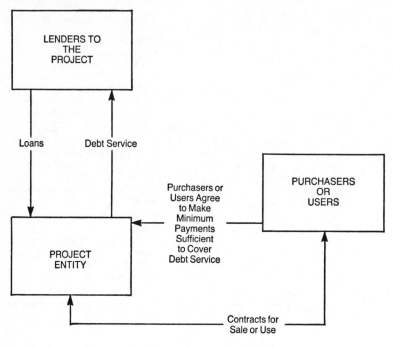

for use of the project facilities or purchase of the project output. The major advantage of this type of financing is that it enables the credit and financial strength of the purchasers or users to be utilized to provide assured debt service for the project.

A minimum payment contract is created when the purchaser of output from a project (or the user of a project facility) agrees to make a minimum payment sufficient to service debt even when the purchaser is not using, or receiving, output from the project. The purchaser or user, in effect, becomes a guarantor of debt service on the loans made to construct the project. Purchasers or users would be willing to enter into such obligations when they have a great need to use the project facilities or to purchase output from the project.

Minimum payment contracts may take a number of different forms. For example, they may involve agreement (1) to supply oil or gas to a project in the case of a pipeline or a refinery and to make a minimum payment for the use of the facilities or (2) to purchase output from a mine or a power station and to make an agreed minimum payment even if the facilities are not operating. Such contracts are sometimes called "hell-or-high-water contracts" because the purchaser must pay under the most extreme circumstances (e.g., a breakdown of the project facility). To mitigate the burdens on purchasers when such a contract is involved, the payments may, in some cases, be treated as partial advances against future output from the project.

Deficiency Agreements (see Exhibit 4)

Under a deficiency payment agreement, a creditworthy party (a government, a central bank, or a corporation) agrees to make up any deficiency between the revenues generated by the project and the debt service. The government or corporation agreeing to make the deficiency payment is, in effect, a guarantor of debt service and provides the security for loans to the project.

There are a number of variations of deficiency payments. One common type involves a pipeline project where the potential users of the

EXHIBIT 4
Deficiency Payment Agreement

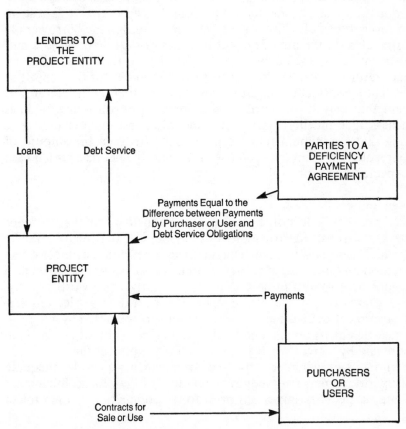

pipeline agree to put a sufficient volume through the pipeline to generate revenues adequate to cover debt service or to make up any deficiency in such revenues through direct cash payment to the lenders.

Other Methods of Credit Support

In some projects, it may be impossible to obtain adequate minimum payment contracts or deficiency payment agreements from creditworthy participants in the projects or purchasers of product output. Furthermore, contractual credit support and deficiency arrangements generally do not cover construction period risks. Thus, in most project financings, additional methods must be used to provide assurance to lenders that debt will be repaid in the event of noncompletion or in cases where the project operates below capacity or not al all for extended periods.

Financial covenants

A common method of providing added credit support is through covenants which impose contractual obligations on the borrower. These include various types of affirmative covenants requiring the borrower (1) to charge rates for the use of project facilities or the sale of project output sufficient to service debt, provide for depreciation, and yield an adequate return on capital; or (2) to pledge revenues for the benefit of lenders. They also include negative covenants restricting the amount of new debt that may be incurred by the borrower or restricting the lines of business that the borrower may undertake; and maintenance tests requiring that a minimum ratio be maintained between the amount of the nonrecourse (or limited recourse) loan and the net discounted cash flow expected from the project.

Direct guarantee

Financial covenants do not, however, cover construction phase risks or provide a real substitute for minimum payment or deficiency arrangements which help ensure debt repayment in all events. The most effective method of providing stronger assurances to lenders is through a direct guarantee of the project debt by a clearly creditworthy party. Under a guarantee, the guarantor agrees to meet debt service requirements on project debt when the revenue stream generated by the project is insufficient to do so. The lender, therefore, knows that the loan will be repaid by a creditworthy party even if the project fails.

Even in cases where contractual arrangements provide adequate credit support, lenders may require guarantees of their loans. Such guarantees are particularly important prior to the completion of the project and the commencement of its commercial operation, because contractual credit support is generally not effective until the project begins operating. In a growing number of projects, lenders are accepting completion risks. However, where they do not accept such risks, sponsors, interested governments, or other project participants often provide guarantees that sufficient funds will be available to complete the project or that debt will be repaid if the project is abandoned prior to completion.

OTHER PROJECT FINANCING TECHNIQUES

In addition to minimum payment contracts, deficiency arrangements, and direct guarantees, a number of other techniques are frequently used in project financings. Some of these techniques are designed to provide protection for the lenders that advance funds to the project (e.g., production payments and trust financing), while others are designed primarily for the benefit of project sponsors (e.g., leasing, construction trust financing, and the project financing partnership facility).

Production Payments (see Exhibit 5)

Production payment financing is a specialized financing technique which is commonly used in mineral- and petroleum-related financing. There are a number of different types of production payment financing, but all involve the same basic concept. Funds are advanced to construct a project against the security of an oil, gas, or mineral reserve. A portion of this reserve is assigned by the project sponsors to the lender. The lender has no recourse to the sponsor, and debt service is then recovered out of the proceeds of the sale of that portion of the reserve. In short, the lender obtains a security interest in the reserve in the ground (or in the output from the project) and uses this interest to help ensure repayment of the loan.

However, the lender does not obtain as complete protection as it would with a guarantee, minimum payment, or deficiency contract from a clearly creditworthy party. If the reserve is underestimated or if there are production or marketing problems, the lender would be at risk and would not have recourse to the credit of the project sponsors or participants.

Production payments are most commonly used to finance production in fields with proven reserves. However, they may also be used to finance exploration. For example, if actual production begins in one field, the reserves in this producing field can be used to raise funds to finance exploration in a different area.

EXHIBIT 5
Production Payments

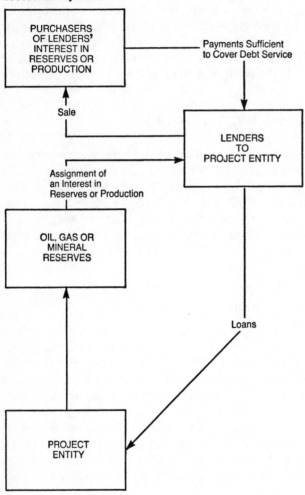

Payment Trust (see Exhibit 6)

In complicated project financings, especially those based on contractual credit support, lenders may insist on trust arrangements designed to isolate the cash flow of the project in such a way that it is available for debt repayment on a priority basis. For example, in a mining project whose output is sold to purchasers in Western Europe, the lenders might require the creation of a trust based in London and might require the purchasers to make payment to the trustee rather than the owners of the project in the host country. The trustee would then segregate in a

EXHIBIT 6
Payment Trust

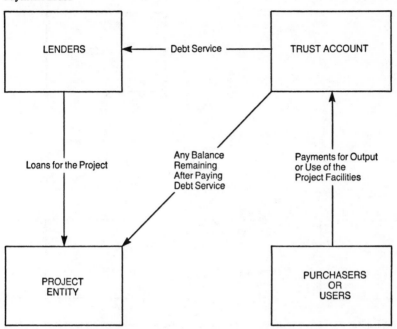

trust account amounts sufficient to service debt and meet other essential obligations of the project. Only if such obligations were satisfied would funds be released to the owners of the project. The trust arrangement does not provide any additional credit support or financial backing for the project, but it does give the lenders additional assurance that they will have a priority claim on project resources.

Occasionally, a payment trust is combined with the deficiency payment concept to create added security for lenders. Under such a combination, if there is a deficit in the trust account created to service debt, a clearly creditworthy party (e.g., a project sponsor or participant) is required to "top up" the trust account by depositing with the trustee an amount equal to the debt service deficiency.

Advance Payment Financing (see Exhibit 7)

This type of financing occurs when a creditworthy project sponsor or other interested party makes an advance payment for output from a yet-to-be-constructed project. The funds are advanced to a separate project entity (usually newly created) which uses them to construct the project. An advance payment account is established, and the funds

EXHIBIT 7
Advance Payment Financing

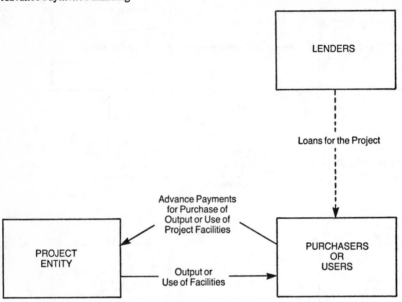

Note: The purchasers of project output or the users of project facilities make payments prior to construction of the project. The project entity uses the funds to construct the project. The purchasers or users then receive output from the project (or use the project facilities) without making payments until their advance payments have been recovered. Lenders make loans to purchasers and users on the basis of their credit and not on the credit of the project entity.

advanced are "repaid" by reducing the account through supplying output from the project.

A common use of advance payment financing involves exploration for new energy sources. For example, a natural gas company may make advance payments for gas that are used to pay the costs of exploration and development. The advance is repaid out of production if the venture is successful. However, if it is unsuccessful, the party making the advance payments would assume the risk of nonpayment by the exploration company.

Construction Trust Financing (see Exhibit 8)

In a construction trust financing, an entity other than the sponsor or ultimate user of a facility arranges for financing and has title to project assets during the construction period. At the end of the construction period, the facilities are sold to the ultimate user. The entity that owns the project assets during construction is generally a newly created cor-

EXHIBIT 8
Construction Trust Financing

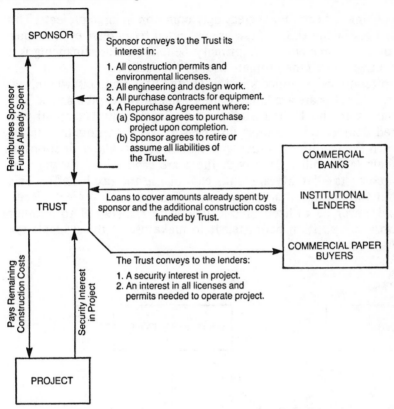

poration or trust. Although it has no operating history, it is able to raise funds because its creditworthiness is established by a purchase agreement with the ultimate user of the facility. The sponsor or ultimate user agrees to purchase (or repurchase) the project facilities at the completion of construction or to assume all financial obligations of the construction entity. The creditworthiness created by this agreement enables the construction entity to obtain capital from a variety of sources, including revolving credit facilities from commercial banks, fixed-rate intermediate-term loans, and commercial paper.

This method of financing does not provide any added security to lenders, which, in the final analysis, must rely on the creditworthiness of the parties assuming the construction entity's debt. It may, however, benefit project sponsors by providing them with increased financing flexibility, potentially lower financing costs during the construction period, and the ability to keep the debt of the project off their balance sheets during construction.

Lease Financing (see Exhibit 9)

Lease financing is becoming increasingly common in large projects. The recent changes in the U.S. tax law are expected to increase even further the use of lease financing. The primary benefit of lease financing is a lower effective cost to the ultimate user of the facility.

In capital-intensive projects in the United States and elsewhere, significant tax benefits are available to the owner of the capital assets. The main benefits in the United States are an investment tax credit and accelerated depreciation. In most instances, project sponsors themselves wish to own the facilities in order to use these credits and deductions to reduce their tax liability. However, there are cases where the sponsor has no income tax liability and thus cannot use the tax benefits. This means that the tax advantages associated with owning a project's facilities would never be utilized unless they were transferred to another party whose tax position permitted it to make use of the available tax credits or deductions.

EXHIBIT 9
Leveraged Lease

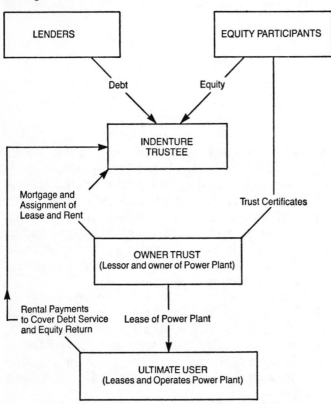

The most common method of doing this is through a lease arrangement in which ownership of the facility to be financed is transferred to unrelated investors that can utilize the tax deductions and credits and are willing to pass some of the benefits back to the sponsor-lessee. The lessee benefits in that the lease rates are lower than the interest rates on debt it would otherwise incur to fund the project itself.

Whether a lease financing is possible and beneficial depends on a complex set of financial, legal, tax, and accounting factors that need to be carefully evaluated in planning any project financing.

Mixed Project Financing and Traditional Joint Venture Financing (see Exhibit 10)

Occasionally, some sponsors of a major project may wish to arrange financing in the traditional manner on their own direct credit, while other sponsors prefer to attempt a project financing. The needs of both groups of sponsors may be met through the use of a specialized financing facility that blends a project financing with a more traditional joint venture financing.

The key feature of such a project financing facility is the creation of a partnership composed of those participants that wish to fund their share of costs through off-balance sheet, limited recourse financing. The partnership would represent their individual and collective interests in the project and would raise funds on the basis of the partners' contractual commitments to purchase output from the partnership. The obligations of the partnership would be backed by a sales and deficiency agreement with each partner. The elements of this technique are shown in Exhibit 10.

Of course, the preparation of a definitive financing plan involving such a facility would require consultation with each of the project sponsors and a careful review of their legal, tax, and accounting requirements.

PROJECT PLANNING AND PREPARATION

Planning to Minimize Project Risks

A successful project financing results from careful planning and management. It is therefore essential to identify potential problem areas at an early stage and to design a comprehensive plan for the project which will ensure its successful completion. As Exhibit 2 indicates, many project risks can be dealt with through contractual undertakings or guarantees. However, a number of risks may also be handled by careful project

EXHIBIT 10
Project Financing Facility

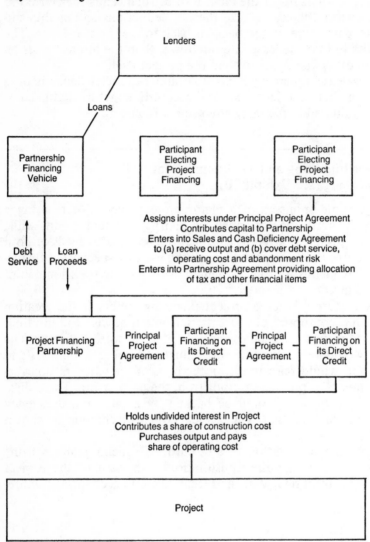

planning and analysis. Several of the key risks and the methods of minimizing them in the planning process are discussed below.

Market risks

Lenders look carefully at basic project economics when they engage in
off-balance sheet, nonrecourse financing. In particular, they need assur-

ance that demand for project output exists and will continue to exist at satisfactory price levels for the duration of their loans. In recent years, a number of major mineral projects have had to be postponed because of soft market forecasts for the project output. Although the problem may be less acute for energy projects, lenders still need assurance that adequate current and future demand at an acceptable price will exist for the output produced. In addition, they will often insist on a study of existing and planned competing sources of supply to make sure that the project in question will not, when aggregated with other projects that are under way, lead to a problem of overcapacity.

At a minimum, lenders will insist on seeing the demand projections and other market studies that have been done in connection with the project. In addition, many of the major financial institutions have their own research groups do independent market studies for a project. Finally, in cases where there may be some doubt, lenders may insist on a third-party feasibility study as a precondition to any lending.

The method of marketing the output from the project will also be of interest to lenders. If the project is dependent on sales to a limited number of buyers, preliminary sales contracts contingent on completion of the project should be arranged to give comfort to lenders and, in some cases, to provide basic security for the project debt.

Resource risks

In major energy or natural resource projects, lenders must be satisfied that the resources dedicated to the project are more than sufficient to ensure successful operation for the duration of their loans. In the most basic sense, the ultimate security for any loan to a natural resource project is the recoverable reserve in the ground. The project may not be able to produce or deliver the quantities anticipated because the recoverable reserves have been overestimated or because construction or production difficulties are encountered. In the case of renewable energy projects, there may be interruptions in the flow of sun, water, or wind to the project site. When this happens, the revenue from such a project may be insufficient to service project debt.

In order to protect against this risk, lenders expect extensive hydrological, meteorological, or geological data from the sponsors and verifications of the sponsors' estimates of the size and nature of the resource by an independent firm of experts. Lenders normally require proved recoverable reserves of at least 1½, and more often 2, times the amount actually needed to supply the planned requirements of the project until debt has been repaid. The quality of the reserves should also be tested to make sure they are of adequate grade to meet the specifications of the buyers. Other methods to minimize the reserve risk include: (1) requiring the producers to make up any shortfall in estimated production from other sources or through open-market purchases and (2) instituting arrangements in which the producer, in effect, warrants the existence of the reserve by agreeing to supply a certain minimum amount of product or to make direct cash payments to purchasers and/or lenders.

Supply and infrastructure

Arrangements for the supply of raw materials and the provision of basic infrastructure requirements, such as transportation, power, and water, are often critical to the success of the project. If the raw materials are to be provided by an unassociated party, a long-term contract for the supply of these raw materials should be sought on terms which are related to the economics of the project. This is to ensure that future prices for raw materials do not increase to the point where the project cannot market its output and the undertaking ceases to be economically viable.

In cases where supply of a key resource is essential to a project (coal for a power plant project), lenders often insist that the project sponsors make adequate provision for a substitute supply source in the event that the basic supply is interrupted or discontinued. Sometimes suppliers will agree to supply product of the same quality from alternative sources. For example, if a loan were being arranged for a coal-fired power plant, lenders would look carefully at the amount and quality of the coal sources for the project, the expected continuity of coal supply for the life of the project, the reliability of the company supplying the coal, and the basic terms and conditions of the coal supply contract.

Many projects in remote areas are dependent on new infrastructure, such as roads, railways, power, and water supply. Problems in constructing or operating a critical element of infrastructure can jeopardize the entire project. Thus, lenders will insist that the construction and financing of these infrastructure facilities be closely coordinated with plans for the project itself.

Regulatory risks

In many project financings, the level and continuity of the cash flow may depend on the existence of an incentive provided by the host government or on a particular regulatory treatment of the project. The most common illustrations are found in the areas of accounting, taxation, and public utility rates. For example, changes in accounting treatment, special incentives, or the way the host country taxes a project may determine whether or not it is profitable. In addition, project financings of energy projects may be dependent on tariff arrangements to ensure cash flow to the project. In such cases, lenders will be hesitant to advance funds if they are not convinced that regulatory approval will be given to the tariff arrangements and maintained in force for the duration of their loans.

Technology

The use of simple, time-tested technology is a major help in mitigating project risks in both the construction and operating phases of a project. Lenders will not assume the risk of providing funds to projects involving unproven technology and will generally insist that the technology used be reasonable when compared to current industry practices and costs. To the extent that high or relatively new technology is involved, lenders often insist that engineering firms with demonstrated experience participate in all phases of the project and/or that manufacturers provide warranties of the technology to be used.

Cost estimates

Since estimated costs influence the planning for the economic, financial, and marketing aspects of a project, the importance of accurate cost estimates cannot be overemphasized. A cost estimate for the project should be made by engineers with relevant experience. The estimate should be as realistic and accurate as possible, and it should be broken down by key components, such as land, construction, installed equipment, and working capital. It should also provide adequate provision for interest during construction, contingencies, and overruns. In the case of a project with a long construction period, an appropriate allowance should be made for escalation due to inflation.

It is very important to assure lenders of the quality of the cost estimate. This is often difficult, especially for large projects with an extended construction period, due to inflation and costs associated with developments in remote areas. A definitive estimate by properly qualified engineers usually entails considerable expense, and sponsors are often reluctant to incur this expense before a final decision is made to go ahead with a project. However, if a project does go forward with unreliable cost estimates, both sponsors and lenders face serious financial risks. Major overruns resulting from inadequate planning can destroy the economics of a project.

In the preparation of a cost estimate, engineers will usually make an allowance for contingencies. Depending on the nature of the project, this allowance can be 10 to 15 percent. The allowance is designed to cover unforeseen occurrences during the construction of the project. In addition to this engineering contingency, it has become customary in project financing to make a substantial financing contingency, often as much as 25 to 30 percent, for overruns. This financing contingency is designed to cover unforeseen delays in completion, higher than expected inflation and interest rates, and the impact of other external events unrelated to the project itself.

Currency considerations

Lenders also carefully analyze the currency and exchange-rate aspects of each project to make sure that undue exchange risks are not involved. Projects should attempt to avoid the problem which occurs when debt service is in a strong currency and project earnings are in a weak currency. If it is impossible to eliminate such a currency mismatch, exposure should be minimized, to the extent possible, by the use of the futures market, currency swapping, or other exchange-financing techniques.

Management risk

A frequently neglected risk which can be addressed in the planning stage is the risk of inadequate management. Many projects are of such a size or nature that experienced, specialized management is needed in both the construction and operational phases of the project. Construction phase management problems can generally be avoided if sponsors appoint experienced architects, engineers, and contractors and create a competent multidisciplinary project team to monitor them. In addition, in the operational phase, it is often necessary to recruit specialized technical, marketing, and other staff to supplement the capability of the sponsors.

Environmental

Major projects are often delayed or even abandoned for environmental reasons. Thus, environmental problems must be identified and dealt with early in the planning process for any project.

Political risk

A major concern of lenders is that a politically motivated act by the government of the territory in which the project is located will affect the project and interrupt the revenue stream. The most extreme examples are war, revolution, and nationalization, but such other factors as foreign exchange controls, denial of export or import permits, denial of work permits, and insistence on local sourcing or local participation can also have a significant effect on a project's overall viability. It is difficult to protect against these risks by contractual arrangements or guarantees by project participants. Therefore, to help lenders overcome their hesitancy to advance funds in the face of political uncertainty, governments have developed insurance schemes to protect against political risks and/ or currency inconvertibility.

Financial Planning

In addition to taking steps to avoid or minimize risks, a number of matters should be addressed in the planning stage that are critical to the financing of major projects. These include the membership of the sponsoring group, procurement sources, and financial feasibility.

Membership of sponsoring group

An early decision regarding the membership of the sponsoring group is of particular importance. As soon as possible, potential members should be identified and agreement reached on the basis of their participation. This may be a critical element in determining the basis of credit support for the project. Other matters that should also be concluded at an early stage include decision making, management, and organizational structure; the basis of apportioning costs, and contributions to cost overrun funding.

Procurement sources

Sources of equipment for major components of the project should be identified, and specific suppliers should be selected. Preliminary agreements with the selected suppliers should be concluded contingent on the final decision to proceed with the project. The availability of supplier credits and export credit financing should be explored and initial arrangements made once procurement sources have been identified.

Financial feasibility

The capability of the sponsors to finance the project at its estimated cost should be reviewed in the light of identified project risks. A capital structure for the project should be selected, appropriate sources of financing identified, and pro forma financial projections made. The objective is to determine the financial requirements and financing risks of the project and whether they are acceptable to the sponsors. If the financing burden is too great, additional sponsors should be sought or an alternative structure devised.

As the matters outlined above are being concluded, a final financing plan should be prepared for submission to, and agreement with, the sponsors of the project. This plan would deal with the following matters:

- Total financing requirements.
- Breakdown of costs into local costs and foreign exchange component.
- Phasing of the financing for both the construction and operational phases of the project.
- Proposed security arrangements to be offered to lenders, including completion guarantees (if any).
- Amount of equity and debt financing.
- Proposed sources of financing.
- General terms and conditions available from expected sources of financing.

Depending on the size and scope of the project, it may be appropriate to make an initial approach to potential lenders concerning both construction and long-term financing. The objective is to familiarize lenders with the project and to discuss the basis on which interest rates and other terms are to be determined and the amount of the funds required. In some cases, an initial commitment may be sought from selected lenders, with final terms to be negotiated during the execution of the financing plan.

SOURCES OF FINANCING FOR MAJOR PROJECTS

Complex projects are generally financed by blending different sources and types of financing to fund different stages or components of the project. A typical financing plan for a major project involves equity, commercial bank loans, export credit, some long-term fixed-rate funds, and perhaps commercial paper. For example, equity funds may be used to finance feasibility studies and preliminary design and engineering; short-term revolving bank credit and commercial paper are frequently used during the construction period; and export credit generally finances major equipment. Long-term, fixed-rate funds are used whereever possible to improve project economics, and commercial bank funding is commonly used to fill gaps in financing plans that cannot be funded from other sources.

The emerging field of left hand financing provides new approaches which will be of increasing importance in raising funds from these sources on the strength of the assets involved and the revenues they produce. The major challenge in any project financing is to combine the various different sources and types of funds into a package that provides the lowest-cost money for the project. (See Exhibit 11 for a schematic summary of relationships among potential participants.)

Three projects in different parts of the world illustrate the potential complexity and difficulty of financing major projects:

1. The Taabo Hydroelectric Project in Ivory Coast was a $302 million project financed with $78 million in equity and $224 million in debt. The debt financing involved 16 different credit agreements covering export credit from five countries; commercial bank loans in U.S. dollars, French francs, Italian lira, and Swiss francs, and an aid loan from the French Caisse Centrale de Cooperation Economique.
2. The Cuajone copper project in Peru involved loans from 10 separate lending groups, including United Kingdom and U.S. equipment suppliers, Japanese and European copper buyers, the U.S. Export-Import Bank, the International Finance Corporation, and a consortium of 29 commercial banks.

3. Fifty-four different agreements were involved in the Selebi-Pikwe copper/nickel project in Botswana. Financing was provided by eight different sources: the mining company sponsors; aid agencies in the United States, the United Kingdom, and Canada; the World Bank and IDA; a West German government agency and a consortium of West German banks; and the South African export credit agency. Insurance cover was provided by governmental agencies in the United States, West Germany, and South Africa.

As these examples suggest, two of the key problems for the sponsors of any project are to determine the available sources of financing and to blend them into the most advantageous financial package. The purpose of this section is to identify key sources of financing and to illustrate the ways in which they have been used to fund major projects.

Project Sponsors

The obvious starting point for funding any major project is the project sponsors. The sponsors normally contribute the equity or risk portion of a project's capital. However, they are frequently called upon to provide overrun funding and completion guarantees in order to make loans from other sources possible.

The providers of equity funds have no assurance that they will ever receive any return on their investment or that they will ever recoup their invested funds. Thus, they have a natural inclination to minimize their cash at risk. Corporate participants often do this by making equity contributions in the form of capitalized equipment or technology, and government sponsors often contribute feasibility studies, preliminary engineering, water rights, mineral concessions, or some other essential asset. For example, in the Selebi-Pikwe copper/nickel project in Botswana, the government received a 15 percent equity interest for contributing mining rights to the mining company.

The percentage of equity funding will vary from project to project, depending on such factors as the degree of risk, cash available from other business operations, availability of debt funds, and project structure. Historically, a very high portion (e.g., 80 to 90 percent) of the financing for natural resource projects was provided by equity or internal cash generation. In recent years, however, a variety of factors have made it impossible for sponsors to contribute such a high percentage of equity. In addition, export credit financing, development bank involvement, and the use of project financing techniques to protect lenders have made much larger amounts of debt financing possible. For example, the percentage of equity in several major mining projects was: Boke bauxite project in Guinea—7.5 percent; Bougainville copper project in Papua New Guinea—35 percent; Cuajone copper project in Peru—36 percent; Samarco iron ore project in Brazil—27 percent; Toquepala copper project in Peru—14 percent; Selabi-Pikwe project in Botswana—23 percent; Ertsberg nickel project in Indonesia—17 percent; Falconbridge nickel project in the Dominican Republic—8 percent; and Gecamines expansion project in Zaire—52 percent.

In addition to providing equity, sponsors often make advances in the form of subordinated loans and provide completion guarantees. In the Selebi-Pikwe project, the mining company sponsors provided overrun funding in the form of subordinated loans and guaranteed the debt of several lenders to the project; in the Falconbridge nickel project, the major shareholders guaranteed loans from U.S. insurance companies; the Boke project sponsors made interest-free advances in the form of subordinated loans; the Toquepala project involved $75 million in advances by equity partners; and shareholders made a $24 million loan for the Lornex copper mine in British Columbia and $10 million in working capital loans for the Nanisivik lead/zinc project on Baffin Island.

Commercial Bank Loans

In recent years, commercial banks have been the most important source of financing for major projects. Funding from commercial banks is generally medium-term (i.e., 5 to 10 years) at a floating rate of interest. The interest rate is generally based on LIBOR, the London Interbank Offered Rate, or the U.S. prime rate, plus a negotiated spread over the prime rate or LIBOR.

The principal advantages of commercial bank financing are its availability and flexibility. Such financing is available for small projects or for large projects running into the billions of dollars; fewer conditions are generally attached to its use than are attached to financing from other institutional lenders; grace periods and drawdowns can be tailored to the needs of a specific project; and its use is generally not tied to procurement from a specific source. The most important disadvantage of commercial bank financing is the fact that the interest rate is floating. This makes project planning difficult, and it may adversely affect project economics if rates increase substantially. Also, the maturities tend to be somewhat shorter than the maturities for some fixed-rate sources, and there can be substantial front-end fees.

Commercial bank funding takes many forms. A common form for major projects is the syndicated bank loan, in which the lead managers seek participation from a large group of other banks which jointly provide funds to a project. Smaller projects are often funded by a single bank or by "club loans" from a smaller group of banks.

Another common means by which commercial banks make funds available involves support from an official export credit program. In the United States, many bank loans to foreign buyers of U.S. equipment are made with the guarantee of the U.S. Export-Import Bank. Bank loans for exports from most other industrialized countries are also commonly subsidized, insured, or guaranteed by an official government agency.

In projects in developing countries, banks are making a growing number of loans in cooperation with one of the development institutions. The World Bank Co-Financing Program, the Inter-American Development Bank Complementary Finance Program, and the International Finance Corporation participation certificates were all designed to increase the flow of private bank funds to projects in the developing world.

Examples of the use of commercial bank financing are myriad, as virtually every major project involves some bank funding. Several projects selected at random from the energy, mining, and industrial sectors illustrate the diversity of use of this source of financing.

1. The British National Oil Corporation borrowed $825 million from a group of 12 U.S. and United Kingdom commercial banks to fund various North Sea oil projects. The loan was unsecured, and it had an eight-year maturity with four years' grace. Part of the loan carried a rate originally set at 113 percent over the U.S. prime rate, and the remainder was made at a rate of 1 percent above LIBOR.

2. A $1.4 billion loan from a diverse group of leading international banks to help finance the first stage of the North West Shelf Gas Project in Australia was arranged by Woodside Petroleum, Ltd., an Australian oil and gas exploration company, Shell Petroleum, Ltd., and Broken Hill Pty.

3. Marathon Petroleum Ireland, Ltd., borrowed $200 million from a group of 10 banks in a production payment financing to help fund development of the Kinsdale Head gas fields.

4. Two Canadian banks made a $150 million limited recourse project financing loan to help develop the Prinos Oil Field and the South Kavala gas field in Greece on behalf of Denison Mines, Ltd.; Wintershall A.G.; Fluor Corporation, and White Shield Greece Oil Corporation (a subsidiary of Basic Resources Corporation).

5. Boru Hatlavi Ile Petrol Tasima S.A., a subsidiary of Turkiye Petrolleri, borrowed $150 million from a group of banks to help finance the Turkish section of the Iraq-Turkey crude oil pipeline system.

6. Commercial banks have been major providers of funds to mining projects throughout the world. Typical examples include a $164 million project loan and a $30 million overrun funding facility to help fund the

Samarco iron ore project in Brazil, a $200 million loan from a consortium of banks to assist in the financing of the Cuajone copper mine in Peru, and a $100 million loan from seven U.S. banks for the OK Tedi copper/gold project in Papua New Guinea.

7. Examples of commercial bank funding for industrial projects include $335 million in Eurodollar loans and a DM 400 million loan for the Acominas integrated steel mill in Brazil and a $78 million credit for the Vitro glass manufacturing facility in Mexico.

8. Among the numerous projects which commercial banks have funded with support from export credit agencies are the Acominas steel project (£150 million with the United Kingdom Export Credits Guarantee Department [ECGD]; £80 million equivalent in French francs with support from the French government agency COFACE; and £120 million equivalent in deutsche marks with support from Hermes); the Cuajone copper project in Peru ($20 million with a U.S. Export-Import Bank guarantee and $45 million with support from the ECGD); and the OK Tedi copper/gold project in Papua New Guinea.

9. Commercial banks have cofinanced with the World Bank in a wide variety of sectors including steel, electric power, and aluminum in Brazil ($105 million, $124 million, and $90 million, respectively); livestock in Romania ($100 million); hydropower in Yugoslavia ($35 million); port construction in Ecuador ($10 million); and hydropower in Thailand ($20 million).

10. Banks frequently provide funds to private sector projects in developing countries by purchasing participation certificates from the International Finance Corporation. In a recent transaction for RO Belisce-Bel in Yugoslavia, the IFC provided $20 million in fixed-rate funds and sold DM 17.8 million in participation certificates to a German bank, AS 104.8 million to an Austrian bank, and U.S. $22 million to a group of European, Middle Eastern, and Indian banks. In a similar transaction involving P.T. Semen Andalas Indonesia, the IFC sold $48 million in participation certificates to a group of commercial banks.

Public Bond Issues

In appropriate cases, funds may be raised through bond issues in the public markets for major projects. For example, a sufficiently creditworthy issuer could issue bonds or notes on the world markets to obtain fixed-rate funds for project financing. However, these sources are available only to the more creditworthy borrowers and are not a universal or necessary feature of project financings. The markets most likely to be used are the U.S. domestic market, the Eurodollar bond market, the deutsche mark market, the Swiss franc market, and the yen market. The precise maturity, interest rate, and other terms and conditions would, of course, vary with the market used and the conditions in that market at the time of issue. The basic advantages of a bond issue are that it is fixed rate and that, in some cases, it may be of long maturity.

Norway's program for financing its share of North Sea oil development provides a good example of the use of the world bond markets to fund major projects. In the late 1970s, Norway borrowed substantial amounts in the dollar, deutsche mark, yen, and Swiss franc markets through a series of five-year note issues. The major portion of the funds was then provided to Statoil, the national oil company, for petroleum development in the North Sea.

The public bond markets have also been used to help fund other major projects in Europe, including the Trans Austrian gasline, the Trans European Natural Gas Pipeline, and the Norpipe gas pipeline from the Ekofisk area in the North Sea. In addition, the supranational institutions associated with the European Economic Community (i.e., the European Investment Bank, the European Atomic Energy Community, and the European Coal and Steel Community) frequently borrow in the international and foreign bond markets to raise funds which they on-lend to help finance industrial, energy, and coal and steel projects. Recently, Pembroke Capital Company, Inc. (owned 50 percent by Gulf Oil Corporation and 50 percent by Texaco Inc.), raised $200 million in a public bond issue in the United States for the construction of a catalytic cracking unit in Wales.

In North America, a variety of public and private entities use the taxable and tax-exempt bond markets to fund major projects. Hydro-Quebec, for example, is a frequent user of the bond markets to help fund the James Bay Project, a multibillion-dollar hydroelectric project on the La Grande River in Northern Quebec. In the United States, public power agencies such as the Washington Public Power Supply System, the Northern Carolina Municipal Power Agency, the Northern California Power Agency, and the Intermountain Power Agency, raise large amounts in the tax-exempt markets to fund major nuclear and fossil fuel power plants. Agencies responsible for port and airport development (e.g., the Virginia Port Authority, the Memphis-Shelby County Airport Authority, and the City of Mobile Industrial Development Board) frequently finance their projects by issuing tax-exempt bonds. One of the larger port financings was a $265 million issue of Tax Exempt Marine Terminal Revenue Bonds by the city of Valdez, Alaska, to finance Arco Pipeline's interest in the TAPS marine terminal in Valdez.

The use of bond markets to help fund major projects is not limited to entities in industrialized countries. For example, major Brazilian

(Centrais Electricas Brasileiras and Companhia Energetica de São Paulo) and Mexican (Comisión Federal de Electricidad) utilities have used the world bond markets to help fund their major projects.

Private Placements

Projects in industrialized countries are frequently funded, in part, through the sale of securities in the world's major private placement markets. The largest such market is the institutional investor market in the United States (e.g., insurance companies, pension funds, savings banks, and trust funds). Private placements are also available in more limited amounts in Eurodollars, yen, Swiss francs, deutsche marks, sterling, guilders, and French francs. The major advantage of the private placement markets is that they have traditionally provided large amounts of long-term, fixed-rate funds.

Most large energy and natural resource projects in North America involve private placements. In one of the largest placements to date, Sohio/BP Trans Alaska Pipeline Finance, Inc., raised $1.75 billion in the form of $10\frac{5}{8}$ percent 15- and 20-year notes to help fund its portion of the Alaskan Oil Pipeline. The private placement markets in the United States also contributed $550 million to the funding of the Churchill Falls hydroelectric project in Labrador and $50 million to the funding of a $300 million power plant for the Syncrude project in Alberta.

Institutional investors are by nature and by law cautious and conservative, and they are generally reluctant to lend large amounts abroad. However, they have helped fund foreign projects in special cases in the past. Institutional investors in the United States provided $104 million to help fund the Falconbridge nickel project in the Dominican Republic and $45 million to help fund the Ertsberg nickel project in Indonesia. In the Falconbridge project, a portion of the loan was guaranteed by the U.S. sponsor companies, and the U.S. government provided insurance against the risk of expropriation and currency inconvertibility. In the Ertsberg project, OPIC provided similar insurance coverage for the loan by the U.S. insurance companies.

There is recent evidence that institutional investors are expanding the scope of their foreign lending. United States insurance companies have lent $140 million to Pemex to help develop the Mexican oil industry and have agreed to lend $25 million to Tubos de Acero de Mexico S.A. to help fund its steel pipe manufacturing expansion project. In other Mexican transactions, they lent $10 million to Industrias Resistol for a particle board plant and $26 million for a glass manufacturing project. Both of these loans were made in conjunction with the International Finance Corporation.

Equity Issues

The public equity markets are also a source of funds for some major projects, although on a much more limited scale than the world's public and private bond markets. A $200 million equity offering in the United States helped COMSAT finance a global commercial communications satellite system; the Lasmo Scot financing for North Sea oil development involved a public equity issue in the United Kingdom; the Bougainville copper project in Papua New Guinea was financed, in part, by a $43.2 million public share offering; and recently, in simultaneous issues in the United States and Mexico, Tubos de Acero de Mexico raised over $67 million to fund the expansion of its facilities for making steel pipe.

Mining companies, especially in the United Kingdom, Australia, and Canada, have traditionally raised equity funds for major projects through rights offerings to shareholders. In the Selebi-Pikwe copper/nickel project in Botswana, a rights offering was used to raise $26 million. (A unique aspect of this offering was the fact that the individual U.S. shareholders had their equity interest insured by the Overseas Private Investment Corporation.) More recently, in 1980, RT-Z issued £126 million in convertible loan stock, Consolidated Gold Fields made a £181 million rights offering, BHP and CRA raised $A 89 million and $A 330 million respectively in rights issues, and Cominco of Canada made a $C 100 million offering to its shareholders.

Commercial Paper

The commercial paper market is a growing source of interim construction finance for large projects in the United States and elsewhere. Commercial paper is a means of borrowing short-term capital funds—usually as an alternative to bank borrowing. Commercial paper is issued in the form of promissory notes with maturities ranging from a few days up to several months. These notes are offered to money market investors through dealers and are sold on a discount basis.

Commercial paper is a general debt obligation of the issuing corporation and is not secured by tangible, corporate assets. Consequently, many issuers are required to maintain lines of credit with their commercial banks to cover commercial paper maturities if necessary. Bank-supported commercial paper can often provide cost savings over other forms of finance that would otherwise be used to fund projects during the construction period.

Construction of the world's largest pumped-storage hydroelectric facility is being financed, in part, by commercial paper issues. The sponsor, Virginia Electric and Power Company, is utilizing construction trust financing and a $220 million commercial paper program to help finance the $1.8 billion dollar project involving six pumping-generating units. The paper is issued by a special-purpose corporation which passes the proceeds to Bath County Hydroelectric Trust for disbursement. The commercial paper facility is backed by an irrevocable letter of credit from two major European banks.

The fuel supply for nuclear projects is also frequently funded by commercial paper programs. Duke Energy Trust was organized to receive and hold title to nuclear fuel and sell the heat produced to Duke Power Company, a large investor-owned utility in North Carolina. Duke Power supports the financial commitments of Duke Energy Trust through a take-or-pay contract for the heat produced by the nuclear fuel. The trust obtains its short-term financing from banks and a $75 million commercial paper program secured by an irrevocable credit commitment from a group of European commercial banks.

Export Credit

Virtually every major project in the developing world and many projects in the industrialized world involve some form of export credit arrangement. Credit may be extended directly by the foreign supplier in the form of a deferred-payment arrangement. Until recently, this method was commonly used by the People's Republic of China to help finance major plant and equipment imports. Deferred-payment arrangements have the advantage of simplicity, but generally mean that the purchaser pays a higher price than normal as the supplier increases price to cover its own financing costs.

The more common form of export credit support is provided by government agencies of the major supplier countries. This support is provided in a number of ways, including direct loans, insurance, interest rate subsidy, and protection against inflation, exchange risk, and arbitrary action on bid and performance bonds. The major institutions providing such support include the U.S. Export-Import Bank; the Japanese Export-Import Bank; the United Kingdom Export Credits Guarantee Department; the Bank of France, the Banque Française du Commerce Extérieur (BFCE), and the Compagnie Française d'Assurance pour le Commerce Extérieur (COFACE) in France; the Canadian Export Development Corporation; and the Ausführkredit Gesellschaft (AKA), Kreditanstalt für Wiederaufbau (KFW), Deutsche Revisions und Treuhand AG, and Hermes Kreditversicherung AG (a private company) in West Germany.

Currently, an International Arrangement on Officially Supported Export Credit among OECD governments establishes guidelines for the terms that can be offered by the export credit agencies. The minimum interest is 10 to 12.4 percent (0.30 percent over the commercial long-term prime rate for yen loans) and the maximum maturity is 8½-10 years, depending on the level of development of the borrowing country. The arrangement does not cover all types of goods and services, and it is often breached by a country particularly desirous of business. In addition, countries occasionally derogate from the guidelines to meet competition from other countries. For example, in a September 1981 loan, the U.S. Export-Import Bank exceeded the maximum maturity established by the International Arrangement by authorizing a loan to be repaid over 20 years, beginning in 1987, to meet French competition for a loan in Ivory Coast. The $95.3 million loan carries an interest rate of 10 percent and will help finance U.S. goods and services for the Soubre Hydroelectric Project.

The degree of credit analysis and security required before an export credit will be made differs from one agency to another. Agencies in some countries, for example, are reluctant to extend export credits on a nonrecourse or project financing basis, while agencies in other countries have no hesitancy in lending to, or otherwise supporting, a complicated project financing. However, as project financing techniques are better understood, there is a growing willingness of export credit agencies to lend in a limited recourse situation.

The main advantages of export credit financing are its ready availability, its fixed rate, and its high degree of subsidization by the governments of the exporting countries. The main disadvantage is that procurement is tied to the country providing the financing. This may, in some instances, result in a higher price and/or lower quality.

Export credit is available for projects of all sizes. For example, the United States recently made an $8 million loan to Cementos Telteca in Mexico to help finance a cement plant, and in 1978, it made a $732 million loan to Korea Electric Company to support the sale of two nuclear reactors. Other large U.S. Export-Import Bank loans have included credits of $480 million and $240 million to help finance LNG facilities in Algeria. The export credit agencies of other countries are also prepared to lend in size. The ECGD recently announced that it was supporting long-term loans for roughly $1.4 billion equivalent (£642 million and HK $1.248 billion) to Castle Peak Power Company, Ltd., to finance turbine generators for a power project in Hong Kong.

Large, complex projects typically involve export credit from a number of different agencies due to the fact that key components are often sourced in different countries. For example, the OK Tedi copper/gold project in Papua New Guinea involves support from five different countries; the Taabo Hydroelectric Project in Ivory Coast also involved credit from five countries (the United States, France, Italy, Belgium, and Switzerland); Belgium, France, West Germany, the United States, and Yugoslavia provided over $60 million in export credits to the Boke bauxite project in Guinea; the Bougainville copper project in Papua New Guinea received $114 million in support from the United States, Japan, and Australia; both the U.S. Export-Import Bank and the ECGD helped fund the Cuajone copper project in Peru and the Vitro glass manufacturing plant in Mexico; and ECGD, COFACE, and Hermes provided support for loans for the Acominas steel project in Brazil.

In addition to funding specific projects, export credit facilities are sometimes established to fund all types of exports to the beneficiary country. For example, since 1978, the People's Republic of China has had over $15 billion in export credit facilities made available to it from 12 different countries.

Bilateral Aid

Projects in certain developing countries may be eligible for bilateral aid. Such aid is provided by most industrialized countries and is desirable in that it is generally offered on highly concessional terms (i.e., low interest rates and long grace and repayment periods). Such aid can be useful in funding feasibility studies, providing technical assistance, or funding infrastructure. The main disadvantage is, of course, the fact that bilateral aid is frequently tied to procurement from the country providing the funds.

Another disadvantage of bilateral aid is that it is generally not available in large amounts to any one country on a continuing basis. However, special circumstances do sometimes mean that aid funding is readily available for major projects. For example, the United States has a large bilateral aid program in Egypt, which has provided substantial amounts for key projects; and the Japanese Overseas Economic Cooperation Fund recently made over $1.5 billion in bilateral, concessionary aid (30-year maturity, 10-year grace period, 3 percent interest) available to the People's Republic of China to help fund transportation and energy projects.

Even in instances where such large-scale funding is not available, bilateral aid can play a useful role in helping finance projects in developing countries. Part of the infrastructure for the Boke project in Guinea was financed by a $22.9 million loan from USAID; the United Kingdom, the United States, and Canada provided $1.5 million, $6.5 million, and $29 million, respectively, to finance part of the water and power supply for Botswana's Selebi-Pikwe copper/nickel project; and the Caisse Centrale de Cooperation Economique provided $17.6 million equivalent in French francs to help finance the Taabo Hydroelectric Project in Ivory Coast.

Bilateral aid is also sometimes used as a means of circumventing the limits established by the guidelines on export credits noted in the previous section. A country blends bilateral aid with funds on export credit terms to create a "mixed credit" with a lower overall rate of interest and a longer average maturity. For example, in 1978 mixed credit facilities were offered to the Cypriot government in connection with an earth satellite station and steam generators for a power project. In the case of the satellite station, the French offered a mixed credit facility which, in effect, reduced the interest rate to 6 percent; and in the case of the generators, the United Kingdom offered to finance 50 percent of the cost out of its aid budget with a 4 percent interest, 25-year maturity, and 3-year grace period.

Development Banks

The international development banks are a potential source of funding for projects in certain developing countries. The major institutions in this category are the World Bank (and its affiliated institutions, the International Development Association and the International Finance Corporation), the Inter-American Development Bank, the Asian Development Bank, and the African Development Bank. The European Investment Bank also has funds available for projects in certain developing countries, as do a number of the Arab development banks.

Development bank funding is broadly divided into soft loan lending (low or zero interest rates and long maturities of 30-40 years) and hard loan lending (higher, but still below-market, interest rates and somewhat shorter maturities of 15-20 years). Hard loans are generally made out of capital resources accumulated through the development bank's borrowing on the international capital markets, member subscriptions, and sales of participations on loans. Soft loan lending is dependent on contributions from members and is therefore more limited in amount. In addition to providing finance, the development banks can provide major assistance in conducting feasibility studies and in helping a host country structure all aspects of a complicated project.

A common role for development banks in a major energy or mineral project is to help the host government fund the basic infrastructure. However, development banks also lend for feasibility studies and preliminary design and engineering, as well as the actual energy or mining facilities. In the Selebi-Pikwe copper/nickel mining project in Botswana, the IDA provided a $3.5 million credit for preliminary design and engineering, and the World Bank provided an initial loan of $32 million to help fund the roads, railroads, housing, and part of the water supply. Other major World Bank loans for mining have included a $66 million loan to the Société Anonyme des Mines de Fer de Mauritanie to fund railway and port facilities, a $35 million loan to Compagnie Minière de l'Ogooué in Gabon for railroad port facilities in connection with a manganese project, a $100 million loan to finance expansion of the Gecamines facilities in Zaire, an $80 million loan for the Cerro Matoso copper project in Colombia, and a $7.5 million loan for feasibility studies concerning a major phosphate deposit in Peru. The Inter-American Development Bank has made a $75 million loan for coal sector development in Brazil and, in conjunction with a $40 million World Bank loan, has lent $33.4 million for a copper mine expansion project in Peru.

The development banks have traditionally been active in providing assistance for the power sector. For example, in fiscal year 1981, the World Bank and IDA provided $1.3 billion for 17 projects in the power sector. More recently, they have dramatically increased their funding in the oil and gas sector. The World Bank has provided the Indian Oil and Natural Gas Commission $550 million to help fund the Bombay High oil field and has made a $107 million loan to Thailand to help fund a major natural gas pipeline. It has, in addition, made loans for oil and gas development in Turkey, Pakistan, Egypt, Peru, and Bangladesh and loans or credits for oil and gas exploration projects in 15 countries.

In the industrial project area, development banks have recently helped fund the development and expansion of the steel sector in Brazil, Egypt, and Portugal; the chemical and fertilizer sectors in India, Turkey, and Bangladesh; the textile industry in Tunisia and Turkey; the paper industry in Egypt; and the glass and particle board industries in Mexico.

Other Official Sources of Finance

In addition to the export credit agencies, the bilateral aid agencies, and the multilateral development banks, a number of governmental and quasi-governmental agencies assist in funding major projects—particularly in the developing world. Three of the most active have been Kreditanstalt für Wiederaufbau (KFW), the Overseas Mineral Resources Development Corporation (OMRDC), and the Overseas Private Investment Corporation (OPIC).

KFW is a West German government agency that has been active in funding mining projects where a portion of the output is suppliedd to West Germany. KFW loans are generally long term (10 to 15 years) at a fixed rate. KFW loans have included a DM 222 million loan (in conjunction with a consortium of West German banks) for the mining facilities at the Selebi-Pikwe copper/nickel project in Botswana, an $8 million loan for the Nanisivak lead and zinc mining project on Baffin Island in Canada, and a $100 million loan for the OK Tedi copper/gold project in Papua New Guinea. OMRDC is a Japanese government entity that helps Japanese mining and trading companies fund mineral projects. It has, for example, helped finance the Mamut copper project in Malaysia and Frieda River copper project in Papua New Guinea.

OPIC is a U.S. government agency that provides insurance, guarantees, and a small amount of direct lending for projects in the developing world. Its activities cover virtually all economic sectors. Recently, it introduced special programs in the minerals and energy area, and in fiscal year 1980 OPIC provided $612 million in insurance coverage for 11 mineral and energy projects. OPIC assistance in this area has included: $27 million in coverage for the Selebi-Pikwe project in Botswana; $20.7 million for a rutile mining project in Sierre Leone; $17.8 million for a silver, lead, and zinc mine in Honduras; $30 million for cobalt mine expansion in Zambia; and $22.5 million and $27.8 million, respectively, for oil exploration and production in the Congo and Egypt.

The European Investment Bank (EIB) is another institution which grants or guarantees loans for projects in EEC member countries and associated developing countries. EIB loans outside the EEC are frequently made in conjunction with such institutions as the World Bank, and a substantial number are made pursuant to the Lome and Yaoundé conventions. For example, EIB made a $20 million loan (in conjunction with the World Bank) to help finance the Gecamines expansion program in Zaire; UA 12 million and UA 10 million loans to the sugar industry in Kenya and Swaziland; UA 14 million for a clinker plant in Togo; UA 9 million for a fertilizer facility in Senegal; UA 25 million for electric transmission and distribution in Nigeria; and UA 25 million for an iron ore project in Mauritania.

A number of Arab financial aid institutions have provided substantial funds for major projects—particularly in Africa and the Middle East. The loans are also frequently made in conjunction with loans from other aid or development institutions. For example, the Libyan Arab Foreign Bank provided $100 million to help the World Bank and EIB fund the Gecamines expansion project, and a $500 million iron ore project in Mauritania was cofinanced by the Saudi Fund for Development ($65 million), the Kuwait Fund for Arab Economic Development ($45 million), the Arab Fund for Economic and Social Development ($35 million), the Abu Dhabi Fund ($20 million); and the OPEC Fund for International Development ($5 million).

Purchasers and Suppliers

Purchasers and suppliers that have a major interest in the success of a project may often assist in financing through loans, guarantees, and, in some cases, equity. Purchasers are also involved in providing credit support for lenders through various types of contractual obligations. In the

Selebi-Pikwe project in Botswana, the major purchaser of the output provided a partial guarantee of loans from KFW and the World Bank. In the same project, the mining companies that used the water and power facilities supported the loans made to finance them through purchase contracts containing take-or-pay obligations. Japanese smelting and trading companies often help finance projects providing output to them. They provided $28.6 million to help finance the Lornex copper mine in British Columbia and a $22.5 million loan to the Ertsberg copper project in Indonesia.

Investment Banks

If the project financing manager is not only an adviser and agent but a full-service investment banker willing and able to make an investment with its own funds, significant integrity can be added to the project. Despite the best planning, an unexpected financing gap can appear. By having the capability to design and make an investment to close the gap, the project financing manager can help ensure the success of a project and therefore the willingness of others to participate.

Local Currency Sources

In international projects, one needs to distinguish between funding local currency costs and funding foreign exchange costs. In many projects with government sponsors, a substantial amount of local currency funding is paid out of the host country's own budget. In addition, the local capital market and banking system may provide funds for the project. This is especially true in developed countries, but it is also true in a growing number of developing nations. In the Acominas integrated steel works project in Brazil, Finame, an agency of the Banco Nacional de Desenvolvimento Economico, provided the equivalent of $881 to finance equipment supplied by Brazilian manufacturers; in both the Cerro Verde copper project and the Centromin expansion project, COFIDE, a Peruvian government agency, provided local cost funding; and a group of Mexican banks provided $19 million equivalent in peso funding for the Vitro glass manufacturing facility in Mexico.

CONCLUSION

Prospects of continued inflation, capital market uncertainties, and weak balance sheets and cash positions mean that potential sponsors are becoming increasingly concerned about their ability to fund major new

EXHIBIT 11
Outline of Relationships among Potential Participants in a Project Financing

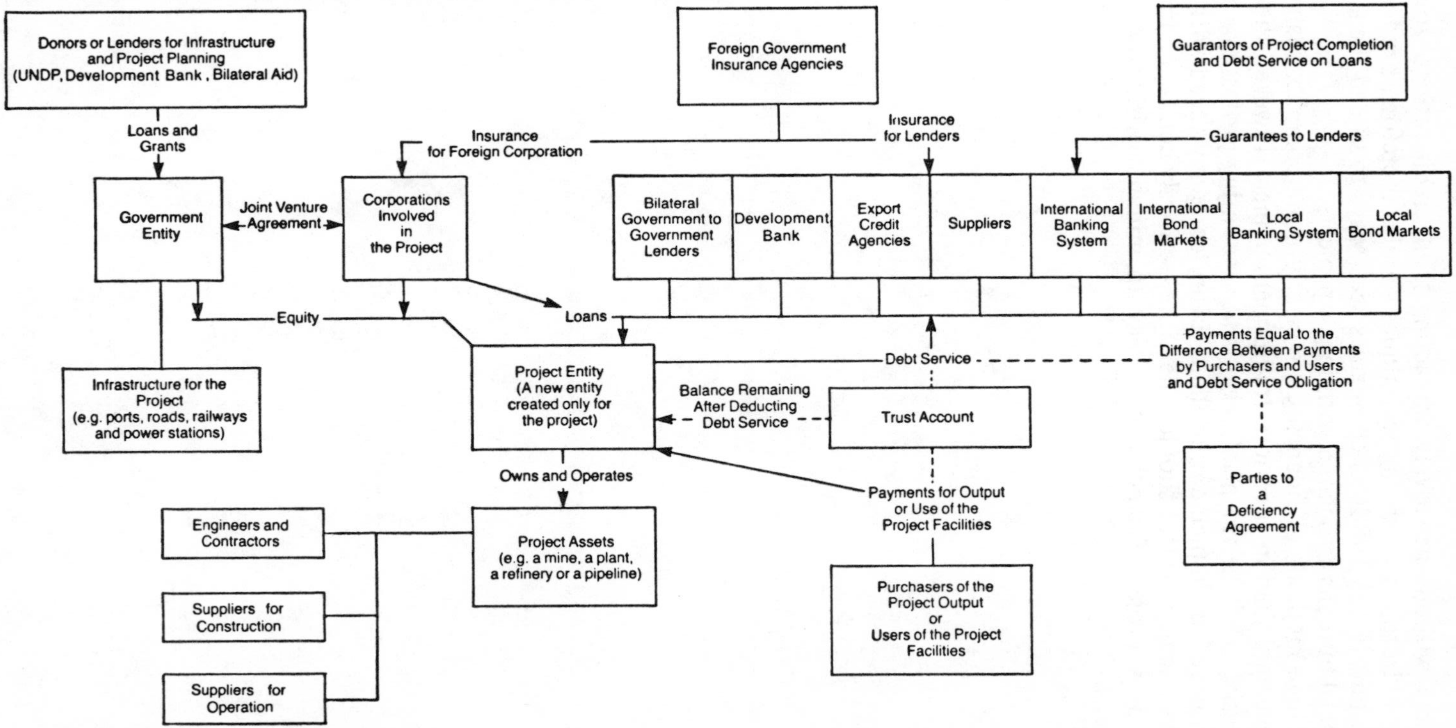

projects without negatively impacting their credit ratings. Joint ventures and project financing techniques should, therefore, become more important in the 1980s as companies seek ways to spread the risks and financial burdens associated with major projects.

These methods of financing are clearly more complex than financing accomplished in the more traditional manner. However, their use is increasing, and the financial, legal, and accounting professions are now experienced in implementing them. Every company faced with undertaking a major project should, therefore, seriously consider a joint venture or a project financing as a way to minimize risk and financial burdens.

CHAPTER 11

Corporate-Related
Municipal Financing

WILLIAM J. GREMP
Merrill Lynch White Weld Capital Markets Group

INTRODUCTION

Corporate-related municipal finance opportunities available to corporations offer a *left hand financing* vehicle. They are permissible because of the public purpose of the assets financed, and lower the cost of expanding the capitalization. This is due to the fact that tax-exempt yields are roughly 70 to 75 percent of taxable yields. The purpose of this chapter is to provide a review of the tax-exempt financing opportunities available to corporations and of the applicable procedures for executing such financings. Corporate-related tax-exempt financing reached record volume in the early 1980s despite historically high long-term interest rates and unprecedented volatility in the bond market. Demand at the short-term end of the yield curve was considerably stronger than at the long-term end, as companies sought to avoid locking themselves into the high interest rates prevailing at long maturities. Strong retail investor interest compensated for slackening institutional participation in the tax-exempt market. Finally, the volume of offerings was affected by the legislative threat of curtailment and by the IRS rulings on composite issues discussed later in this chapter. Such issues were subjected to restrictive tests as of August 1981.

In response to the sharply rising yield curve and the changing investor composition, investment bankers developed innovative financing techniques, primarily short-term, three-year issues, adjustable-rate long-term issues carrying put options and priced as short-term maturities, floating-rate issues with coupons based on a percentage of the prime rate, offerings secured by letters of credit, and the exploration of uses for original issue discount bonds.

Since tax-exempt rates are 70 to 75 percent of taxable yields, corporate interest in tax-exempt financing will be strong. An active market will depend on continued retail demand, especially if institutional participation remains weak. If high interest rates prevail, the corporate-related group will pursue short-term offerings and long-term variable-rate alternatives. However, a growing momentum in legislative circles to reduce the volume and uses of industrial revenue bonds under $10 million makes their future uncertain.

In general, income received as interest on the debt obligations of states or political subdivisions is not included as gross income for federal income tax purposes. This "tax exemption" is provided in the Internal Revenue Code of 1954.[1] An exception to this exemption is "industrial development bonds," which are defined as bonds issued by states or political subdivisions (1) the proceeds of which are to be used in a trade or business and (2) the payments of principal or interest on which are derived from payments in respect of property or secured by any interest in property used in a trade or business.[2] The circumstances under which an industrial development bond would qualify for tax exemption are then listed:[3]

1. If the proceeds are to be used to construct "exempt facilities," which currently are:
   a. Residential real property for family units.
   b. Sports facilities.
   c. Convention or trade show facilities.
   d. Airports, docks, wharves, mass commuting facilities, parking facilities, storage facilities, or training facilities directly relating to any of the foregoing.
   e. Sewage or solid waste disposal facilities or facilities for the furnishing of local electric energy or gas.
   f. Air or water pollution control facilities.
   g. Facilities for the furnishing of water if the water is available on reasonable demand to members of the general public.
2. If the issue qualifies as an "exempt small issue," under either the $1 million exemption or the $10 million exemption. Bonds issued under this section are generally referred to as "industrial revenue bonds." Qualifying requirements are discussed later in this chapter.

---

[1] Section 103(a).
[2] Section 103(b)(1).
[3] Section 103(b)(4)-(6).

There is also an exemption for issues to finance the acquisition and development of land for industrial parks.

The two provisions most commonly used by industrial corporations are those relating to pollution control facilities and exempt small issues (industrial revenue bonds). Hence, the more detailed discussion that follows is focused on these two provisions. However, much of the material relating to financing techniques and the structuring and marketing of issues applies to industrial development bonds generally.

INDUSTRIAL REVENUE BONDS

Qualifying an Issue as Industrial Revenue Bonds

Industrial revenue bonds (IRBs) are bonds issued by states or political subdivisions, the proceeds of which are used to finance the acquisition and construction of industrial facilities for private companies. For these bonds to be eligible for the tax exemption, they must meet the terms of a number of major restrictions imposed by the federal government which limit:

— The total amount of bonds which may be issued for a company in any locality.
— For certain larger issues, the overall size of the facility for which such bonds may be issued.

These restrictions are contained in Treasury regulations and the Internal Revenue Code.[4]

There are *two* types of bond limits:

— A $1 million limit issue for which there are very few restrictions.
— An alternative $10 million limit issue to which there is a separate limitation on capital expenditures.

Basic Structure of Industrial Revenue Bond Financing— Local Requirements

Industrial revenue bonds may be issued by municipalities, counties, or state or local authorities (the "issuer") in accordance with state enabling legislation or local ordinances. The state and local laws generally determine:

— The types of projects eligible for bond financings.

---

[4] Section 103 (b) (6).

— The form of the financing (through loan, lease, or installment sale agreements with the company).

— The required security for the bonds.

Most enabling acts allow bonds to be issued for manufacturing plants as well as warehousing and office facilities. The issuer is usually required to show that the project will increase local employment. Further, the bond statutes of some states prohibit bond financing of a plant relocation *within* the state. Occasionally, approval by an agency, such as a state department of commerce or a local industrial development commission, is required.

Limitation on Size of Issue

$1 million issues

The Internal Revenue Code permits the issuance of bonds in an amount of up to $1 million with very few restrictions.[5] Under this provision, up to $1 million in bonds outstanding at any one time may be issued for projects of a company located within the same incorporated municipality *or* within the unincorporated areas of the same county. Projects must be combined if they cross municipal or county lines which are contiguous or functionally integrated.

The project financed must consist of land or depreciable property. However, bonds may also be used to pay for certain "soft costs," such as fees of bond counsel and printing expenses.

Items which may *not* be financed by bonds include working capital, inventory, and research and development expenses. However, despite the prohibition on financing working capital, if preliminary approval for the bond issue is obtained from the issuer, a company may initially finance construction with its own working capital pending issuance of the bonds and later reimburse itself from bond proceeds.

There are *no* capital expenditure limitations for a $1 million issue. A $1 million issue may also be combined with an issue of pollution control facility bonds of any size.

$10 million issues

Up to $10 million in bonds may be issued for a project, provided the company is able to meet certain limitations on capital expenditures. Under the alternative $10 million bond limit, the company may not incur capital expenditures with respect to *any* of its facilities located within the boundaries of the issuer in excess of $10 million during a six-

[5] Section 103(b)(6).

year period beginning three years before and ending three years after the date of issuance of the bonds. Expenditures counted against the $10 million capital expenditure limitation include:

- Capital expenditures financed with bond proceeds.
- Capital expenditures financed in any other manner or paid for from the company's working capital.
- Pollution control expenditures financed with tax-exempt bonds.
- Capital expenditures on any other facility that is within the boundaries of the issuer and is owned by the company or any affiliate of the company.
- Capital expenditures that are made on facilities within the boundaries of the issuer by any other "principal user" of the bond-financed facilities (which would include a lessee of 10 percent or more of the property).
- Expenditures with respect to the facility by "any person" other than the company, including (1) a government agency (except for certain utility installations), (2) any 10 percent lessee, and (3) *any* lessee to the extent that the expenditures ultimately benefit the lessor company.

A "capital expenditure" is defined as "amounts properly chargeable to the capital account" of "any person" with respect to the facility and has been interpreted by the IRS to include:

- Expenditures by a contractor under a "turnkey project."
- Trucks "based at" the facility.
- Research and development expenses related to plant, equipment, or products—even if the company elects to deduct such expenses for tax purposes.
- The cost of equipment moved to the facility which is incurred within the six-year period.
- Prior capital expenditures by any acquired corporation on facilities located within the boundaries of the issuer.

Capital expenditures do *not* include:

- Public utility expenditures of a public utility company or governmental unit that are normally paid for from the periodic fees of users.
- Leased property under a "true lease."[6]
- Expenditures made to replace property damaged or destroyed

---

[6] See Chapter 7 for an explanation of a "true lease."

by fire or other casualty, but not in excess of the fair market value of the property replaced.

- Expenditures required by a *subsequent* change in state law or regulations.
- Expenditures of up to $1 million which arise out of circumstances that could not reasonably be foreseen on the date of issuance of the bonds or which arise out of a mistake of law or fact.

The capital expenditure limitation is increased to $20 million if the Department of Housing and Urban Development issues an Urban Development Action Grant in connection with the project. The bond limit, however, remains at $10 million.

If a company exceeds the $10 million capital expenditure limitation within three years after issuance of the bonds, the bonds become taxable from the date on which the limitation is exceeded. For this reason, such bonds typically contain provisions which require either an increase in the interest rate or a mandatory redemption if the bonds become taxable.

Requirement for Preliminary Bond Resolution prior to Commencement of Construction

The Treasury regulations require some kind of "official action" by the issuer (such as a preliminary bond resolution) prior to commencement of construction or acquisition of the project. This provision reflects an attempt to ensure that the issuance of tax-exempt bonds is an inducement for the project. "Commencement of construction or acquisition" may be the date of execution of the binding purchase contract, ground breaking, or the commencement of fabrication by a contractor.

POLLUTION CONTROL BONDS

Qualifying an Issue as Pollution Control Bonds—Definition under Proposed IRS Regulations

Pollution control regulations proposed by the IRS on August 20, 1975, define an air or water pollution control facility as a discrete unit of property which (1) has been certified by the appropriate agency as furthering the control of pollution or (2) has been designed to meet applicable pollution control requirements and "is used in whole or in part to abate or control water or atmospheric pollution or contamination by removing, altering, disposing, or storing pollutants, contaminants, waste, or heat."

Property is excluded from qualification as a pollution control facility to the extent that it avoids the creation of pollutants, is designed to prevent accidents or injuries, or previously controlled such material or heat as a customary practice for reasons other than compliance with pollution control regulations.

Therefore, the regulations provide that when a pollution control facility "also has a function other than the control of pollution," only the incremental cost of the facility shall be treated as a qualifying expenditure for pollution control facilities. The incremental cost is determined by subtracting from the total cost of the facility an amount determined by multiplying the total cost of the facility by a fraction whose numerator represents the present value of the economic benefit of the facility over its useful life and whose denominator represents the facility's gross capital costs (adjusted for its burden of federal income taxes) plus the present value of expenses to be incurred in the operation of the facility over its useful life.

"Economic benefit" is defined to be "gross income or cost savings resulting from any increase in production or capacity, production efficiencies, the production of a by-product, the extension of useful life of other property, . . . and any other identifiable cost savings such as savings resulting from the use, reuse, or recycling of items recovered." The proposed regulations also identify as cost savings capital expenditures for and operating expenses of any property which have been rendered unnecessary by the construction and use of the pollution control property. Under the proposed regulations, the only costs which may be deducted from this economic benefit are the selling expenses incurred in the disposition of by-products.

Arbitrage Regulations

An aspect of the Internal Revenue Code that is applicable to *all* tax-exempt financings concerns the investment of bond proceeds during the period between issuance of the bonds and application of the proceeds.[7] The IRS has issued "arbitrage regulations" which limit the extent to which the proceeds of an issue of tax-exempt bonds may be invested in securities at a yield higher than the yield on the bonds.

In general, if certain conditions are met, the proceeds of tax-exempt financings may be invested in securities for a period of not more than three years without regard to the yield restrictions of the regulations.

---

[7] Section 103(c).

The regulations permit the three-year period to be extended to five years on the basis of an engineer's or architect's certificate (submitted as part of the arbitrage certificate at the closing) without an IRS ruling. Moreover, in general, a maximum of 15 percent of the bond proceeds can be invested in higher-yielding securities without regard to the aforementioned three- or five-year periods.

General Tax-Exempt Financing Considerations

Tax-exempt industrial development bond financing is only possible to the extent that it is authorized by enabling legislation of the state where the project is to be located. This legislation specifies the types of political subdivisions that are authorized to issue industrial development bonds and the manner in which the bonds may be issued. Within the framework of the applicable state enabling legislation, the selection of a financing method is based on numerous factors, which include (1) compliance with federal, state, and local pollution control standards; (2) the company's rights and obligations under controlling local statutes; and (3) internal company policies.

No Registration Requirement

Under the federal securities laws, there is no registration requirement for the issuance of tax-exempt industrial development revenue bonds. In 1970 Congress amended the Securities Act of 1933 and the Securities Exchange Act of 1934 specifically to exempt most revenue bonds, including pollution control bonds, which qualify as tax-exempt obligations of the Internal Revenue Code of 1954, as amended. A later amendment to the Trust Indenture Act of 1939 exempted from qualification any indenture written for this type of security.

Basic Financing Techniques

In industrial development bond financings, a subdivision or instrumentality of the state where the facilities are located (the "issuing authority") issues tax-exempt bonds whose proceeds are used to pay for the facilities. The company then causes the construction of the facilities and provides the funds for the payment of principal and interest on an issue of tax-exempt bonds. The bonds are paid only from revenues provided by the company pursuant to an agreement with the issuing authority and not from any public funds. Depending on state law, the issuing authority for industrial development revenue bond financings may be a county, city, or town or an agency, such as an air quality board or an industrial development authority.

Structure (Method) of Financing

All types of industrial development bond financings are structured to create an obligation of the company to make payments which are sufficient to cover the principal and interest on the bonds. Generally, the structure of industrial development bond issues falls into one of the following three categories: (1) a direct loan from the issuing authority to the company, (2) an installment sale of the facilities to the company, or (3) various leasing arrangements.

The following provisions are normally present in all three methods:

1. Substantially all (90 percent) of the "net proceeds" of the bond issue must be used to pay the costs of qualifying facilities. Up to 10 percent of such net proceeds of the bond issue may be used for any purpose permitted by the laws of the issuer's state. The net proceeds of the bond issue are those proceeds which remain after payment of the costs of issuance (underwriters' discount, attorneys' and engineers' fees, printing and engraving costs, rating agency fees, etc.).

2. A commercial bank with trust powers is appointed trustee to collect payments from the company and to pay principal and interest on the bonds, to hold bond proceeds pending disbursement for construction or other purposes, and to perform the other duties normally assigned a trustee under a corporate indenture.

3. Excess bond proceeds are held for the redemption of bonds; the company is obligated to complete construction if the bond proceeds are insufficient; and the company covenants to operate and maintain the facilities.

4. The company supervises the design and construction of the facilities and is able to make changes as work proceeds.

Direct loan

With the direct loan method, the issuing authority issues tax-exempt industrial development bonds and lends the proceeds of the bond issue to the company. The company obligates itself to repay the loan in installments corresponding to the principal and interest payments which the issuing authority must make on the the tax-exempt bonds. The company delivers to the issuing authority written evidence of its obligation to repay the loan, normally in the form of a loan agreement which may or may not be accompanied by a promissory note.

Installment sale

In the case of an installment sale, the issuing authority issues tax-exempt bonds and acquires the facilities either by purchasing partly completed facilities from the company and completing their construction or by constructing the facilities from the start. The company then purchases the facilities from the issuing authority and obligates itself to pay a purchase price in installments equal to and simultaneous with principal and interest payments that the issuing authority must make on the tax-exempt industrial development revenue bonds. The company's obligation to make such payments is evidenced by its undertaking in the installment sale agreement, which may or may not be accompanied by a promissory note, to make the scheduled payments of the purchase price.

Lease

Under the lease method, the issuing authority issues tax-exempt bonds and acquires the facilities by purchasing them from the company, by constructing them, or by leasing them from the company. The facilities are then leased (or leased back) to the company for a specific period (usually matching the term of the bond issue) with or without options to renew the lease. Rental payments under the lease are equal to and simultaneous with the payments of principal and interest on the bonds. This lease agreement could be (1) a lease between the issuing authority and the company with or without a guarantee of the bonds, (2) a lease from the company to the issuing authority with a subsequent leaseback to the company by the issuing authority with or without a guarantee, or (3) a leveraged lease.

The lease may give a lessee the right to purchase the property for a nominal amount at the expiration of the term, and thus be regarded as a financing lease, or it may provide that the lessor retains rights to the property, in which case the lease may be a true operating lease.

Leveraged lease

A leveraged lease is used when the company's tax position is such that it can advantageously transfer to an outside investor the investment tax credit and accelerated depreciation tax benefits relating to the facility. In such situations, the leveraged lease method can result in substantial savings to the company in terms of both cash outflow and noncash charges to the income statement. Leveraged leasing is discussed in Chapter 7.

Balance Sheet Accounting Treatment

The choice among the lease, installment sale, and loan methods influences whether the obligation represented by dock, wharf, and related storage facility revenue bonds will appear on the company's balance sheet as a liability. The obligation will almost certainly have to appear as a liability if the installment sale or direct loan method is used. If a lease is used, the obligation represented by the lease may or may not be capitalized and treated as a borrowing transaction, depending on the nature of the transaction.

Credit Rating Agency Considerations

One of the factors to be considered when choosing a basic financing technique is the obtaining of a credit rating. The principal legal instruments that are used to help achieve such a credit rating include a guarantee and first-mortgage bonds.

Credit rating under lease method—effect of guarantee

Where the obligation of a company or its subsidiary is in the form of a lease, a guarantee of the bonds is used in view of federal bankruptcy statute provisions that under a lease of real property a bankrupt lessee's liability may be limited to rent for one year or, in the event of a reorganization, for three years. The credit rating agencies considered a company's lease obligations to be of a lesser quality than its other unsecured general obligations. A guarantee of the bonds has been used on the theory that it would not be subject to these federal bankruptcy limitations.

Such a guarantee is normally an agreement to guarantee the payment of the bond principal, premium (if any), and interest to the trustee for the benefit of the bondholders. Where a subsidiary is the primary obligor, a guarantee by the parent corporation will place the parent's credit behind the bonds.

When a transaction is in the form of a lease accompanied by a guarantee, the general practice has been to accompany the guarantee with counsel's opinion as to the effect of the federal bankruptcy limitations on it. Given such a guarantee and a satisfactory opinion, a credit rating equal to the company's senior unsecured debt obligations is normally granted.

Credit rating under installment sale and loan methods

When an installment sale is used, the company's obligation is evidenced by its undertaking in the installment sale agreement to make the scheduled payments of the purchase price. Although perhaps not required, a promissory note may be given by the company. When the direct loan method is used, the obligation is evidenced by a loan agreement which may be accompanied by a promissory note. In both of these methods, a guarantee may be used if the primary obligor is a subsidiary and it is desired to place the parent's credit behind the industrial development revenue bonds. Provided that the credit rating agencies are satisfied that the company's obligation on the financing ranks equally with any other senior unsecured debt obligations, the effect of an installment sale or a loan is normally to secure a credit rating equal to the credit rating which is or would be given to the company's senior unsecured debt obligations.

One of the credit rating agencies may reqire an opinion of counsel confirming that a bare installment sale financing makes the bondholders unsecured general creditors of the company. This requirement might be waived if the rated company delivered a guarantee or perhaps a note in favor of the trustee with respect to the debt created under the installment sale agreement.

Basic Financing Terms

The terms of an industrial development bond offering are an important part of the structure of the issue. The basic financing terms of an industrial development bond issue are outlined below. Except for specialized redemption provisions, these terms generally do not vary with the type of facility financed. The terms may also be used as a guide to the terms available in the private placement market, although the form of delivery may differ. In some of the terms, there is considerable latitude in what the market will accept; in others, there is little latitude. This list is not meant to be all-inclusive, and it is subject to change due to market conditions.

Type of Issue	Terms of Issue
Security	The bonds will be limited obligations of the issuing authority payable solely from a pledge of revenues to be received from the company under the financing agreement (and guarantee, if applicable) and secured by a pledge of revenues plus such other security as the company may determine to provide (e.g., a mortgage on the facility).
Structure	Typically one or more term bonds.
Maturity	Term bonds generally mature in either 25 or 30 years, though a term of 10 to 20 years has become more common with institutional buyers. All terms are normally subject to sinking-fund redemptions, resulting in an average life 1.5 to 5 years shorter than term.
Interest payments	Semiannual.
Form	Generally issued in denominations of $5,000 as coupon bonds registrable as to principal only, or in fully registered form in multiples of $5,000.
Principal payments	Annually upon maturity of serial bonds or mandatory redemption of sinking-fund obligations.
Redemption (1) Sinking fund	Normally begins 5 to 10 years prior to maturity; dollar amount maturing in final year is subject to total issue size, type of marketing distribution contemplated, and industry characteristics.

Type of Issue	Terms of Issue
(2) Optional	Noncallable for first 10 years. Thereafter, callable at 103 percent of the aggregate principal amount outstanding and declining annually by one-half percent to 100 percent.
	Callable at par at any time as a result of the occurrence of certain extraordinary events. The following are among the events which have appeared in recent issues:
	(1) Damage or destruction.
	(2) Condemnation.
	(3) Imposition of unreasonable burdens or excessive liabilities on the issuing authority or the company with respect to the facility, including new ad valorem or other taxes.
	(4) Changes in economic conditions relating to operation of the plant.
	(5) Company prevented by judicial or administrative action from carrying on its normal operations at the facility for a period of six consecutive months or other agreed-upon period.
(3) Mandatory	Callable at any time upon a determination that interest on the bonds has become taxable (because the company has failed to observe IRS regulations). Pollution control bonds: No penalty. Industrial revenue bonds: Penalty generally equals interest paid on the bonds from the date the bonds became taxable to the date of redemption.

A basic strategy on the terms of an issue is to seek an average loan life that is as long as possible, consistent with market constraints and the company's preference. Thus, the company would be able to take maximum advantage of the tax-exempt interest rates while securing 100 percent financing of the qualifying facilities. The precise terms, however, would depend largely on industry characteristics, the company's credit standing, and market conditions at the time of the offering.

Additional financing techniques which could prove advantageous in periods of high interest rates are short-term financings of either fixed-rate or floating-rate debt which can be refunded when long-term rates improve. If so desired, floating-rate bonds can be issued on a long-term basis on the theory that the average interest cost over time will compare favorably to the current rates for long-term fixed-rate financings.

PROCEDURES FOR POLLUTION CONTROL OR INDUSTRIAL REVENUE BOND FINANCINGS

Internal Revenue Service Ruling Application

For any piece of equipment whose status as a pollution control facility is questionable, a ruling application should be prepared and submitted to the Internal Revenue Service. Such applications are normally submitted to the IRS by bond counsel after drafts have been reviewed by the various parties associated with the financing. It is difficult to give any estimate as to how much time will elapse before a decision is received from the Internal Revenue Service. The time involved may be six months or longer.

Selection of Issuing Authority

The issuing authority should be selected as provided within the applicable state enabling legislation, and the company should confirm with that authority its willingness to issue the proposed bonds.

Preliminary Bond Resolution

The next important procedural step is to ensure that the issuing authority adopts a satisfactory preliminary inducement bond resolution or other similar official action. The resolution should be drafted by bond counsel. Work can begin on it shortly after the issuing authority is determined. It is important that this resolution be adopted before the construction of the facilities is initiated. Unless the inducement resolution is adopted before the start of construction or acquisition, the company cannot finance the project through tax-exempt securities, provided construction did not commence prior to September 2, 1972.

Certification

In a pollution control financing, the next procedural step is to make sure that the equipment to be financed is certified, as designed, to be a pollution control facility under existing rules and regulations. The IRS requires that a certification be obtained from the appropriate federal, state, or local agency either (1) that the equipment is "in furtherance of the purpose of" pollution abatement or (2) that the equipment is designed to meet or exceed federal, state, and local pollution control standards.

Legal Opinion

An unqualified approving opinion by a recognized bond counsel is required to the effect that the bonds are valid obligations of the issuing authority and that under the Internal Revenue Code interest on the bonds is exempt from present federal income taxes.

To convey an idea of the overall time schedule for a tax-exempt industrial development revenue bond financing and the various steps to be undertaken, a sample public offering timetable is presented below.

Timetable for an Underwritten Offering of Tax-Exempt Pollution Control or Industrial Revenue Bonds

The following is a summary of the principal steps and procedures in a tax-exempt pollution control or industrial revenue bond financing. The preliminary steps are:

- Ensure that a properly established issuing authority has been selected.
- Company selects managing underwriter.

Days before Offering	*Procedure*
0 – 95	Company, the underwriter, and all counsel study the pollution control equipment list to be sure that all the items on the list are pollution control facilities. Any questionable facilities (including those which it is planned to finance through an industrial revenue bond) require a ruling from the Internal Revenue Service. Facilities which require an IRS ruling may be financed separately to avoid delaying the initial financing.
	Determine whether a ruling request on any of the facilities being financed is required; if so, submit ruling request.
	Company, the underwriter, and counsel select method of structuring the financing.
0 – 90	Company (working with its counsel), counsel for the issuing authority, bond counsel, and counsel for the underwriter obtain authorization from the issuing authority to issue up to a certain amount of tax-exempt bonds.
	Issuing authority, before construction of the facilities commences, takes necessary inducement action required by Internal Revenue Service regulations.
	Bond counsel begins preparation of documents such as the trust indenture and the loan agreement or lease, coordinating its efforts with other counsel.
	Company, the underwriter, and all counsel begin preparation of official statement.
	Counsel for the underwriter prepares drafts of the contract of purchase, the blue-sky survey, and the legal investment survey (if applicable).
	Conferences with all parties held as required on drafts of the documents.
	All parties meet to resolve open questions and finalize drafts of documents.
0 – 21	Request of ratings from credit rating agencies (with presentation if necessary). Invitation to other prospective underwriters to participate in the financing, if syndication is planned.
0 – 14	Distribution of preliminary official statement.
0 – 1	Negotiation of price and spread between the company and the underwriter. Company approves terms.
Offering day	Issuing authority approves terms.
	Signing of contract of purchase by the underwriter, the issuing authority, and the company.
	Signing of letter of representation.
	Commencement of offering.
0 + 21	Closing. Issuing authority receives payment from the underwriter.

- Select bond counsel.
- Develop detailed list of proposed facilities and their estimated cost.

Marketing Strategies for Tax-Exempt Offerings

The market for long-term tax-exempt securities is principally banks, casualty insurance companies, tax-exempt bond funds, and individuals. For high-quality borrowers, the institutional market is dominated by the casualty insurers. Banks generally restrict their investments to maturities of 15 years or less, which is generally shorter than the maturities corporations prefer. Bond funds seek higher-yielding bonds of equivalent credit rating, such as those issued by housing finance agencies or hospital authorities.

Most institutional buyers prefer to purchase publicly offered, underwritten issues for several reasons. The buyer usually has a small staff of investment officers who manage a large volume of transactions. As a consequence, the investment officers purchase rated underwritten issues so as to take advantage of the analytical work and due diligence of the rating agencies and the underwriter. This frees up staff time and allows the investment officers to be portfolio managers. In addition, institutional purchasers are very active in the secondary market and therefore prefer the added liquidity that a publicly offered, underwritten issue provides.

Limited Public Offering

In order to gain access to the institutional market at costs comparable to those of a conventional private placement, a method of sale has been devised which is generally known as a "limited public offering." This is an underwritten offering which is directed solely toward institutional purchasers and utilizes an abbreviated, typewritten offering circular with financial information on the company comparable to that contained in an S-16 registration statement. Because of the reduced printing costs and the lower sales credit required on institutional orders, the underwriting spread charged and the expenses incurred are considerably smaller in a limited public offering than in a full public offering and more in line with the costs of a private placement.

The limited public offering device is recommended when the size of the issue relative to the potential institutional demand indicates that the additional spread and costs involved in a full public offering will not be repaid by a reduction in interest rate. Offerings of up to $40 million to $50 million or more can be handled in this manner in the right institutional climate.

Private Placement

As public offerings of tax-exempt securities are, in general, exempt from registration, the principal advantage of the tax-exempt private placement is the discreet manner in which the sale of the bonds is accomplished. There is no public record of the bond issue, and only a select few institutional purchasers are offered the bonds. This financing method is desirable for companies that do not wish to disclose information in a public document. It is quite possible, however, that the selected buyers would request more information than is typical in a public offering. No ratings are usually required for private placements.

Public Offering

A conventional public offering is recommended when the size of the issue or the state of the institutional market indicates the advisability of securing at least some retail support for the issue. Such support can arise for relatively small offerings when, as in the first half of the 1970s and at the time of this writing, low casualty underwriting profitability reduces the casualty insurers' appetite for tax-exempt income. It can also arise when, due to peculiarities of state law, taxpayers within the state where the bonds are issued benefit from purchasing locally issued securities.

A method for further reducing financing costs, especially in the case of projects less than $5 million in size, has been to "bundle" into a single offering all such projects under consideration for financing in the near future. While each issue remains legally separate and fully documented, a composite offering statement is used. This approach reduces both out-of-pocket costs and especially professional time spent per dollar raised.

Recent IRS rulings question the ability to bundle. These rulings most likely render composite offering statements unusable for the foreseeable future. Effective alternative techniques are being studied by bond counsel firms.

INNOVATIVE FINANCING TECHNIQUES

Investment bankers and their corporate clients are devising numerous innovative financing techniques to help postpone selling long-term issues during difficult market periods. The principal techniques that have evolved are short-term bonds, bonds backed by letters of credit, insured bonds, commercial paper, floating- and adjustable-rate bonds, and put bonds, and consideration is being given to convertible and deep-discount bonds. Following is a description of these techniques and of their advantages and disadvantages.

Short-Term Bonds

The principal tax-exempt financing technique now being used by companies to finance projects on an interim basis is short-term fixed-rate bonds. Due to the highly positive slope of the yield curve, short-term issues provide substantial coupon savings, ranging from 200 to 400 basis points lower than long-term fixed-rate issues.

In addition, short-term issues offer:

— Substantial arbitrage earnings on temporary investments of unexpended proceeds from the original short-term issue and, potentially, the long-term refunding issue.

— Modest optional redemption premiums (generally, three-year issues provide one year of call protection followed by optional calls at 100½ percent after one year and 100 percent after two years).

— Simple document preparation and flexibility in restructuring the issue to a long-term financing should market "windows" appear.

Most short-term, fixed-rate issues have a three-year maturity. Longer maturities are possible, and under certain circumstances, these may be more attractive. Higher rates and more restrictive call features are necessary to market such issues. Also, IRS regulations require issues with maturities longer than three years to be refunded in whole within six months from the initial issue date of refunding bonds.

Short-term issues are extremely attractive to both retail and institutional investors. Where long-term issues may encounter marketing difficulties, large corporate-related short-term offerings continue to attract purchaser interest.

The major disadvantage of short-term financing is the possibility that permanent refinancing on a tax-exempt basis will be restricted or prohibited by prospective legislation. However, should such legislation be enacted, it is expected that the refunding of short-term issues which have already been completed will be allowed. It is felt that an orderly transition period for issues in progress will also be permitted.

Bonds Backed by Letters of Credit

Tax-exempt financings secured by letters of credit (LOCs) issued by commercial banks rated Aaa/AAA or Aa/AA can provide companies with substantial interest rate savings and, in most cases, wider access to the market. Depending on corporate and bank ratings, companies using LOCs may realize annual savings, net of LOC fees, ranging from 25 to 50 basis points.

Over the last year, the structure of LOC-backed issues has evolved to a fairly standardized form. LOCs are easily obtained by most companies and are evaluated under a simplified rating procedure, thereby avoiding an extended presentation of the company's financial position. By acquiring an LOC, companies can also avoid securing their issue with first-mortgage bonds. This feature is particularly attractive to investor-owned utilities and to companies having low mortgage coverage ratios or only limited bondable property available.

One of the few disadvantages of LOC-backed issues is the need to deposit refunding bond proceeds in escrow three months in advance of the maturity or redemption date. This advance deposit, required by the rating agencies, ensures that payment of principal to bondholders cannot be declared a preference payment by a trustee in a bankruptcy proceeding. Although these deposits may be reinvested at unrestricted taxable rates, this earlier funding requirement shortens the refunding period available to companies.

LOCs are generally much less advantageous when good market conditions prevail, since yield spreads between rating categories narrow and interest rate savings to the company are reduced.

To date, many short-term tax-exempt financings have used LOCs because of their numerous advantages. A few 10-year LOCs have been issued, though banks are generally reluctant to extend their LOCs for long periods of time and charge higher rates for doing so.

Insured Bonds

Insurance for municipal bonds has been offered for many years by two companies: Municipal Bond Insurance Association (MBIA) and American Municipal Bond Assurance Corporation (AMBAC).

Until recently, neither organization had a policy of extending its program to corporate-backed tax-exempt issues. In mid-1981, both MBIA and AMBAC reversed this decision. At the time of this writing, one publicly offered corporate issue has been insured by AMBAC and several other issues are under consideration.

Standard & Poor's now rates both MBIA and AMBAC insured bonds AAA. Moody's does not recognize municipal bond insurance when assigning its ratings. AMBAC's fees, payable in a lump sum at closing, are computed as a percentage of the total debt service (principal and interest payments) insured. The percentage generally ranges between ½ percent and 1½ percent. For a 30-year bond, the annual effective cost of this fee arrangement is roughly one half of the percentage rate set by AMBAC.

Insured bonds receiving an AAA rating from S&P are viewed by the market as less creditworthy, and therefore, the yields of such bonds are comparable to those for an AA-rated bond with an equivalent maturity. The interest savings from using insurance are highly dependent on market conditions and must be carefully evaluated against the insurance costs.

The disadvantages of municipal bond insurance programs for companies are:

— The insurer might require restrictive covenants (e.g., maintaining certain financial ratios) and, under certain conditions, mandatory deposits into escrow funds.
— High premium costs.
— Loss of expected interest rate savings due to improved market conditions when the issue is sold.
— Limitations by AMBAC and MBIA on the amounts of insurance coverage that they will extend to any one company.

The credit enhancement provided by insurance and the potential interest savings net of insurance fees make the AMBAC and MBIA programs attractive for lesser-rated companies considering long-term issues, particularly in difficult markets.

Commercial Paper

Tax-exempt commercial paper is another short-term interim financing option that is now available to companies. Sold in a coupon or discounted form, commercial paper offers maturities which typically run from 7 to 90 days. Depending on market conditions, maturity, and rating, interest rates on tax-exempt commercial paper range from 100 to 200 basis points lower than the rates on three-year short-term revenue bonds.

Other advantages offered by tax-exempt paper programs are:

— Inexpensive placement fees (generally running ⅛ percent annually) required to manage the program.

 — Almost unlimited refunding flexibility due to the short-term
   nature of the program, and consequent avoidance of redemption
   premiums.
 — Lower annual interest costs due to the periodic issuance of notes
   in amounts as needed, based on the progress of construction.

Offsetting the lower interest costs of a commercial paper program
are:

 — The need in most cases to provide a revolving line of credit.
 — The additional supervisory and administrative costs incurred to
   maintain an interim financing program.

Although only a few corporate tax-exempt commercial paper programs have been established so far, issuers seeking interim financing are
likely to use this technique more frequently in the future.

Floating- and Adjustable-Rate Bonds

From mid-1980 to the present, several long-term corporate-related tax-
exempt floating-rate issues have been publicly sold. Designed so that
the coupon rate rises or falls with the higher of a long- or short-term
index, these issues appeal primarily to companies which expect major
downward trends in interest rates to occur in coming years.

Floating-rate bonds allow a company to raise long-term funds at
initial rates below those for fixed-rate issues of comparable rating and
maturity. For the floating-rate issues already sold, the initial coupon
savings have ranged from 50 to 150 basis points.

Companies may find other advantages to this alternative, including:

 — Potential for additional interest savings should interest rates
   move lower.
 — Earlier call dates than for long-term fixed-rate issues.
 — Protection from extreme upward interest rate moves through
   the use of coupon "ceilings" and a weekly averaging method of
   calculating the interest.
 — Greater purchaser interest in the company's bonds due to the
   scarcity of floating-rate issues or to heightened demand when
   buyers perceive that rates will continue to increase for some
   time to come.

The major disadvantages of floaters are:

 — Potential for additional interest costs should rates move to and
   remain at higher levels.

- The generally higher cost associated with this technique as compared to short-term fixed-rate issues. (The latter are more marketable and have earlier refunding dates, lower call premiums, and lower underwriting and issuance costs.

In addition, dramatic changes in market conditions between the time of the financing decision and the time of the bond offering may reduce anticipated interest savings or, worse, the marketability of the issue. While the risk of sudden turns in interest rates exists for all types of financings, the expected delays and restructuring costs are greater for floating-rate issues than for other types of financings.

Adjustable-rate bonds, a variation of the floating-rate concept, are long-term bonds whose interest rate is reset at specified intervals, for example, on a monthly or yearly basis. Issues combining fixed short-term rates and subsequent adjustable rates have also been introduced in the municipal market.

In summary, most companies consider variable- and adjustable-rate issues unattractive because this financing alternative exposes them to higher interest rate potentials and possible limited investor appeal caused by unpredictable moves in the market.

Put Bonds

A tender or "put" option is another technique used by companies seeking lower interest rates on long-term issues. A put allows the purchaser to redeem bonds at par at any time or at a specified time interval early in the life of the issue. This right reduces the interest rate to the company because the offering is priced as though it matures on the first date on which the investor may exercise his put option.

Use of a remarketing agreement with put bond issues allows them to be reoffered to new buyers in the secondary market rather than retired. Remarketed put bonds can carry fixed or adjustable interest rates, depending on the structure of the issue.

Many other variations have been considered by investment bankers and companies when structuring such issues. The terms of an issue (and its attractiveness to the company) will depend on pricing methods, put and redemption features, and the security provided.

Offsetting the advantage of lower initial interest rates are the high interest rates that may confront companies as put bonds are tendered and remarketed. In addition, a company that issues put bonds risks the loss of proceeds if tendered bonds cannot be successfully remarketed. Finally, in some cases, refunding flexibility may have to be sacrificed in the design of a put bond issue.

Convertible and Deep Discount Bonds

Two types of long-term financing options are now being considered for use in the tax-exempt market: (1) convertible bonds and (2) original issue discount (OID) and zero-coupon bonds (i.e., deep-discount bonds).

Technically, tax-exempt convertible bonds would differ little from conventional taxable bonds convertible into common stock. Tax-exempt OID and zero-coupon bonds would be similar to those popularized in the taxable market in 1981, except that the annual accretion of the discount is exempt from federal income taxes. As a result, tax-exempt OID and zero-coupon issues are expected to have much broader investor appeal, particularly with retail buyers, than taxable discount bonds (which are sold principally to nontaxpaying pension funds). Use of these two alternatives in corporate tax-exempt financings is dependent on favorable review by the Internal Revenue Service.

Tax-exempt OID and zero-coupon bonds are especially attractive long-term options for companies financing in a high-interest-rate environment. Investors seeking to establish bond swap tax losses or to lock in assured yields guaranteed by the discount, or both, will accept lower yields on such issues than on par bonds.

Depending on the specific structure and timing of the issue, the yield savings on OID and zero-coupon tax-exempt bonds may reach 50 to 150 basis points annually. Deep-discount bonds are also attractive to companies because a yearly pro rata portion of the discount is tax deductible. As the amount of the discount from a cash-coupon bond of comparable maturity is increased, the effective financing cost of deep-discount bonds is reduced dramatically by this tax shield.

One of the principal disadvantages of deep-discount bonds is that the issues sold to date have been either (1) nonrefundable or (2) callable at par, or premiums to par. However, discount issues with below-par redemption schedules (providing yields approximating or somewhat above those obtained with traditional coupon bonds when called) might be salable.

Although deep-discount issues effectively lose their refunding flexibility when par redemption schedules are demanded by investors, the combined yield and tax-saving benefits of OID and zero-coupon bonds make such issues highly attractive alternatives to traditional coupon-bearing issues.

Other disadvantages of OID bonds include:

— The size of the final interest and principal payments required at the issue's maturity.
— Limits on the proceeds and maturity of such issues as the coupon discount from par is increased.

– For tax-exempt industrial development bonds, the loss of the ability to include accrued noncash construction interest in bond-sizing calculations.

Investor-owned utilities must also consider the need to seek approval from their regulatory commissions (1) to include accrued noncash interest expense in rate-making proceedings and (2) to "normalize" rather than "flow-through" interperiod tax benefits. Already, several state regulatory commissions have approved the use of this technique.

SUMMARY

When reviewing tax-exempt financing alternatives, companies should take into account the possibility that future legislation might curtail their financing flexibility. Congressional and Treasury Department opponents of corporate tax-exempt financing are expected to continue efforts to curb its future use. Opposing restrictions on tax-exempt financing are those who stress the employment and capital formation benefits historically associated with tax-exempt industrial development bonds (IDBs), particularly the public purpose served by special-facility issues (e.g., those for pollution abatement projects, resource recovery projects, and marine and airport terminals).

Although special-facility tax-exempt issues seem secure from legislative elimination for the time being, small-issue ($10 million and under) IDBs may be significantly restricted or eliminated. Small-issue IDBs used for recreational and commercial purposes (e.g., golf course, ski resort, tennis club, and fast-food facilities) are likely to be curtailed, partly because they have received a great deal of adverse publicity.

Congress is expected to consider other legislation that may reduce corporate interest in tax-exempt financing, including (1) the institution of much tighter state and local IDB approval procedures and (2) the elimination of recently enacted accelerated cost recovery system depreciation for facilities financed with tax-exempt bonds. Even without further action, the volume of small-issue IDB financing may be reduced because of a 1981 Treasury revenue ruling which restricts the combining of several small-issue IDBs into a composite offering.

CHAPTER 12

Vendor Financing

DANIEL W. WEST
Macrolease International Corporation

We have seen in rather clear terms that the asset side of the balance sheet can be used to generate funds without severely diluting corporate equity. The hypothetical examples cited in Chapter 1 briefly describe some of the alternatives that are available to industry groups which utilize their assets to generate capital. This chapter will highlight the *left hand financing* alternatives as they specifically relate to a user obtaining financing directly (1) from an equipment vendor; or (2) from an independent, third-party financing source. This chapter will also look at these financing alternatives from the vendor's perspective. It will be shown that the utilization of outside financing generates cash to the equipment seller and significantly limits the amount of equity that the equipment user must provide.

Vendor financing can come in a variety of nicely packaged units. In some cases, large manufacturers of leasable equipment have formed subsidiaries to handle the financing and leasing needs of their customers. These subsidiaries are captive relationships and, in more cases than not, draw on the financial resources of the parent. The captives, as they are known in the industry, perform dutifully in many cases and, as competitors to third-party lessors, are a strong economic force with which to contend. From the point of view of the customer (user), captives often provide highly attractive financing rates, although they are often restrictive as to terms. These rates provide a major selling impetus and frequently are the single most significant factor in the ultimate decision to acquire equipment from a specific vendor. Terms, including down payment requirements and the amortization period, are often more restrictive, however, due to lack of competition and historic resale experience.

Many examples of this selling approach can be described. For example, major equipment manufacturers, such as North American Rockwell, Xerox, McDonnell Douglas, and RCA, to list but a few, have heavily invested in subsidiary financing and leasing operations. The manufacturer's motivation for making these substantial investments is primarily to help increase sales, although the tax shelter aspects and profit potential of the leasing industry certainly are additional factors.

Equipment users have learned that the suppliers with captive financing arms are often well worth listening to and may be willing to assume credit risks not acceptable to independent parties on a selective basis. In addition, the buyer often feels that the manufacturer's financing represents more leverage should the equipment fail to perform up to expectations. The parent company can utilize captive financing capabilities by providing their equipment sales force with attractive programs, including deferred rentals, below-market interest rates, favorable termination/trade-in provisions, and so on, to encourage the lessee to acquire the parent's product. In many industries, financial statements of the small- to medium-sized companies typically reflect a leveraged condition, and financing is often difficult to obtain. The parent's financing subsidy relationship provides an additional benefit to the prospective lessee in that many credit decisions on marginal risks are made easier when operating with the knowledge that their parent company would support and remarket the equipment representing their collateral in the event of default.

In some cases, the captive financing company may benefit through recourse agreements from the manufacturers which are not available to outsiders. This arrangement allows approval of transactions that outside sources would find unacceptable. The manufacturers and the captive working together as one entity are able to maximize the resale effort in a default situation.

From the user's point of view, utilizing the vendor to provide financing may be advantageous. From the vendor's point of view, however, the issue of providing long-term financing to its customers can be involved and complex. Not only is the manufacturer concerned about funding a leasing/financing subsidiary, exposing itself to a new type of credit risk, and supporting the overhead of a new subsidiary, it must also now concern itself with the problem of recognition of income on sales that are being financed by an affiliate.[1] The financial reporting requirement to defer income as a result of financing its own sales has caught more than one equipment vendor by surprise.

Assuming the vendor makes the decision to establish a captive finance company after evaluating the business impact of each of those concerns, it has a number of options available to deal with future events

---

[1] Financial reporting concerns are discussed in Chapter 4.

which may cause it to reevaluate the decision. One of these options, the sale of all or part of the captive, involves the vendor in left hand financing for its own account since the investment in the captive is reflected as an asset on the vendor's financial statements.

The captive can generally be sold for an amount equal to a present value of the portfolio at a competitive rate plus a premium equal to the present value of the customer list. The customer list can be expected to generate some residual new business. Situations occur where financing companies can generate capital by merely selling off a part of their portfolio. The seller can select specific transactions or can liquidate the entire portfolio. The company stays intact, and when circumstances change for the better, the company can begin providing financing again with little effort.

INDEPENDENT, THIRD-PARTY FINANCING

Although the formation of captive financing/leasing companies is continuing at an accelerating pace, especially since the enactment of the "safe harbor" lease provisions of the Economic Recovery Tax Act of 1981, many manufacturers and equipment suppliers are utilizing independent, third-party leasing sources as financing alternatives. Third-party financing sources do not have common ownership with the supplier and provide financing through independent channels; however, a captive leasing company to one manufacturer may be a third-party lessor to an independent and unaffiliated manufacturer.

Many equipment suppliers, for some of the previously cited reasons, utilize third parties in their selling programs. Because of the expense of forming, financing, and operating a captive, the number of nonaffiliated, third-party lessors far exceeds the number of captives. It is also safe to assume that the volume of business written annually by entities providing third-party financing for vendors is substantially greater than that of captive finance companies.

Financing programs offered by captives and by nonaffiliated third parties are very much interchangeable, and the same or similar programs can be offered by either. (Many programs are much more effective from an accounting/tax treatment standpoint when operated at "arms length" by a nonaffiliated third party.) When a potential buyer has to be turned down by the captive for credit reasons, the equipment sale may be lost because the customer is left with the impression that the equipment supplier is rejecting the sale. Because of the alternative of seeking another third-party financing source, a third party may reject a potential customer as a bad credit risk while making it easier for the equipment salesperson to retain the customer. From the vendor's perspective, the vendor may be better able to retain capital and to use that capital more efficiently by using nonaffiliated, third-party financing sources.

THIRD-PARTY FINANCING

Benefits to User

The substantial benefits an equipment user often receives from the introduction of a third-party financing source go beyond those that would be realistically available through a captive. For example, in many cases, a third-party source faced with extreme competition does provide terms which are more aggressive than the captive operation where no such competition may exist.

Still further, a third-party source of financing is in a better position to provide a total project financing package, including equipment, from more than one supplier. In most cases, this is not possible with the captive.

Once again, because of competition, the third-party source may be better prepared to provide special services, including personal visits and advice on complicated tax matters. Manufacturer's captive personnel are probably less experienced in many of these financial areas.

From a geographic viewpoint, many equipment users prefer that the finance/leasing company have local representation. Local representation is more common when dealing with a decentralized, third-party source. Many captives are centralized and operate only at the manufacturing headquarters.

PRICING OF VENDOR FINANCING PROGRAMS

Up to this point, we have concentrated on concepts and transactions that have not expressed any relationship to tax benefits or residual values. We have seen that third-party lessors can offer unique and valuable services to both a vendor and a lessee. The third-party lessor transactions previously cited were basically finance oriented and were created primarily as sales tools. However, the leasing industry exists today in significant part because of available tax benefits. Third-party lessors offer the same basic financing services in the true lease and safe harbor lease marketplace and are used extensively by equipment vendors.

When pricing lease transactions where some or all of the tax benefits[2] are transferred from the user to the lessor (that is, "true leases" and

---

[2] As explained in Chapter 3, a lessor may elect to pass through the investment tax credit to the lessee.

safe harbor leases), the lessor will consider not only its marginal tax rate but also the date that the tax benefits become available. For example, a calendar-year taxpayer looks to December 31 as the optimal date for closing a given transaction. If a sizable lease is closed on October 15, the lessor will calculate the 76-day differential into its yield, thus increasing the coupon rate to the lessee. (The coupon rate is the effective interest rate without considering the tax benefits and residual value.) The basis of paying estimated taxes, be it based on prior-year or current-year earnings, is also significant in evaluating the coupon rate. By recognizing the lessor's tax-paying characteristics, the lessee may be better able to control the delivery of equipment to obtain a more attractive leasing arrangement.

The most significant variable among leasing firms is that of residual valuation. In a true lease, the purchase option price at termination may not be less than fair market value at the time the purchase option is exercised. With a safe harbor lease, on the other hand, a nominal purchase price is allowed. Lessors can have common year-end closings, pay taxes at the same rate, pay estimated taxes on the same basis, and seek the same return on cash, and yet one lessor can offer a more attractive lease rate because that lessor gives more credence to the residual value.

Residual valuation has been and probably will continue to be both the bane and the spark in transactions involving true leases. A lessor that assumes a piece of equipment is going to be worth 15 percent of its original purchase price at the end of its lease term, say of five years, and that is willing to give the lessee the benefit of the 15 percent assumption can offer a discounted coupon rate over a lessor who assumes that the equipment will not have any value at termination. It is important to note that the lessor is not guaranteeing to the lessee that the purchase option will be 15 percent. The lessor is merely creating an internal formula that will allow the lessor to comfortably charge a competitive rate while hopefully remaining conservative in terms of residual valuation.

The residual valuation is a major factor in pricing lease financing. The equipment vendor who is seeking third-party leasing sources looks for a company that understands and has had experience in handling the vendor's industry. In many cases, that understanding gives the vendor a meal ticket to an aggressive marketing program. Equipment suppliers seek leasing companies with an understanding of the vendor's market, which generally permits the lessor to take greater residual risks thus providing lower coupon rates and more competitive selling terms. Remember, however, that determining residual values is a function of the type of equipment and the use it is to receive, and to date, there is no formula for determining such a value.

The lessee, while most likely benefiting from an attractive coupon rate, does assume a residual risk except in a safe harbor lease with a nominal purchase option. In order for the lessor to satisfy both its yield requirements and the IRS guidelines for a true lease, it is difficult if not impossible to predetermine the purchase price at termination of the lease. The lessee risks the possibility that the equipment may have a very high value at the end of the lease term. If that equipment is worth 75 cents on the dollar and the lessor is seeking that amount, the options are rather clear cut: (a) the equipment can be purchased at the asking price; (b) the lease can be renewed for an additional period of time at a negotiated rental; or (c) the equipment can be returned to the lessor.

The machine tool industry is a very dramatic example of a market where residual values remain very high and financial leases with pre-determined nominal purchase options are the order of the day. The computer industry, on the other hand, is at the opposite end of the spectrum. Due to the dramatic, state-of-the-art changes that are made almost seasonally in the industry, older-generation equipment tends not to have high residual value, and thus true lease financing is popular.

The automobile and truck leasing industry is one where prospective customers have determined that the benefits of ownership are question-able and that leasing may be the more economical route to go. Lessors have utilized the residual valuation concept to the apex of their abili-ties, and because of the high resale value of most vehicles and the high cost of maintenance, vehicle users are using the leasing route with increasing regularity. Lessors, in some cases, not only provide relatively inexpensive terms but also handle the maintenance, insurance, licensing, and resale of the vehicles. The ability to use capital assets, such as motor vehicles, for an extended period of time while keeping debt off the balance sheet is considered by many to be a major accomplishment. The fact that a vehicle is usually discarded or replaced after a two- or three-year period coincides with the general terms of the vehicle leasing industry. There is no better example of the utilization of lease financing for the preservation of corporate equity.

SUMMARY

The approach of using the equipment vendor or third-party financing sources to finance the seller's product is not a new one. It is, however, a concept that is becoming increasingly popular inasmuch as many manu-facturers have recognized that they must offer imaginative, flexible, and less costly financing/leasing terms to compete in today's markets. The use of the vendor's captive financing company or an independent third-party financing source has been demonstrated as a viable alternative to diluting equity through direct participation in the financing. Equipment vendors also benefit from utilizing their assets to generate capital. The example of selling captive financing portfolios or an entire captive company present financing options available to a vendor with a captive finance company. The use of a third-party source reflects one more avenue that is available for the equipment seller in utilizing its assets.

Vendor financing can add a new dimension to the corporate financial plan. Equipment shoppers evaluate their financing options in the same thorough manner that they evaluated their equipment options. Equipment vendors consider their customer financing options as thoughtfully as they review their internal financing alternatives. Each of these options provide real opportunities to avoid expanding the corporate equity base by utilizing the left hand financing concept.

CHAPTER 13

Secured Short-Term Financing

MAYNARD I. WISHNER
Walter E. Heller & Company

The ratio of debt to equity in manufacturing and distribution companies continues to rise steadily, as it has for more than a decade. Corporate balance sheets are well into a period of sharp decline of retained earnings. New-issue equity financing is essentially prohibitive in cost. Yet, the demands for credit continue to press.

Our larger business entities are engaging in strategic financial planning. Is this the time to commit to long-term fixed rates, or shall we stay short and float? Shall we increase our dividend, or shall we keep earnings to avoid as much as we can of high money costs? Shall we lean on our suppliers for a two- to three-day additional investment in our accounts payable (their receivables), or are they insufficiently dependent on us to accept being forced to make us a non-interest-bearing loan? Are we in a position to move from bank borrowings at the prime rate to the commercial paper market, where we will enjoy reasonable acceptance at some rate below prime?

The luxury of being able to select among options diminishes as we move down the ladder of corporate size and down the scale of corporate strength. We are now in the unhappy process of discovering that size and strength are not as synonymous as we once supposed.

While large may not be the equivalent of strong, being small or medium in the business world imposes its own set of realities. Whatever may be true about increasing debt-to-equity ratios among the large corporations is even more so among the small. Significant equity infusion has been unavailable. Venture capital sources once in vogue virtually disappeared, and to the extent that they returned with appetite, it was only on a highly selective basis where projected growth curves made some sense on the potential reward side of the risk/reward equation.

Old formulations which contemplated going public in three to five years at 15 to 20 times earnings have no reality in light of our current equity markets.

In the meantime, the steady press of inflation has taken its toll. Just standing still, that is, producing the same units of product after a year of, say, 10 percent inflation, has meant a 10 percent increase in investment in inventory and in accounts receivable. Just to stand still, more credit is needed than was required last year. While normal payables will pick up some of this pressure, the rest will have to come from lenders.

Carry this process through even a fairly short-term cycle of double-digit inflation, and we see a significant increase in the requirement for borrowed funds not only in absolute terms but in relation to underlying net worth if retained equity has not had a commensurate growth.

A company experiencing not merely "monetary" growth but *real* growth, in unit terms, has even greater appetite, indeed need, for external financing to carry an accelerated investment in inventory, receivables, and probably some additional fixed assets to accommodate growing production requirements.

This continuing push of need for credit in growing ratio against net worth has created some problems for unsecured lenders, essentially the banks. As limits imposed by conventional rules of thumb which have constituted hallowed guidelines for unsecured lending are being breached, the banker is faced with having to say "no" to a valued customer or having to "stretch" to provide the requested accommodations.

Debt to worth, current assets to current liabilities, clean up the loan once a year "so we do not have a permanent investment in your business" are all under growing pressure even with growing successful businesses. Comes recession, a year or more of declining profits, or the first encounter with a loss, and the unsecured lender begins to have problems. Unsecured does not mean insecure. Indeed, one can be unsecured and feel quite secure. But to be unsecured and insecure at the same time means that something has to change.

The taking of security in furtherance of trade and commerce is an ancient and hallowed practice. The revolution in financing that the "invention" of the mortgage made possible is part of the saga of the industrialized nations. Envision our cities today without the device of the real estate mortgage. Which structures would now be standing if all borrowing for real estate development had to be done on a balance sheet basis against the net worth of the developer?

We have been seeing an exploding use of security interests in the assets making up the left hand side of the balance sheet to facilitate the financing of ordinary business activity. These techniques are making possible the growth, acquisition, and, in many cases, survival of tens of thousands of business enterprises which otherwise would find debt markets inaccessible or severely limited.

By looking to the assets of the business, the lender is able to apply a wholly different set of considerations in determining his willingness to accommodate financing requirements. These assets provide a basis for the lender's advances, to which he can look for repayment should matters not go as planned.

The assets generally involved in such secured corporate lending or asset-based lending are the accounts receivables, inventories, machinery and equipment, and real estate of the company.

It has been possible to perfect security interests in all these types of assets for some time. Yet, we did not see the widespread use of these devices until relatively recently. The pioneering was done by the independent commercial finance companies that developed and applied the techniques which are now increasingly becoming part of mainstream financing.

The relatively sudden burgeoning of the use of these techniques is attributable in part to the growing need arising out of the pressures referred to earlier.

Of great significance has also been the adoption of the Uniform Commercial Code developed in the early 1960s. Prior to that time, each of the states had evolved its own approach to the question of perfecting security interests and assuring (or limiting) the priority lenders might enjoy. For the most part, these approaches were judge-made and tended to follow different rationales in trying to cope with the problem of how third parties dealing with the company could know or be presumed to know that its non-real estate assets were assigned or pledged to a lender (or other creditor).

Whether it was a legend to be posted on the books and records of the company or a theory of a possessory security interest which required the assertion of "dominion" over the accounts, the approaches used were not nearly as satisfactory as the procedure of filing on the public records that had long been available to real estate lenders.

The Uniform Commercial Code now adopted by all of the states, provides, with some variations, for a method of filing a notice, alphabetically indexed under the name of the debtor, that a security interest may exist in favor of a named secured party in those assets of the debtor described in the document filed. A search of such records, whether under a county system or a statewide system, provides the device for notice to those interested. The fictions of possession and dominion were set aside, and a straightforward security interest was created, which, save for some exceptions as to purchase-money obligations, gave priority to the first to file.

With some of the legal uncertainties out of the way (problems of conflict between the Uniform Commercial Code and bankruptcy law still remain), the path was opened for lenders to move more confidently into the secured lending arena with considerably more surefootedness as to their legal position.

What does all this mean to the borrower? The secured lender is in a position to extend credit to an extent not appropriate to the unsecured bank lender. In good times for growth, in more difficult times, through a turnaround situation, the borrowing capacity of a company is increased. The company's assets provide the basis for financing, and the borrowings expand and contract daily in accordance with the creation and liquidation of current assets.

ACCOUNTS RECEIVABLE FINANCING

The secured lender will look first to the accounts receivable of the client. In general, one can expect advances to be made to the extent of approximately 80 percent of the receivables that the lender deems acceptable. This rate of advance can vary from company to company, depending on the quality and nature of the receivables, the type of customer the client sells to, the terms of sale, and the extent of returns and allowances characteristic of the business.

Not all receivables in a portfolio are deemed acceptable. Various criteria may be used to determine acceptability.

Most secured lenders will ordinarily not accept foreign receivables, although international factoring networks make it possible to qualify these receivables as well. Government receivables may require special handling.

The lender will clearly disqualify "stale" receivables, that is, those which are delinquent to the extent of an agreed number of days past the due date. He may also apply a 10 percent rule that will disqualify all receivables owing from an account debtor where 10 percent or more of the amount owing to the client is over 90 days past due.

He will also be looking at concentrations of risk where open-account credit is being extended by his client beyond what the lender believes is warranted based on the financial condition and creditworthiness of the client's customer. Here the client may find an unexpected benefit from working with the professional secured lender. He may well find himself looking at the quality and turn of his receivables with a discipline that he had not brought to bear in the past. He may focus on delinquencies in a more organized way as he recognizes the impact on his business of a portfolio turning more slowly than it would need to if it received the necessary attention. If the lender raises questions about a concentration of risk in a questionable credit, shouldn't the client be even more worried about it? After all, he will still have to repay the debt incurred by borrowing against the receivable. Moreover, he retains the risk of collectibility and the impact of bad debt losses. (This would not be true in the case of factoring, to be discussed later.)

The mechanics of receivable borrowing are generally quite simple. The borrower can, on a daily basis, or weekly, if that is the understanding, submit to the lender a schedule of receivables representing shipments made since the last schedule. Copies of invoices are generally attached, and some sort of shipping evidence may be required. Upon receipt of the schedule, the lender will transfer to the client's account up to the agreed percentage of the face of the invoices. The client is not obligated to borrow the 80 percent. He need not borrow any more than he needs. He must schedule all of his receivables to the lender, all of which secure the total indebtedness, but he borrows (and pays for) only what he needs for his cash requirements.

In the meantime, collections are coming in. In accounts receivable lending arrangements, the client's customers are generally not notified of the existence of the lender's interest and continue to make payments to the borrower. However, since all of the proceeds have been assigned to the lender, the client receives these payments in trust and is required to deposit all collections to the lender's account. Cash realization may be accelerated by a lockbox arrangement, the account being under the lender's control. The lender will want to see copies of the customers' checks so as to have a full understanding of the behavior of the portfolio.

Cash received is applied toward reduction of the loan. This is important to the borrower since charges on the loan are computed on the basis of daily outstanding balances. Excess cash, that is, cash which brings the loan down so that the loan is brought below the formula availability, is available to the borrower.

By way of example, assume a portfolio of $500M of eligible receivables supporting a $400M loan on an 80 percent advance formula. Now suppose collections of $100M come in on a given day. If no new receivables are assigned, the outstanding gross receivables now amount to $400M, but the loan, after clearance of the account debtors' checks, has been reduced to $300M. Since the borrower is entitled to an 80 percent advance, he could have a loan of $320M and, therefore, can call upon the lender for $20M or, by prearrangement, have the $20M forwarded to him. What has actually happened is that the lender has made an $80M loan against $100M in receivables. When the $100M is collected, $80M is used to retire the advance, and the other $20M, sometimes referred to as a collected reserve, is refunded to the client.

With the ebb and flow of shipments and collections, the client has a virtually automatic program for realizing substantial cash as goods go out his door, with a lending resource structured to accommodate his daily needs and with loan reduction taking place as collections are received.

The loan goes up and down in relation to the accounts receivable asset, enabling the client to deal with his trade payables and other obligations by drawing the available cash as he needs it and reducing his loan as collections come in during the normal monthly cycle.

The financing provided under these programs does not require amortization. Loan agreements are generally entered into for from one to three years, and if all goes well, they can, in fact, continue indefinitely without ever having to be "repaid."

INVENTORY FINANCING

Inventory represents the other current asset against which revolving loans may be made. Here valuation and administration present more problems to the lender than in the case of receivables. We must remember that the lender is looking at the assets assigned to him as collateral which secures his position in the event of failure. Being thus secured is what enables the lender to extend accommodations in excess of the accommodations that an unsecured lender can extend. He therefore must look at the inventory in terms of what he can realize through its liquidation on a nongoing business basis.

While the face value of receivables is a good starting point for valuation, liquidation of inventory will not bring the same proportion of book value as amounts duly owing from third parties for goods had and received.

Raw materials of a standard nature are relatively easy to value. Once a coil of standard steel has been cut to prepare it for the client's manufacturing process, its value upon liquidation has been destroyed and it may only be realized upon for scrap value. Generally, work in process will be given little value for lending purposes. Finished goods are susceptible to some form of liquidation at a price, provided the mix of goods on hand is reasonable and has not been picked clean of more salable items, leaving behind odds and ends, off colors, partial runs, or obsolete items not in the current product line. Depending on the business, the expectation of customers for support of warranties, part replacement, and the general good name of the manufacturer will impact the realization possibilities of inventories that need to be disposed of at a time of distress.

For these reasons, rates of advance are less against inventories than against receivables and vary industry by industry and company by company. Advance rates may differ between inventory that is being built in hopes of acceptance for items in a new line and inventory that is being prepared for shipment against firm orders. Advance rates may be higher during the period of inventory buildup for seasonal requirements with an expectation that the requirements will be reduced during the shipping season, with the inventory loan brought down through the creation of receivables generated by sales. The receivable loan expands as the inventory loan contracts, again matching the ebb and flow of the asset side of the balance sheet.

FIXED ASSETS AND SECURED FINANCING PACKAGES

Frequently, loans against the company's fixed assets are part of the secured financing packages. The techniques involved are fairly straightforward. Since the lender needs to feel secure as to his realization if the debt is not repaid from operations, he will generally require an auction value appraisal and will lend some percentage of that value, setting an amortization schedule with repayments generally called for over a five-year term.

Since the lender is interested in realizable value, book value will not necessarily provide a useful guideline as to loan value. Fairly standard machine tools and other equipment may well have been written down over time to a level well below the current liquidation value. That will not concern the lender who is looking to the liquidation value for his security and will be comfortable lending well in excess of book. On the other hand, a company may show substantial book values for its machinery and equipment but may find that pipes, wiring, conveyor systems, furnaces, ovens, and other built-ins—are not assets which can be sold to someone who is not going to continue the same operation in place. With a solid liquidation valuation provided by a sound appraiser, the lender can be reasonably aggressive in meeting the client's needs.

COST OF SECURED BORROWING

What about cost? Since dealing with revolving current asset collateral (receivables and inventory) requires almost daily active handling by the lender, the costs of secured borrowing will tend to be higher than the costs of unsecured bank debt. The differences, however, will not be fully understood if the borrower's treasurer does not undertake a more in-depth cost analysis that takes into account the realities of this bank relationship with an almost universal requirement for the maintenance of compensating balances and the characteristics of his company's use of cash.

Price is not the equivalent of cost. It is illusory to view the cost of borrowing in terms of the expressed rate of interest if the company is permitted to make use of only 80 to 90 percent of the amount of the loan. Interest is paid on the total amount of the loan. Therefore, under a 20 percent compensating balance requirement, the interest cost of the borrowed money which is actually put to use in the borrower's business is 125 percent of the expressed rate of interest. When balance requirements can be met from the normal minimum cash reserves which a well-run enterprise ought to have available for its daily needs, we are not dealing with the additional costs described above. However, the artificial maintenance of balances to meet borrowing requirements represents a real cost ingredient.

A key component of borrowing costs is the time basis for charging interest. An analysis should determine the extent to which the company actually makes use of its borrowed money.

In the typical company, the requirements for borrowed cash are not at a constant level. There are periods of the month which are characterized by heavy cash demands, such as the classic challenge of meeting the payroll. There are other periods during which the inflow of collections operates to relieve cash pressures. Similarly, in many businesses, there are seasonal characteristics which impose requirements for borrowed funds that are at sharply different levels during the course of the year. If a chart is prepared showing the need for borrowed cash on a daily basis, that need will appear as a series of peaks and valleys, the slopes of which will vary greatly, depending on the type of business.

Unsecured bank borrowings will generally appear as a flat amount for a stated period. Interest is paid on the full amount of the loan for every day it is outstanding. The secured lender charges for the use of funds on a daily basis. Here again, the stated interest rate is clearly not the sole determining factor in a cost comparison between the two differing methods of charge. The following process may be used to obtain a fair comparison of the true costs of these two types of short-term borrowing.

To begin, note the amount of the bank loan. This is generally arranged to cover both the company's peak requirements during a 60- or 90-day cycle and the required compensating balance. Using the expressed per annum rate, compute the actual dollar cost of interest for the full loan period. That amount may now be measured against the cost of borrowing only the daily funds actually required during the period, without having to maintain compensating balances. To compute that cost, determine the amount of funds actually required for each day and total them. Divide the total by the number of days in the cycle, and the resulting figure will represent the average daily loan amount required by the company for the period. Apply to the average loan amount, the interest rate which would be charged on a secured loan for the period and the result will be a dollar cost which can be compared to the dollar cost of the unsecured bank accommodation. The higher of these two figures obviously represents the more expensive borrowing. In many cases, the program which expresses the highest annual rate will not be the most expensive in actual cost.

FACTORING

A financing method which should be mentioned in any listing of "short-term" methods is factoring. While factoring serves some of the purposes of short-term borrowing, it is primarily a specialized, professional service. It is not simply another way of lending money. Factoring can include an arrangement to accelerate cash flow, but this is only an optional service that a factoring client may elect to employ.

Because of the increasing use of factoring as a form of financing, a detailed discussion of this service is provided. Hopefully, this will serve to clarify a common misconception. Quite often, one hears people refer to commercial finance firms as "factoring houses." By this, they are implying that everything these firms do is factoring. They are incorrectly applying the term *factoring* to both lending against receivables and the purchase of receivables. Only the latter relates to factoring. Lending against receivables, which has been discussed earlier, is a fundamentally different service known as accounts receivable financing or pledging of receivables.

There are some general observations which should be made before beginning a detailed description of factoring. First, factoring is suitable and productive for manufacturers and wholesalers; its use is widespread in lines of business ranging from lumber mills to steel tube welders, from toys to scientific instruments, and from textiles to electronics. Second, the service benefits alone have special appeal to well-financed, established firms that do not need the cash advances which are available, if wanted, before maturity of the accounts.

The factor becomes the credit and collection department of the client and assumes the risk of credit losses.

The factor establishes lines of credit for the customers of his clients and approves shipments up to those amounts at the factor's credit risk. When shipments are made, the factor will, at the client's option, immediately advance up to 90 percent or so of the net invoice value to the client. This is merely an advance payment for the receivable since the factor has actually purchased the accounts. It is in no sense a loan which must be repaid. The factor then ledgers the receivables and collects them. The 10 percent or so of the net value of unpaid receivable is retained by the factor only as a reserve for protection against merchandise disputes, the risk of which he does not assume. If this reserve exceeds 10 percent of the outstanding receivables, it is refunded at the end of each month or more frequently if desirable.

The combination of services and quick payment is known as "old-line" factoring. Without the early advance, it is called "maturity" factoring. Under a maturity arrangement, the factor performs all of the service functions and takes the same risks as in old-line factoring, but he does not advance money at the time of shipment. Instead, the factor pays for the receivables around the time of their average maturity date. Hence, there are no interest charges in maturity factoring.

In both types of factoring, a charge is made for the factoring services, that is, setting the credit lines, ledgering the receivables, collecting, and assuming the credit risk. This charge is called the factoring "commission." In old-line factoring, interest is charged for the period between the date of the advance at the time of shipment and an agreed-upon date after the maturity of invoices.

A factoring relationship can involve a loan as a supplement to the basic services provided. For example, firms in lines of business with heavy seasonal demands may need funds to build inventory. Most factors will provide loans for this purpose. In addition, factors will also make equipment loans or meet other unusual cash needs of their clients. These loans, however, are not part of the factoring process. They are handled separately and are most often provided merely as an accomodation to the client.

Because factoring is not a loan, its effect on the client's balance sheet is unlike that of any other type of financing. For example, assume that a company has a current ratio of about 2 to 1, is not factoring, and has current assets and current liabilities as follows:

Current assets:		Current liabilities:	
Cash	$ 10,000	Payables	$160,000
Receivables	100,000	Net worth	150,000
Inventory	200,000		$310,000
	$310,000		

Now suppose that the same company is factoring its sales, with a 90 percent advance, and is able to reduce its payables because of accelerated cash flow. The balance sheet changes to reflect a current ratio of better than 3 to 1.

Current assets:		Current liabilities:	
Cash	$ 10,000	Payables	$ 70,000
Due from factor . . .	10,000	Net worth	150,000
Inventory	200,000		$220,000
	$220,000		

Companies which use factoring think of it as a sales-minded service. This capability has to be carefully developed by a factoring firm. Its credit staff has a delicate job. The factor must master the art of making credit judgments and collections in a way that not only avoids customer dissatisfaction but also develops growing, profitable users of the clients' products. This necessitates bringing credit lines to the customers' full credit capacities, as well as paying special attention to increasing the buying power of customers or prospects with marginal credit standings. It does not mean that factors are foolishly liberal with credit. Their credit staffs do develop expertise and special advantages that are not usually shared by the credit people of the normal business firm. Factors have wide-ranging experience in the industry served by the client, augmented by frequent trips out in the trade to keep abreast of industry trends. The availability of the factor's own tremendous store of current credit files on business firms is also beneficial. The result of all this, of course, is that credit becomes an important sales tool for the client, to the advantage of both the client and the factoring firm.

What a company pays for factoring may be no more, and may often be less, than what it would cost the company to perform all credit and collection functions on its own. If the company handled its own credits, it would be required to maintain its own credit and collection departments and to buy credit information, pay collection and attorneys' fees, incur inevitable bad debt losses, and absorb a variety of other miscellaneous overhead items.

It is interesting to note that the reader is closer to factoring than he or she may know. Each time a personal credit card is used, the holder is participating in a form of factoring. The cardholder is the "customer," the store or restaurant is the "client," and the credit card issuer is the "factor" who does the credit checking, bookkeeping and risk taking. The store or restaurant is charged a "commission" for those services.

CONCLUSION

The secured lending and factoring devices discussed above are now an established set of tools for companies that have a need of financial support and cannot be accommodated by unsecured bank sources. This need may exist because things are too good, that is, when growth is outstripping the financial base of the company. It may arise when things have gone bad and a lender is needed who will help keep the company alive while it works out its problems.

A growing use of these techniques has arisen in the area of financing *leveraged buy-outs.* We are in a period when many larger companies are seeking to rationalize their product lines in a reaction to the period of conglomeratization when it was the fashion to acquire almost any kind of entity that showed profit potential, ability to manage effectively, and market image. Return on assets employed is among the considerations that have led to a period of "de-conglomeratization."

Among the buyers have been the specialized entrepreneur, the management group, or another company in the same industry which can profit from the "fit." Since such transactions are basically asset acquisitions, asset-oriented lending has been a most effective tool for making such buy-outs possible for buyers who are not basically "monied." Substantial enterprises have been acquired with relatively modest equity and with programs in place to support continued growth.

In summary, secured lending is here to stay. It can do what other forms of lending cannot do, and it has become an important contribution to the growth and strength of American trade and commerce.

Index